EVOLVING STAGES

EVOLVING STAGES

A Layman's Guide to 20th Century Theatre

Tony Cottrell

THE BRISTOL PRESS

A CIP catalogue record for this book is available from the British Library

© Tony Cottrell, 1991

First published in the UK (1991) by:

The Bristol Press
226 North Street
Bedminster
Bristol BS3 1JD

ISBN 1 85399 148 1

The Bristol Press is an imprint of Bristol Classical Press

Printed in Great Britain by
Billing & Sons Ltd, Worcester

CONTENTS

INTRODUCTION

It must be said from the start that this is not an attempt at an exhaustive examination of this century's new drama. To try to achieve that between the covers of a single book and by a single author would be foolhardy, if not impossible. Inevitably, this book will be both subjective and incomplete and is likely to infuriate the various specialists in their specific fields of excellence. However, it is not aimed at scholars; the body of expert opinion in all the areas briefly visited by this book is enormous and this is not intended to increase it; it is, however, hoped that this book will act as a guide for the amateur, the drama student, the interested theatre-goer who, like me, wants to know how one thing relates to another, how the side-streets and byways join up those bits of the map with which we are well acquainted. Brecht and Shaw, Beckett and Miller, Pirandello and Lorca, Pinter and Bond – these are perhaps the names we've heard of, whose work we know, but we would also like to learn something of their background, about their mentors and peers, contemporaries, disciples, competitors and colleagues. We'd like to know what was going on in British theatre before *Look Back In Anger*. Who invented 'Theatre of the Absurd'? What was 'Theatre of Cruelty'? Who influenced Brecht? Who were the founding fathers of American theatre? Why are the Irish so influential in English-speaking theatre? Who *else* wrote plays in Spanish or Italian? And how does it all fit together? These were the sort of questions that I wanted answers to, the last one in particular.

While I cannot claim to have plotted every pathway and may have even unwittingly omitted a motorway and metropolis or two, I trust that the following chapters will help to colour in the map and encourage you to explore hitherto unknown places.

1: THE STATE OF THE ART

Until the emergence of the movies early this century, it was impossible to have objective documented proof of any actor's performance and despite the enormous development in, not to mention mass-production of, celluloid, acting on stage is still an ephemeral art and impartial judgment of it an impossibility; a student must balance the exaggeration of friends and the derogation of enemies and, even then, an actor's work can only be known through reputation.

We have no way of knowing how good were Aeschylus' performances in his own plays but we can still read the *Oresteia* and judge him as a playwright; Roscius may have been Rome's finest actor but it is the scripts of Terence and Plautus that survive. Burbage and Kempe may well have taken the plaudits but it is only because of Shakespeare's plays that the memory of these actors is still with us.

And so, although it is the art of the actor that makes the moment extraordinary, it is almost always the playwright, alone or in collaboration, who provides the vehicle, assembles the ideas and orders the words; although it is impossible to ignore the actor or that recent refinement, the director, it will be on the authors and their creations that this introductory guide to the most productive century in the two and a half thousand year history of the theatre will concentrate.

In order to guess where we might be going, it helps to know where we have come from. An examination of the twentieth century's contribution to the theatre cannot begin baldly at 1 January 1900 but must step back into the nineteenth century for a while. Obviously, art is no respecter of calendars and artistic movements do not confine themselves to temporal restrictions, but the end of the nineteenth century witnessed the heyday of at least three memorable theatrical *genres*, the Melodrama, the Operetta and the Comedy of Manners as epitomised by Wilde's *Lady Windermere's Fan*; and it was as a reaction to this sort of comfortable, escapist work that the movement that was to be called Naturalism developed.

The nineteenth century was the century of revolution and the theatre witnessed its own share of upheaval accompanied by the inevitable manifestoes. August Strindberg (1849-1912) provided one of the most inflammatory:

> The Theatre and indeed art in general has long seemed to me a *Biblia pauperum*, a Bible in pictures for the benefit of the illiterate...I

2

feel that the theatre, like religion, is on the way to being discarded as a dying form which we lack the necessary conditions to enjoy. This hypothesis is evidenced by the theatrical crisis now dominating the whole of Europe; and not least, by the fact that in those cultural strongholds which have nurtured the greatest thinkers of our day, namely England and Germany, the art of writing plays is, like most other fine arts, dead.

Thus wrote Strindberg in 1888 in the preface to his play, *Miss Julie*. And yet at the same time as Strindberg and other visionaries were prematurely bewailing the death of theatre, in Britain, for example, the institution had never been healthier.

Encouraged and, until the death of her husband, actively led by their Queen, the Victorians went to the theatre in droves. It may have been to a music hall at the back of the local pub or one of the growing empires being established by Moss and Stoll; it may have been to the immensely popular melodrama, the 'sensation' drama, the operetta as epitomised by the works of Gilbert and Sullivan; it may have been to the farce, the pantomime, the extravaganza, the burlesque, to Shakespeare as performed by Sir Henry Irving and Ellen Terry at the Lyceum or even the new and abominable Naturalistic theatre that so revolted and appalled many of its original audience; it may have been to one or any of these. But without doubt, to the theatre they went.

In Volume V of his *History of English Drama*, Allardyce Nicoll presents a list of new works for the stage produced in the latter half of the nineteenth century; it is some six hundred pages long and contains thousands of entries, from Charles Harrie Abbot's *Captain Kidd or the Bold Buccanneer* to Madame Zoblinsky's *Annie of Tharau*; it includes eighty-eight separate anonymous versions of *Cinderella* – not to mention all the attributable ones – and sixty-five different works by W.S. Gilbert, including *Foggerty's Fairy* and the immortal *The Merry Zingara or the Tipsy Gypsy and the Pipsy Wipsy*. Faced with the content of such offerings, the funereal announcements of a serious dramatist such as Strindberg may well be understandable, with 'self-indulgence' as the probable cause of death, but, despite Strindberg's contradiction, performances of sorts in theatres of sorts were taking place on a remarkable scale.

During the last two decades of the century, over one hundred and forty theatres were functioning in and around London and this figure does not include the music halls. Elsewhere, the figure was in excess of three hundred and fifty, including nine theatres in Edinburgh, five in Merthyr Tydfil and, among the prodigious crop of Theatre Royals, one each in Attercliffe, Bilston, Brierly Hill, Goole, Seaham Harbour, Wednesbury and Wigan.

When we think of the plays of the nineteenth century, we inevitably think of the melodrama, that enormously popular *genre* summed up by Michael Booth:

> Essentially, melodrama is a dream world inhabited by dream people and dream justice, offering audiences fulfilment and satisfaction found only in dreams…an allegory of human experience dramatically ordered as it should be…uncomplicated, easy to understand and immeasurably exciting.[1]

It is interesting to note that words like 'dream' and 'allegory' are going to be used in descriptions of the work of two of the major opponents of melodrama, Ibsen and Strindberg, interesting if only to help us toward the eventual realisation that, in spite of all the talk of 'avant-garde' and revolution, nothing really changes and revolutions go full circle.

Also, it is no coincidence that Booth's last phrase – 'uncomplicated, easy to understand and exciting' – could well be used to describe the products of Hollywood at its height; a white hat meant a hero, the heroine would be saved no matter how much the audience tried to convince itself that she might not be and a 'good time was had by all'.

Much of that need for blatant, exciting and simplistic entertainment with an easily-digested moral – a need that goes back to the roots of man, religion and theatre, a need that melodrama fulfilled and the early morality plays and the gorier aspects of Jacobean tragedy gratified – is now being catered for by the cinema and its sanitised companion, television; indeed, it was the rise of the movies that finally killed the barn-storming melodrama tours.

The basic structure of the *genre* was very straightforward with easily-recognisable characters that were often interchangeable. The Hero, the Heroine and the Villain were essential, very often accompanied by a Good Old Man and a Good Old Woman – usually parents of the heroine – while a Comic Man and Comic Woman added light relief. These were all familiar types, closely related to figures from the Harlequinade, the Pantomime and, originally, Italian Commedia dell'Arte.

Where these nineteenth-century melodramas differed from their ancestors was in the intensity of the sufferings of the guileless hero and luckless heroine. Every sort of fate, from simple death to the one supposed to be far worse than death, befell the heroines, usually while the hero was unconscious, tied up, wrongfully imprisoned for the foul deeds of the villain or, preferably, all three. In the end, the villain always received his just deserts, thereby permitting managers to argue that these were infinitely moral works; however, it seems more than likely that the audiences enjoyed the vicarious terrors and perverse pleasures of the protagonists just as much as they did the supposedly uplifting conclusions. Booth summarises the contents of these plays thus:

> The shootings, stranglings, hangings, poisonings, drownings, stabbings, suicides, explosions, conflagrations, avalanches, earthquakes, eruptions, shipwrecks, trainwrecks, apparitions, tortured

heroines, persecuted heroes, and fearsome villains are only a lengthy prelude to inevitable happiness and the apotheosis of virtue.[2]

Be this as it may, one cannot help wondering what today's moral vigilantes would make of such explicit sex, violence and degradation, even in the cause of moral enlightenment!

The audiences for such fare were essentially urban and working-class, buying a little relief from the new-found tedium of factory labour with the increase in wages that accompanied it. Initially, these pieces dealt with simple subjects, painted large, but with the development of technical expertise and stage machinery, coupled with the increasing demands of an ever more blasé audience, the settings and subjects became more and more spectacular. (Some would argue that the 'hi-tech' musicals of the late 1980s are products of the same demands.)

The ensuing 'Sensation Drama' as epitomised by the work of Dion Boucicault and Augustin Daly more than matched the melodrama in popularity. Boucicault (1820-90) established the Sensation Scene with his *Poor of New York* (1857), the title of which would vary with the venue of the performance. Boucicault's considerable influence on a number of *genres* will be considered elsewhere but the summary of just one subsequent sensation drama, *The World* by Augustus Harris and Paul Meritt (1880), encapsulates the sort of thing that was demanded, a spectacle that would have taxed the ingenuity of the stage machinists far more than the technique of the actors:

> Returning from South Africa to inherit his estates, Clement Huntingford sails in a ship sunk by a bomb planted in the hold by two swindlers who have heavily insured a consignment of diamonds that does not contain diamonds at all. Huntingford puts the heroine, Mary, returning to England to marry his brother, safely in a boat but himself suffers fearfully on a raft with a thirst-crazed passenger, whose frantic attempt to drink the remaining water results in the water being spilt; luckily a ship sights them. In England, Huntingford's brother, Harry, denounces him as a mad impostor when he claims the estates and has him locked up in a lunatic asylum run by two insane doctors. Although he is already married, Harry also pursues Mary. Clement escapes. In attempting to seize Mary, Harry is locked in a lift shaft and crushed to death by the descending lift; two other villains – the play is remarkable for having seven – are arrested at a fancy dress ball.[3]

It is hardly surprising that audiences which had come to demand and expect such sensationalism might find the subtleties and apparent passivity of Chekhov's work rather tame by comparison.

To stage such pieces demanded considerable improvement in production techniques from those satirised by Charles Dickens fifty years before in

Nicholas Nickleby. Vincent Crummles, the actor-manager, instructs Nicholas to write a play:

> 'We'll have a new show-piece out directly,' said the manager. 'Let me see – peculiar resources of this establishment – new and splendid scenery – you must manage to introduce a real pump and two washing tubs.'
> 'Into the piece?' said Nicholas.
> 'Yes,' replied the manager. 'I bought 'em cheap, at a sale the other day; and they'll come in admirably...It'll look very well in the bills in separate lines – Real pump! – Splendid tubs! – Great attraction...'

The attractions available in the London theatres were remarkable indeed; at Sadler's Wells there were tanks of water so that the stage could 'house' a sea battle; cascading waterfalls and erupting volcanoes appeared on stage, trap doors opened, backdrops rose and fell, gauzes created magic transformations and, with the introduction of the 'diorama', the scroll-like moving backcloth, the impression of armies marching or horses galloping could be produced on stage.

In spite of these technical innovations, there was also a move towards more controlled, 'directed' playing of the less fantastic plays, so that the development of a theatre that was more realistic in both style and content was evident in Britain even before the conscious theorising of naturalism was heard and its end products seen.

While the content of much of his writing may have been light-weight, W.S. Gilbert was viewed by his actors as 'a dreaded director' and he ascribed the instigation of such direction, called 'stage-management' at the time, to T.W. Robertson, a nineteenth-century playwright of rather mediocre talents but one who insisted on as realistic as possible reproduction of everyday activities in his plays, albeit for comic effect.

'It was an unknown art before his time,' wrote Gilbert:

> Formerly, in a conversation scene, for instance, you simply brought down two or three chairs from the flat and placed them in a row in the middle of the stage, and the people sat down and talked, and when the conversation was ended the chairs were replaced. Robertson showed how to give life and variety and nature to the scene by breaking it up with all sorts of incidents and delicate by-play.

'Realism', which has been described as the representation of unheroic everyday life, was appearing without anyone really knowing it, but the desire for melodrama was still strong.

Viewed with the assumed sophistication of hind-sight, melodrama may often appear comic; eventually, this is how many of the plays came to be taken, with the obvious result that the *genre* was actively burlesqued. *Gentle*

Gertrude, or Doomed, Drugged and Drowned at Datchet by T.E. Pemberton, and *Pure as the Driven Snow* by Paul Loomis, were among those written as intentional parodies of an infinitely 'parodiable' form. However, with such original lines as:

'Ha! Baffled! And by a woman too! Confusion!' (*The Tempter*, 1833)

and:

'Rage on, beautiful tigress, rage on! Your scorn but adds fresh charms
to your perfection – fresh zest to my desire!' (*Khartoum*, 1885)

it is very difficult for us now to imagine how they could ever have been uttered in earnest.

However, the reason why they *were* accepted – and, co-incidentally, why Chekhov's *The Seagull* failed initially in Moscow – was a style of acting which matched and on occasions surpassed the demands made by such unrealistic dialogue. In an actor's manual *The Actor's Art* by Gustave Garcia published in 1882, the enthusiastic thespian, in order to display Anger, is advised: 'All the muscles of the body acquire a convulsive power. The eyes become fiery and roll in their orbits. The hands contract violently, the mouth foams, the teeth grind fiercely. The whole body, equally the soul, is in convulsions. The veins of the neck and temple swell; the blood rushes to the face; the movements are violent.'

Grief, on the other hand, should be: 'Sudden and violent; expresses itself by beating the head or forehead, tearing the hair and catching the breath, as if choking – also by screaming, weeping, stamping the feet, lifting the eyes from time to time to Heaven and hurrying backwards and forwards' (The *Thespian Preceptor*). One dreads to think what actors trained in such a school would have done to the superficial calm and torpor of Chekhov, or how Masha's line: 'I am in mourning for my life. I am unhappy' must have fared at the hands of exponents of such Grief.

It is said that, at such a distance, we cannot really know how these pieces were played, what *Maria Martin* or *The Demon Barber of Fleet Street* were like, how the legendary line from *East Lynne* – 'Dead! And never called me "Mother"!' – was delivered, but a glance at the acting in early silent films proclaims their indebtedness to the melodramas of the previous century. The heavily-mascara'd, doe-eyed heroines tied to railway tracks by vast, hirsute and dastardly villains were direct descendants, daughters if not actual sisters, of the heroines of melodrama who nightly suffered the same fate on stage. Thomas Erle's description of a villain from the London stage of 1860 could well fit some of Chaplin's adversaries some fifty years later: '...corked up to such a pitch that his face rivals in blackness that of a metropolitan statue' while 'his forehead is ploughed with...prodigious wrinkles, indicative of his "haggard mind" '.

This simplistic, obvious characterisation was adopted and developed by the early cinema, but while cinema was a new medium, a new art form, ready and able to grow, the stage melodrama was, by the beginning of the new century, on the decline. While the cinema might well be called the child of the melodrama, it was, like many healthy and ambitious offspring, later to usurp and eventually destroy its progenitor.

However, it was not only the cinema that caused the decline of melodrama; throughout Europe, the momentum that had encouraged Gilbert and Tom Robertson to be more life-like in their direction was growing. The movement away from the heroic and romantic towards more commonplace subject matter that was evolving in other areas of literature was gradually being felt in the theatre

It was in the French novel that this transition was first experienced; Flaubert, Balzac, Maupassant and the Goncourt Brothers all contributed influential works. *Madame Bovary* dealt with the provincial bourgeoisie while *Boule de Suif* actually had a common prostitute as its heroine. However, it was the younger Emile Zola (1840-1902) who was to experiment even further with the characters and language in his novels, taking the working-class bars of Paris or the mines and the peasant farms of the countryside as settings for his novels, works that would eventually be described as Naturalistic. It was not just that he was attempting a more 'realistic' depiction of life but also dealing with the lower social classes and their inherent problems, subjects and settings that hitherto were considered not worthy of such interest.

Not all the experiments were successful; there were attempts to dramatise some of Zola's novels and an examination of the picture of the set for *L'Assommoir* (see illustrations) will show the dangers that excessive attention to realistic detail can have on a production. However, in his Preface to the published dramatisation of *Thérèse Raquin*, Zola states his faith in the new movement:

> ...painting has become completely real...the novel, that individual social study, of such a supple form, now infinitely enlarged, has completely established itself...These are facts that none can deny...that is why I am absolutely convinced that soon we shall see naturalism imposing itself upon the theatre, bringing to it this power of reality, the new life force in modern art...The drama will die unless a new vigour rejuvenates it. The body needs blood. People claim that the operetta and the spectacle have killed the drama. That is wrong; the drama is dying its own death, dying of extravagance, lies and platitudes...there should be no more literary schools, no more formulae, no more pundits of any sort; there is only Life, an immense field where everyone can study and create after his own fashion...I have the deep conviction – and I insist upon this – that the experimental, scientific spirit of the age will reach the theatre and that it can be the only possible regeneration for our stage...Drama will either die or be modern and realistic...

Despite Zola's theories and ideals, his dramatisation of the novel is not particularly impressive, as it inevitably indulges in over-long monologues to put across the story line while the multiple suicide of Thérèse and Laurent, drinking prussic acid under the vengeful eye of Madame Raquin, is worthy of the most hackneyed melodramatist. However, his theories and his novels inspired others.

Across Europe, from Moscow to Dublin, men who were eventually to be regarded as revolutionaries were at work. The names of Ibsen, Chekhov, Strindberg, Stanislavsky, Hauptmann, Shaw and Synge may now appear to be engraved alongside those of Aristophanes, Shakespeare, Molière and Goethe in a Dramatic Hall of Fame but, at the turn of the century, they were the 'angry young men' of their time, reacting against a trite and light-weight theatre, daring to examine new and perhaps shocking subjects in innovative and exciting ways.

Revolutions need leaders, even ones that are unaware of their disciples. They may simply be figure-heads, outstanding or charismatic enough for the populace to rally round, or else they may be theoreticians whose manifestoes disseminate subversion. In the case of the new movement in the theatre, the Norwegian poet and playwright, Henrick Ibsen (1828-1906), was hailed as this leader. In Britain, what was eventually called 'Naturalism' started under the name of 'Ibsenism' – George Bernard Shaw's 1890 defence being called *The Quintessence of Ibsenism* – and Ibsen is often credited with the paternity of the school. His play *Ghosts* (1881) appears regularly as *the* seminal piece that inspired many of his younger disciples, although, given its subject of hereditary venereal disease, perhaps 'seminal' is an unsuitable description.

However, while he was content to accept the eventual admiration of the 'avant-garde', Ibsen was not one to wait for the crowd to catch up so that he might lead the rabble in their assault on the Establishment. Like many innovators, Ibsen was ahead of his time and consciously so.

He was not the theoretician that Strindberg and Shaw were to become and nothing could have been less naturalistic than his early verse dramas, *Peer Gynt* and *Brand*. Ibsen saw himself as a poet and these unwieldy masterpieces were not initially intended for the stage. When he was eventually persuaded to have them produced, they ran for up to seven hours each!

However, the publication of *Brand* was a considerable commercial success, which provided Ibsen with the wherewithal to survive in self-imposed exile in Rome where he found the freedom to write *A Doll's House* (1879), *Ghosts* (1881) and *An Enemy of the People* (1882). They each dealt with powerful social themes and, despite his insistence that such was not the case, were viewed respectively as effective attacks on the restricted role of women in society, venereal disease and commercial exploitation versus the demands of public health.

Unfortunately, Ibsen would not stay within the new Naturalistic pigeon-hole that critics and acolytes alike had constructed for him; his later work, such as *The Master Builder* and *When We Dead Awaken*, displays a healthy disregard for such categorisation. The early works, for example, were not only in that most 'unnatural' of all speech forms, verse, but were also full of allegory and symbolism, a word which, when presented as a proper noun, was to characterise a future movement that was to be a reaction *against* Naturalism. In his introduction to his translation of *Brand*, Dr Gathorne-Hardy summarises the last act thus:

> The concluding scenes...must similarly be judged as poetic allegory. A literal interpretation can only see Brand's action as sheer madness. To start a revival movement by leading a flock of untrained and ignorant peasants, without thought of food or shelter, into a wilderness of uninhabited mountains must seem, in cold prose, the act of a dangerous lunatic; but it becomes a most impressive picture if regarded as poetic imagery – a heroic trumpet call to forsake the cramped and sunless security of a rock-bound cleft, and to struggle towards the light and breadth of vision attainable on the heights nearer heaven!

The earlier, better-known piece, *Peer Gynt*, is full of equally evident allegory, from the onion with no heart that the old Peer likens himself to, to the mysterious Button Moulder with his ladle for melting down human souls; hardly the sort of material that should incite such criticism as: 'a dramatist who, apart from the non-construction of his alleged plays, deliberately selects his subjects from the most sordid, abject, even the most revolting corners of human life, relieving the crushing effect of their hideous monotony only by a mechanical joyless mirth like the crackling of thorns.' Or a review of *Ghosts* from the *News of the World* which proves that not much has changed in the realms of populist journalism in the past century: 'The work of a crazy foreigner which is neither fish nor flesh but is unmistakably foul.'

In fact, the change in the content and style of Ibsen's work from the 'poetic' to the 'realistic' was not as drastic as some critics may suggest. Ibsen was an innovator, albeit of genius, who was motivated by instinct rather than theory, moving on to subjects that interested him rather than fulfilled any specific criteria of a new literary movement that had to run along prescribed and obvious rails. When replying to Georg Brandes on the subject of Dr Stockman, his hero of *An Enemy of the People* (1882), Ibsen applied the same argument to himself:

> I maintain that a fighter in the intellectual vanguard cannot possibly gather a majority around himself...the majority, the mass, the mob will never catch up with him. As regards myself, at least, I am quite aware of such unceasing progress. At the point where I stood when I wrote each of my books there now stands a tolerably compact

crowd; but I myself am no longer there. I am elsewhere; farther ahead, I hope.

He is aware of his position but he is also insistent that he is ahead of the crowd. Dr Stockmann's final line is: 'The strongest man in the world is he who stands alone!' and while Ibsen dilutes the supremacy of this claim with a little cosy comedy in the last few lines of the play, it is evident that this is also how he saw himself.

His works were both condemned and extolled for their content; *Ghosts* deals with the effects of inherited venereal disease; *An Enemy of the People* with industrial pollution; *A Doll's House* with the role of women in society – all good, meaningful issues to be presented in the new, naturalistic manner. However, it is not difficult to discover the moral behind these dramatised sermons or to grasp the allegorical meanings of the symbols: the venereal disease is destroying the son's brain in *Ghosts*, a blatant example of the sins of the father being visited on the son, epitomising the moral ills that are destroying society; the effluent from the tannery that pollutes the public baths in *An Enemy of the People* is a similar image, while the very title of *A Doll's House* underlines Ibsen's implication. Such themes are not inexplicable changes in artistic direction for the creator of the Button Moulder, the Boyg and Brand. Some of Ibsen's works can be seen as flagships for the Naturalistic movement but they are essentially stages in the progression of a remarkable writer, and while Ibsen remained the 'fighter in the intellectual vanguard', his later plays refused to fit easily into the new Naturalistic category; however, he had sown seeds, particularly with *Ghosts*, that were to influence a whole generation of writers, producers and theatre-going audiences.

Anton Chekhov (1860-1904) is the other playwright to whom the fathering of the Naturalistic movement is often attributed, although this is partly because Stanislavsky and Nemirovich-Danchenko at the Moscow Art Theatre used his mature works – *The Seagull* (1896), *Uncle Vanya* (1899), *The Three Sisters* (1901) and *The Cherry Orchard* (1904) – as vehicles for their developing theories on more realistic styles of playing. Chekhov had a great respect for the works of Ibsen and insisted on seeing whatever of his he could. In a letter to A.L. Vishevsky, he wrote: 'As I am soon coming to Moscow, please keep a ticket for me for *The Pillars of Society*. I want to see the marvellous Norwegian acting and I will even pay for my seat. You know Ibsen is my favourite writer.'

Chekhov, like Ibsen, dealt in allegory: what else is the dead seagull? Or the cherry orchard, beloved of the decadent aristocratic family, bought by the 'nouveau-riche' and chopped down for development? He also confined his work to the portrayal of a privileged circle, far away from Zola's peasants and similar to the society in which the British 'Comedy of Manners' was set; indeed, he insisted that his plays were social comedies. What made the work different and exciting was a style of writing, of implication rather than explanation, of action between and behind the lines, all of which necessitated a new style of playing, a style which previously had not existed.

It was, however, not a development that happened overnight. In 1895, after the first performance of *The Seagull*, Chekhov wrote: 'The actors played more than stupidly!...I shall never either write plays or have them acted.'[4] But four days later, common sense, along with a touch of self-diagnosis, prevailed; we tend to forget that Chekhov was a country physician who, to begin with, simply wrote as a pastime. 'When I got home, I took a dose of castor oil, had a cold bath and am ready to write another play.'[5]

From his plays and letters, we see Chekhov as a mixture of astute critic and naive provincial; the unworldy innocence is reflected in Vanya, Nina, even Madame Ranevsky, while each piece is a gentle, comic, sad but unrelenting critique of a society in decline.

When it came to viewing his own creations, the innocent and the critic were both in evidence. Summarising *The Seagull*, he described it as 'a great deal of conversation about literature, little action, tons of love',[6] and this the piece that contains the role of 'Nina', one that young actresses place alongside Juliet in their tragic repertoire! Equally, there is no hint of false modesty when writing of his masterpiece: 'At the first performance of *The Cherry Orchard* on the 17th January, they gave me an ovation so lavish, warm and really so unexpected that I can't get over it even now.'[7]

Much has been made of Chekhov's debt to Stanislavsky and his co-director of the Moscow Art Theatre, Nemirovich-Danchenko. True, they provided – eventually – a style of playing that suited Chekhov's subtleties and – eventually – Chekhov's praise was lavish: 'Please do just as you like about the scenery (for *The Cherry Orchard*) I leave it entirely to you; I am amazed and generally sit with my mouth wide open at your theatre. There is no question about it, whatever you do will be excellent, a hundred times better than anything I could invent.'[8]

However, he was not always so enthusiastic about the actors. He wrote of the Moscow Art Theatre that: 'it is the most ordinary kind of theatre, and things are managed there pretty much as elsewhere, only the actors are intelligent, very sensible people; true, they do not burst with talent, but they try, they like their work and they study their parts.'[9]

Elsewhere he describes actors as: 'a good lot but uneducated topers', while he firmly puts them in their place in an 1888 letter: 'The public, however stupid, is generally more clever, more sincere and more sympathetic than...the actors.' And he has a theory for this limitation: 'Sazonov plays abominably in *The Bear* (an early short play of Chekhov's). That is very comprehensible. Actors never observe ordinary people...On the other hand, they can represent to the life mistresses, empty sharpers and, in general, all those individuals whom they observe by chance roaming about the eating houses and bachelor companies. Their ignorance is astounding.'[10]

Chekhov had very definite views about how his plays should be played. He recognised the ability of Stanislavsky, whose attention to naturalistic detail in characterisation helped the realistic staging of Chekhov's work. (It was also to metamorphose into the mumblings and slouchings that were the worst aspects of the 'Method' school of acting as epitomised by the Marlon Brando lookalikes in American films of the 50s.) Chekhov, however, never allowed theory to oust technique and would contradict Stanislavsky when his insistences were in danger of unbalancing the whole. 'Do not spend much time on it', he wrote to an actor about the nervousness of the character he was to play; 'present it as only one of many typical traits. I know Konstantin Sergeyevich (Stanislavsky) will insist on this superfluous nervousness; he exaggerates it but do not yield; do not sacrifice the beauty and power of the voice for the sake of such a detail as the accent. Do not make the sacrifice because in this case the irritation is only a detail!'[11]

However, while he was capable of practical opposition to Stanislavsky's schemes, he also allowed himself moments of theorising, even at the expense of contradicting himself. As early as 1887, he explained that: 'artistic literature is called so just because it depicts life as it really is, the aim is truth, unconditional and honest'[12], while six years later he claimed 'writers are the children of their age and therefore like the rest of the public, ought to surrender to the external conditions of society. Thus they must be absolutely decent. Only this have we the right to require of the realists.'[13] This is hardly the advocacy of artistic anarchy and it is to be doubted whether he would have approved of Ibsen's *Ghosts*, or of the decapitation of the finch in Strindberg's *Miss Julie* – let alone the seduction of Julie by the valet, Jean – while the subject of prostitution raised by Shaw in *Mrs Warren's Profession* would hardly have been 'decent' in Chekhov's eyes. His so-called realism was not a brash naturalism, the product of rebellious and youthful revolutionaries; in fact, it can be argued that Chekhov's plays are exceptionally stylised. And while the society depicted in his plays may be seen as ripe for revolution, it is difficult to be sure that such judgements have not been made with the invaluable help of hindsight. Those revolutionaries who do appear in the plays are essentially comic, while the pervading humour is not one of anger and violence but more of sadness, sensitivity and wry criticism. Michel Saint-Denis, one of the most influential men in mid-century European theatre, wrote of *The Cherry Orchard* that 'it is impressionistic art and you can't take a written line at its face value. The elementary meaning is given by the very story told by the play: the theme is simple, but it is played upon, from act to act, in so many ways, by so many characters, in so many shades, that its material aspect disappears; the story is a pretext, well chosen, to make us discover...an unforgettable vision of laughing, suffering and lovable humanity.'[14]

More definite demands for revolution were being made, though. When we think of French theatre prior to this century, we automatically picture the staple three-course diet of Corneille, Racine and Molière with occasional *entremets* and *amuse-gueules* such as those provided by Beaumarchais and Feydeau. Of course, this, like any other generalisation, is unfair, but for the English amateur, such is the restriction. However, the French have always possessed a radical spark ready to oppose conservatism. From the marvellous monk who gave the world Gargantua and Pantagruel, Molière ready to depict and deflate the various pomposities of man, Voltaire with his innocent Candide reflecting on bigotry, avarice, and excessive, unfounded optimism, right up to the revolutionaries of 1789 and the idealists of 1968, this crusading zeal has been a part of the national character. In André Antoine, a Parisian gas company worker with theatrical aspirations, France produced a figure who was to be as influential practically as Ibsen and Chekhov were textually in this pan-european move towards a more naturalistic theatre.

In 1887, Antoine opened 'Le Théâtre Libre', a move that was to be copied in Berlin with 'die freie Bühne' and, eventually, in England with J.T. Grein's 'Independent Theatre Society'. 'Le Théâtre Libre' provided a venue for the work of the new generation of playwrights that was following Ibsen's lead and Zola's exhortations. To accompany this, Antoine made fresh demands of his actors, demands reminiscent of Chekhov, though made in true manifesto style:

> In view of the hoped-for generation of new playwrights, there will be needed a new generation of actors...the actor will no longer 'speak his lines' in the classical manner; he will say them naturally, which is just as difficult to learn...Purely mechanical movements, vocal effects, irrational and superfluous gestures will be banished. Dramatic action will be simplified by a return to reality and natural gestures...feelings will be expressed by familiar and real accessories; a pencil turned round, a cup overturned, will be as significant and have an effect as intense...as the grandiloquent exaggerations of the romantic drama.

And this only five years after the publication of Gustave Garcia's dictates on the portrayal of Anger on stage.

Antoine's 'hoped-for generation of new playwrights' did indeed appear, with the fervid person of August Strindberg at their head. He shared Antoine's views on staging plays, reflecting the undercurrent of dissatisfaction with the technical state of European theatre, and saw in himself, the necessary messiah. He was not hampered by an excess of modesty; he boasts of his play-writing prowess in a letter to an actor-friend: 'There need never be any shortage of material, for I can write a one-act play in two days.'[15] Although his early masterpiece *Miss Julie* took more like two weeks than two days to complete, Strindberg's manic energy and achievements were astonishing: 'He wrote sixty-two plays...in violent and spasmodic bursts of activity punctuated by years of, as far as the theatre was concerned, silence...In addition, he composed innumerable novels, volumes of essays and short stories, memoirs, poems, and theses on science, philosophy, and philology; his collected works fill over fifty volumes.'[16] As an example of his play-writing fury, he wrote twenty-six separate pieces in the five years between 1898 and 1903.

He was writing under the immediate influence of the works of Nietzsche, whose theories on the Superman can have done little to quell Strindberg's messianic complex, and it is interesting to note that, despite his ignorance of Freud's contemporaneous work, Strindberg was, more than any of the others collected under the fortunate umbrella of Naturalism, the explorer of 'the dark corners of the human soul which most of us seal off like poisoned wells'.[17]

In his Preface to *Miss Julie*, Strindberg offers an angry and honest view of the state of the art. The whole of it is worth close examination, expressing as it does his views on the suitable contents of a play, but he also examines the technical aspects of the theatre, from the dimensions of the auditorium to the make-up on the actors' faces. He is particularly scathing of contemporary actors: 'I do not dream that I shall ever see the full back of an actor throughout the whole of an important scene but I do fervently wish that the vital scenes should not be played opposite the prompter's box as though they were duets milking applause.'

Obviously the natural tendency of many a bad actor to find himself down-stage centre is not a new phenomenon; he adds, 'a word about make-up; which I dare not hope will be listened to by the ladies who prefer beauty to truth...In a modern psychological drama, where the subtler reactions should be mirrored in the face rather than in gesture and sound, it would surely be best to experiment with strong side-lighting on a small stage and with the actor wearing no make-up, or at best a minimum.'[18] While these may have been dismissed at the time as the rantings of an obsessive maniac, perhaps such a magnificent obsession would not be amiss today.

Strindberg even proposed radical changes in the auditoria themselves, many of which have since been effected.

> If we could then dispense with the visible orchestra, with their distracting lampshades and faces turned towards the audience; if we could have stalls raised so that the spectators' sightlines would be above the actors' knees; if we could get rid of the side-boxes (my particular 'bête-noir') with their tittering diners and ladies nibbling at cold collations, and have complete darkness in the auditorium during the performances; and, first and foremost, a *small* stage and a *small* auditorium – then perhaps a new drama might emerge, and the theatre might once again become the place for educated people.[19]

The arrogance may be reprehensible but the enthusiasm is admirable, an enthusiasm which translates theory into practice in his plays.

However, Strindberg's plays, like those of Ibsen, were not written to a formula and, like Ibsen, Strindberg cannot be categorised simply, even though some of his work can fit some of the '-isms' some of the time. He was to continue to change throughout his tortured life and to be viewed as an ally and mentor by many in the varying vanguards of the 'avant-garde', the very existence of which was testament to the questioning and experimentation that he had inspired.

Following Antoine's example of 'Le Théâtre Libre' in Paris, Otto Brahm founded a society called 'die freie Bühne' in Berlin and introduced Ibsen's *Ghosts* in September 1889. A few months later and the first work of the major German contributor to the Naturalistic movement was given its world premiere.

Gerhart Hauptmann (1862-1946) had been greatly impressed by a production of Ibsen's *Nora* that he had seen at the Deutsches Theater, describing it as 'a flourish of trumpets'; he moved away from his novel-writing, where he had been influenced by that other great force, Zola, and wrote a piece for the theatre. *Vor Sonnenaufgang* (*Before Dawn*) (1889), trod the same sort of paths as Zola and Gorki, dealing as it did with heredity, alcoholism and the new feeling of Socialism. It has to be said that, like Zola's dramatic attempts, it smacks more than a little of the melodrama but Hauptmann's champion, Professor Behl, writes that 'it was, however, more than a copy of reality; it was vigorously moulded, poetically magnified realism'.[20]

It also led to Hauptmann's naturalistic masterpiece, *Die Weber* (*The Weavers*), also staged by 'die freie Bühne'. Here, Hauptmann was again dealing with abject poverty and social injustice but what makes it remarkable in the context of theatrical history is that it not only presaged Brecht's 'epic' style but was also 'hero-less' or, rather, had a whole group of people, the exploited cottage-weavers of Silesia, as its main character. This piece, written when he was only thirty, proved to be the high point when one looks at Hauptmann's contribution to modern theatre for, while he was to continue writing for almost fifty years and to be awarded the Nobel Prize for Literature in 1912, his work, like that of Ibsen and Strindberg, moved away from the realistic towards the allegorical, the spiritual and – as it so proved – the less theatrically effective; this inclination is evident even in an early piece, *Hanneles Himmelfahrt* (*Hannah's Ascension*) which deals with a dying child's vision of Heaven and is distinctly 'fey'.

Die Weber, however, aroused great interest. Fontane, the German poet, wrote to Hauptmann in guarded support of a work the content of which was more than dubious for its time: 'Because I admire the vigorous and the honest, the unvarnished truth...I can disregard entirely the social and political aspects of your work' for 'there is in that which to the layman merely appears as a true copy of life a degree of art greater than can be imagined.'[21] It is this so-called copying of life while at the same time producing a valid work of art and, what is more important, an effective piece of theatre that makes these early works of Hauptmann so special. In fact, Behl goes so far as to claim that: 'the first performance of *Die Weber* was undoubtedly the greatest and most stirring event in the more recent history of the German theatre',[22] a claim made in 1956, one supposes, in the light of the entire canon of Brecht's work, not to mention that of Wedekind, Sternheim, Kaiser, Zuckmayer, Dürrenmatt and their peers.

Britain, as was so often to be the case in theatrical innovation, lagged behind Europe and it was not until 1891 that a Dutchman, J.T. Grein, began the private club, the Independent Theatre Society, which aimed to 'give special performances of plays which have a Literary and Artistic, rather than a commercial, value'. (Why 'Literary' and 'Artistic' should merit capital letters and 'commercial' should not, and why the latter epithet should be mutually exclusive to the two former is by no means obvious, but alas, it would seem that 'twas ever thus!)

The Independent Theatre Society, as elsewhere, opened its assault upon the Establishment with *Ghosts* which appears to have been designated the battering ram of the 'new' theatre against the portals of the old, offending many of its first audiences. However, as with many offences, the result was to leave the defences down, open to subsequent incursions, the most significant of which was the metamorphosis of George Bernard Shaw (1856-1950) from critic to creator.

The end of the century saw the transformation of the Independent Theatre Society to the Incorporated Stage Society (soon to lose its 'Incorporated') and this organisation was the first to stage Shaw's early plays, *Widowers' Houses*, a tract opposing slum-landlordism, and the better-written and far more controversial *Mrs Warren's Profession* which dealt with one of the many taboo subjects, prostitution.

These were the first two pieces of work that were *for* the theatre rather than *about* it from the pen of one of the major influences on the theatre of the twentieth century. Arguably the finest English playwright of that century – and in his own opinion, of any century – he was, of course, an Irishman and his influences will be examined further in later chapters. However, by the beginning of the twentieth century, Shaw had become positively involved in play-writing, Ibsen had written his last play *When We Dead Awaken*, Strindberg was moving towards an obsession with the occult, dreams and death, while Chekhov was at the height of his powers, having already written *The Seagull* and *Uncle Vanya* and soon to produce *The Three Sisters* (1901) and *The Cherry Orchard* (1904). 'Ibsenism', Naturalism, Realism – whatever the name might be for the movement that had opposed the excesses of the operetta, the sensation drama and the melodrama – was firmly established

alongside its opponents and was, indeed, already attracting young denigra-
tors of its own. In fact, melodrama, sensation drama, romantic drama,
naturalistic drama, drama of allegory, symbol and dream, not to mention
vaudeville, music hall, pantomime, operetta, musical comedy and burlesque,
were all pretty well patronised in these first years of the new century. In spite
of Strindberg's obituary, the reports of the death of the Theatre seemed
somewhat premature; what needs to be seen is whether, one hundred years
later, his warnings may not at last be coming true.

Ten plays for further consideration

1. Dion Boucicault, *The Poor of New York*
2. Various, *Sweeney Todd – the Demon Barber of Fleet Street*
3. Henrik Ibsen, *Peer Gynt*
4. Henrik Ibsen, *Ghosts*
5. August Strindberg, *Miss Julie*
6. August Strindberg, *To Damascus*
7. Anton Chekhov, *The Seagull*
8. Anton Chekhov, *The Cherry Orchard*
9. Gerhart Hauptmann, *The Weavers*
10. George Bernard Shaw, *Mrs Warren's Profession*

Notes

1. Michael Booth, *English Melodrama*, p. 14
2. ibid.
3. ibid., p. 141
4. A.P. Chekhov, *Collected Letters*, ed. Blom, p. 147
5. ibid., p. 148
6. ibid., p. 145
7. ibid., p. 163
8. ibid., p. 162
9. ibid., p. 188
10. ibid., p. 193
11. ibid., p. 184
12. ibid., p. 275
13. ibid.
14. Michel Saint-Denis, introduction to *The Cherry Orchard*, p. viii
15. Letter from August Strindberg to August Lindberg, Strindberg, *Collected Works*, trans. Meyer, p. 91

16. Strindberg, op. cit., p. 8
17. ibid., p. 11
18. ibid., Strindberg, Preface to *Miss Julie*, p. 111
19. ibid., p. 112
20. C.F.W. Behl, *Gerhart Hauptmann*
21. Fontane, quoted by Behl, op. cit.
22. Behl, op. cit.

2: THE GERMAN LEGACY

If the average student of the theatre were asked to name a twentieth-century German playwright, it is likely that, in spite of Hauptmann's Nobel prize, the answer would be Bertolt Brecht (1898-1956). Brecht, like Shaw and Pinter, has such an individual and original style that his name has come to be used adjectivally in describing other authors' work. As with a play by Beckett, a piece of Brecht's mature work is instantly recognisable; there is the didactic element, the socialist polemic, the use of rough song and stark characterisation and, most distinctive, the constant awareness of its own theatricality. However, although he issued authoritative and even authoritarian edicts upon the Theatre and possessed an undeniable genius, it is not as though Brecht sprang immaculate and complete into this world. He, like every other artist, had influences and ideals, heroes and abominations, all of which went towards his development.

Brecht was born in 1898 and grew up in a pre-war Germany that was experiencing one of the most exciting artistic movements of this and perhaps any other century. As with other so-called revolutions, Expressionism – a name borrowed from the world of graphic art – was a reaction of the young against what they thought to be the status quo, the Romanticism and Naturalism of the end of the previous century. The movement was to reach a peak in the years after the First World War and not only affected the theatre but also the worlds of art, opera and the cinema; in fact, 'stills' from *Nosferatu* and *The Cabinet of Dr Caligari* help us to envisage other work in the movement.

'Expressionist' has become to mean a certain 'non-realistic', almost surreal, technical style; this ignores the philosophical content that many of the early writers saw as the more important aspect of their work. It is the style that interested and influenced such American playwrights as Eugene O'Neill, Clifford Odets, Elmer Rice, Edward Albee, even Arthur Miller and Tennessee Williams; however, before it is possible to examine the movement more fully, it is necessary to look at two earlier originals whose work has not only proved more lasting than much of the ephemera of Expressionism but which also stimulated the new movement and influenced much of subsequent European theatre.

The life of Georg Büchner cannot by any stretching of the calendar be placed chronologically within the twentieth century but his few plays and fragments were so far ahead of his time that they were not staged until this century and so must be considered here.

He was born in October 1813 and died of typhus in February 1837. His only experience of the theatre was through the reading of plays, where his heroes were Lenz and Shakespeare; he never heard a word of his spoken on a stage but in *Danton's Death* (written in 1835 but not staged until 1903), and more especially in *Woyzeck* (written 1837, staged 1913), he wrote two remarkable pieces which are refreshing even now, some century and a half after their creation; with their inter-cut structure, abandoning any notion of the unities of time or place, they not only presage Brecht but are more reminiscent of film-scripts than conventional stage plays.

Büchner intended to follow a career in medicine and, at the time of his premature death, had just been appointed to a lectureship in anatomy at the University of Zürich. Coupled with his arduous medical studies and his spare-time reading of the classics, he was also intensely interested in politics, a propensity that was encouraged during his student years in Strasbourg.

In order to practise medicine in Germany, it was necessary to have studied in a German university and so Büchner went to Giessen. The repressive atmosphere of that small state, after the comparative freedom of Strasbourg, brought his subversive views to the fore. His first publication was a political pamphlet, *The Hessian Courier*, which demonstrates the intensity of Büchner's commitment more than the wisdom of his judgement: 'The life of the rich is one long Sunday... the people lie before them like dung on the fields. The peasant walks behind the plough: but the rich man walks behind peasant and plough, driving both him and his oxen, taking the grain and leaving the stubble!' This may not appear to be anything particularly original from the distance of 150 years but if one considers that Büchner was dead before Karl Marx had started work, then perhaps we achieve a fairer perspective on his radicalism.

The pamphlet was printed but never properly distributed; a number of Büchner's friends were arrested for attempting its distribution but Büchner escaped, returning to the family home in Darmstadt where he continued with his studies, all the while working on his play *Danton's Death* in secret. Legend has it that his brother would keep watch on the stairs while he wrote and that he would hide the manuscript under his medical books whenever his father came into the room.

It has to be admitted that *Danton's Death* is rather static and, with thirty-two scenes, more than thirty named characters and a list of extras that includes: 'Ladies at gaming tables...citizens, citizen-soldiers...Jacobins, presidents of the Jacobin club and the national convention: turnkeys, hangmen and carters...grisettes, a ballad singer, a boy etc.', it would take a considerable company to stage it today. There are indeed productions, and effective ones at that, but the main lesson to be learned from *Danton's Death*, perhaps, is that the theatre can often be a far more effective political weapon than any pamphlet, no matter how forcefully written.

The lack of dramatic conflict in *Danton's Death* has been taken by some to be not so much a weakness but more a positive strength, although such advocates do seem to view any aspect that supports their theses as inevitable and that the coming of their Messiah, Brecht, was the obvious culmination of, and only reason for, the existence of these earlier authors:

> The absence of genuine conflict contributes to making *Danton's Death* as formally significant as it is in the history of epic theatre. To say...that the play lacks conflict as well as crisis and struggle, and to say so disappointingly, is not to be fully alert to the anti-Aristotelian vantage point from which Büchner wrote. Like Brecht, he sought a dramatic form to emphasise the extent to which character does not control reality, but vice versa. The result would be less dramatic in the conventional sense, but this is wholly deliberate. Undramatic should not become a pejorative here; at stake is a cooled off concept of dramatic experience that Brecht would champion a century later.[1]

Faced with such advocacy for Büchner as the John the Baptist to Brecht's Messiah, it seems heretical to suggest that perhaps such theories may not have been so firmly established in a twenty-one year old medical student but may actually be weaknesses, attributable to inexperience.

Whatever the case may be for *Danton's Death*, Büchner's incomplete masterpiece *Woyzeck* has indeed proved itself to be seminal not only in German twentieth-century theatre but throughout Europe and America. Apart from serving as the libretto for Alban Berg's 1925 opera, it is a work of such originality of content and structure that it has provided models for much later experimental work.

At first sight, particularly to the traditionalist, the subject matter is uninspiring. Based on the true story of a soldier-cum-barber-cum-dogsbody who killed his woman and was hanged for it, the piece appears scrappy; it was written in dialect, has characters that Büchner will only label with a rank or occupation rather than a name, is an amalgam of songs, stories and inarticulate meanderings, especially from the mouth of the protagonist himself, and yet, as Dr Spalter has said, Woyzeck 'is the the most intense character Büchner created, the first nobody in the history of drama whose dimensions disprove the view that tragedy is exclusively for the highborn'.[2]

Woyzeck is a loser, arguably a paranoid schizophrenic. Although such terminology was not coined until the end of the nineteenth century and many commentators prefer to enhance his tragedy by insisting that he remain on this side of insanity, the 'voices' that Woyzeck hears from the walls and the ground – in other words, auditory hallucinations – coupled with the strange lights that he sees in the sky are nowadays recognised as classic symptoms of the illness. Schizoid or not, he is certainly the victim of his social superiors and here Büchner allows himself full rein in his attack on the upper classes as epitomised by the Doctor and the Captain. These characters are not permitted the humanising luxury of a name – a ploy used by later Expressionist writers to imply a reduction in human standing; the one persistently mocks Woyzeck while the other treats him purely as an object of experiment, insisting that he live on a diet of peas and infuriated when the poor man has to relieve himself before arriving at the Doctor's, thereby doing him out of a day's sample for examination.

The only thing of value in Woyzeck's life is Marie, the mother of his child. His is a simple inarticulate love but when Marie, a sensuous, unsubtle girl, is attracted by the animal presence of the Drum Major, Woyzeck's love turns to jealousy. He tries to fight his rival but is easily beaten (hardly surprising for one subsisting on peas); Marie recognises her weakness in a very effective little scene when she quotes from the New Testament story of the woman taken in adultery but also recognises her desires and admits that she cannot change. Eventually, Woyzeck stabs her, is hounded out of a tavern because of the blood on his hands and in an ambiguous final scene wades into a pool to wash away the blood and we are left to decide whether he drowned himself or not.

If ever a man loved 'not wisely but too well', it is Johann Woyzeck, but this is not a great exotic general, the Moor of Venice, but a little private soldier from Leipzig. For such a one to become a figure as tragic as Othello, without even the agency of an Iago to ensnare him, is remarkable indeed. It is not just Büchner's choice of social status for his hero that is revolutionary but the style of the presentation as a whole, in the use of the grotesque caricatures with their implicit social criticism, the fragmented scenes (some twenty-four in as many pages), the use of the fairground and tavern settings that would be much loved and copied by Wedekind and Brecht, the mixture of dialect, regular speech, song and storytelling, all touched with a nihilistic despair more suited to the twentieth rather than the nineteenth century, that makes Büchner's *Woyzeck* so remarkably precocious.

The order in which the scenes are to be played is uncertain, and depends upon which of the versions one consults, but however they are ordered, they produce a sequence of impressions that provide the portrait of the main character. The structure has been likened to that of the early morality plays, such as *Everyman*, the 'Stationendramen' that showed the various stations on the way to the death of the protagonist. This format was to become very popular with the Expressionist playwrights and aspects of 'Epic' theatre also have their roots in this form.

The caricatured characters condemn themselves out of their own mouths. The inhumanity of 'the Doctor' – not even permitted the courtesy of a definite article before his name in the original – is blatant in his examination of the Captain:

> Hm. Puffy. Fat. Thick neck. Subject to apoplexy...Of course you
> may only get it down one side. You may just be half paralysed. Or
> with a bit of luck it may only affect the brain. Then you'll live on like
> some sort of vegetable...if the good Lord decides to paralyse one
> side of your tongue, we'll conduct experiments that will make our
> name go down in history.[3]

Woyzeck himself displays an inarticulacy that would have delighted any student of the Actors Studio. Translating his dialogue or, rather, monologues into any form of intelligible English causes much of the sparsity of the original to disappear; the original dialect drops many of the inflected verb endings of normal German and almost entirely ignores subject pronouns, but the raw poetry of his anguish comes across in the following speech, delivered while contemplating Marie after he has discovered her unfaithfulness:

> Hm. Can't see anything. Can't see anything! O, you should be able
> to see it, should be able to grab hold of it in your fists!...such a big
> fat sin – it stinks so much you could smoke the little angels out of
> Heaven with it. Your mouth is red, Marie – no blisters on it? Oh,
> Marie you're as beautiful as sin. Can mortal sin really be so beautiful?[4]

In the fairground scene with the barker's 'spiel', we have a direct link with the next major figure to influence the Expressionists, a man who was to end his career singing in cabarets with a young Bert Brecht, Frank Wedekind (1864-1918). In *Woyzeck*, the barker shows off a monkey dressed in human clothing, saying: 'Examine this beast as God created him. Nothing to him, see? Then observe the effect of art: he walks upright and has a coat and trousers. Also a sword. The monkey's a soldier – not that that's much, the lowest form of animal life...';[5] in the Prologue to Wedekind's *Erdgeist (Earth Spirit)* (1895) the Animal Tamer does the reverse, introducing his characters as if they were the animals in a menagerie, with Lulu, the main figure in both *Earth Spirit* and its sequel, *Pandora's Box* (1904), carried on and displayed before the audience like a beast. He describes her as a snake and introduces her thus:

> She was created for every abuse,
> To allure and to poison and seduce,
> To murder without leaving any trace

(Tickling Lulu under the chin)

> Sweet creature, now keep in your proper place,
> Not foolish nor affected nor eccentric,
> Even when you fail to please the critic.

You have no right with miaows and spits inhuman
To distort for us the primal form of woman,
With clowning and with pulling stupid faces
To ape for us the childlike simple vices.
You should – I discuss this today lengthily –
Speak naturally and not unnaturally.
For since the earliest time the basic element
Of every art is that it be self-evident.[6]

At a stroke in this Prologue, Wedekind rejects the paths of his contemporary Naturalists and makes claims for stronger stuff. This was written in 1895, at a time when many were still unaware of the works of Ibsen and Hauptmann, let alone preparing to reject them. Earlier in the declamation from the Animal Tamer, a part played by Wedekind himself in early performances (see illustrations), we are told;

The times are bad. Ladies and gentlemen
Who once would crowd before my cage's show,
They honour farces, dramas, operas, Ibsen,
With their most estimable presence now – very meagre stuff.
What do these plays of joys and griefs reveal?
Domestic beasts, well-bred in what they feel,
Who vent their rage on vegetarian fare
And then indulge in a complacent tear,
Just like those others – down in the parterre.
This hero cannot hold his liquor in,
That one's uncertain if his love is genuine.
You hear the third despair of this earth-ball
(For five long acts he groans about it all),
None gives the coup de grâce to do him in.
The wild and lovely animal, the true,
Ladies and gentlemen, only I can show you.[7]

These are, of course, extravagant, controversial claims, but Wedekind was no stranger to controversy. His first play, *Spring Awakening*, was written in 1891 but not performed until 1906 because of its theme of sexual repression, the 'spring awakening' being the traumas of puberty, while the 'Lulu' plays were the subject of an obscenity trial in 1905, not simply because of the crudity of the pun implicit in the German title of the second play, *die Buchse der Pandora*.

Wedekind had worked as an actor, a singer and also in a circus, a medium for which he had great affection, reflected by his choice of setting for the Prologue to *Earth Spirit*. While his earliest influences may have been the Naturalist theatre, the circus with its animals and clowns gave him a taste for the grotesque, which is amply displayed in his plays. The very act of hauling on Lulu as if she were some puppet immediately destroys any pretence at realism, displays the author's attitude towards the character and is as 'alienating' as any effect later to be devised by Brecht.

Class, money and sex are the three major themes dealt with in the German theatre of the first two decades of this century, with war soon to become an inescapable fourth. Poverty had combined with sexual jealousy to drive Woyzeck to his death but, in these early plays of Wedekind, socio-economic forces take a back-seat when faced with the elemental sexual enigma that is Lulu, Wedekind's agent of destruction. To describe her as a heroine would be wrong because she is a sexual cipher, almost a symbol with little or no attempt at characterisation in Wedekind's writing; as such, it must be difficult for an actress to play the part, particularly in the later piece, when Lulu becomes little more than an impersonal weapon of destruction.

She is all things to all men – and women; indeed, her most pathetic fellow victim is the lesbian, Countess Geschwitz, the inclusion of whom is another bold innovation in the play. Lulu's pre-history is non-existent and even her name appears to be arbitrary. Schigolch, her aged and repulsive 'protector' who may also be her father but who certainly is one of her earliest conquests, 'knew' her at twelve and calls her 'Lulu', but she is also variously called 'Mignon', 'Eve' and 'Nelli' – a diminutive of 'Helen' – all names evoking various sexual stereotypes or legends. She is the child-bride, the mistress, the erotic dancer, the prostitute – her death at the end comes at the hands of one of her customers, Jack the Ripper – and she is always the object of desire with never a hint at the procreative element that there is in sexual relations. Sex, as envisaged by Wedekind and embodied by Lulu, is always destructive; during *Earth Spirit*, Goll, her first husband, dies of apoplexy; the artist Schwarz, her second husband, cuts his throat because he believes she has been unfaithful; she herself shoots Schön, the one man who appears to attract her, and in the course of the cluttered and less satisfactory *Pandora's Box*, Rodrigo the acrobat is murdered at her behest, Hugenberg the schoolboy commits suicide, Alwa, reduced to the role of pathetic voyeur, is beaten to death by one of her clients, and finally both Lulu and Geschwitz are stabbed by the psychopath Jack.

Reduced to such a précis, the destruction becomes comic and it is inescapably true that Wedekind descends into the type of melodrama that would have delighted the customers of the Grand-Guignol. It is not possible at this distance to say whether this was intentional parody or unconscious plagiarism, but it is certainly possible to criticise the later play for a loss of effect through such excess. Possibly an edited combination of the two plays, such as Alban Berg used for the libretto of his opera and Peter Barnes produced in his 1971 adaptation, would prove the most effective way of staging them. It should be noted that both the French pantomime that inspired the work and Wedekind's original version of the Lulu plays managed to contain the theme within one evening's performance.

Despite their flaws, the Lulu plays performed a service far in excess of their comparable artistic merits. As Elisabeth Boa writes:

> Whatever the ideological positions, the connecting link between Wedekind, Brecht, Beckett, the Theatre of the Absurd and many other modern playwrights has to do with quintessentially theatrical matters. Wedekind is a technician who appeals to other writers and men of the theatre... Wedekind avoids that naive naturalism which presents the mediated image as if it were a necessary truth or a fact of nature, immutable and independent of interpretation. He exploits the language of the stage. In subverting dramatic convention, Wedekind turns everything into theatre which mixes clownish slapstick, heightened melodrama, jolting gearshifts of verbal style and a sensuous language of things and bodily movement. Theatre itself becomes a metaphor for culture as a language which we can interpret and manipulate to rewrite ourselves or change the world.[8]

As well as being an author, Wedekind was also a performer, both an actor and singer of songs in cabaret, actually influencing the young Brecht in his style and choice of song. But as well as providing places for the ageing Wedekind and the youthful Brecht to perform, the cabarets were also venues for plays and playlets opposed to the complacency of turn-of-the-century Wilhelmine Germany and inspired by the growing anger that bubbled under the surface and burst out among the young. Pieces like the painter Oskar Kokoschka's *Murderer Hope of Womankind* (1907) were little more than 'happenings', the one in question being staged at an art exhibition, written overnight and probably baffling the players as much as the audience.

In the face of mass-production, urbanisation and growing militarism in Germany, Expressionism started out simply as the assertion of the individual, the perennial youthful need for opposition and recognition, the desire to shout, 'Oi, look at me! I exist!' in as startling and subjective a manner as possible. The attitude appeared before the label, an attitude described by R.S. Furness:

> The outlook known as expressionism combines the following: a movement towards abstraction, towards autonomous colour and metaphor, away from plausibility and imitations; a fervent desire to express and create regardless of formal canons; a concern for the typical and essential rather than the purely personal and individual; the grotesque; a mystical, even religious element with frequent apocalyptic overtones; an urgent sense of here and now, the city and the machine seen not from any naturalistic point of view but 'sub specie aeternitatis'; a desire for revolt against tradition and a longing for the new and strange.[9]

These last two aspects are applicable to most adolescent reactions, while the whole has the feel of youthful idealism, an idealism which was not to survive the First World War, even though many of the other aspects of Expressionism did not come to fruition until after the conflict. J.M. Ritchie's distillation of the essence of the movement in the theatre is more specific:

> Perhaps the most striking formal feature of Expressionist drama is abstraction. Essentially this means that the Expressionist dramatist is not concerned with projecting an illusion of reality on stage; instead he gives something abstracted from reality, that is, either something taken from the real world but reduced to the bare minimum, or something totally abstracted from reality in the sense that the norms of time and place and individuation have been completely abandoned.[10]

Quite understandably in a young, angry, 'alternative' theatre, many of the central butts of the early plays were father-figures, representing authority, reaction, conservatism – the 'status quo' that the writers were attacking. In Reinhard Sorge's play, *Der Bettler* (*The Beggar*) (1912), the poet son poisons his insane father, a direct reversal of the situation in *Ghosts*, the standard bearer of the Naturalist movement, where, through inherited syphilis, the father can be seen to have poisoned the insane son. It is interesting to note that Max Reinhardt, the leading German director for the first thirty years of the century, had opened his small Kammerspiele theatre in Berlin in 1906 with *Ghosts* and ten years later was staging *The Beggar*.

While the styles of the plays ranged from Carl Sternheim's comic *Scenes from the Heroic Life of the Middle Classes* through such apocalyptic visions as Carl Hauptmann's *War: A Te Deum* and the final scenes of Georg Kaiser's *Gas Trilogy* to the anarchic rampages of Iwan Goll's splendid descendant of Pere Ubu, *Methusalem*, the unifying theme is of explicit opposition to a stultifying society and a plea for something better.

Carl Sternheim (1878-1942) aspired towards, and achieved, the title of 'the modern Molière', producing comic social satires based on stereotypical bourgeois characters. The sequence of plays *Scenes from the Heroic Life of the Middle Classes* traces the fortunes of the Maske family, whose very name implies falseness and pretence. It starts with *Die Hose* (*Knickers/Bloomers*) (1911), the very mention of which was likely to produce apoplexy in the target classes and did in fact cause the play to be banned. In it, Theobald Maske exploits the fact that his pretty wife loses her knickers in public, in the sight of the emperor. The fame or infamy of this event attracts lodgers and so Maske is seen to be capitalising on the prurient imaginings of his customers.

In *Der Snob* (1914) the chronicle moves on to the story of Christian Maske, the son, who does away with his parents in order to facilitate his social climbing. The saga continues in *1913* with the grandchildren now on show, effete and decadent, and the final hammer blow, a long way on from the light comedy of *Bloomers*, comes in *The Fossil* where the last surviving member of the family is shot by her father, a Prussian militaristic tyrant named Traugott (or 'Trust God'). The murderer rejects safety in flight from authority, insisting that he give himself up:

> Form and breeding to the bitter end...What can happen to me in this day and age?...well, then. By the right, quick march! Above all, there must be order and justice in Germany. Hurrah!

There is no doubt that Sternheim's cycle is criticising the present order, but in the cynical destructiveness of the final play it is impossible to find any positive solution, a fault that is often evident in Expressionist work. While theorists may state that the new movement embodies a search for 'the New Man', it is easier to see what is wrong with the old than to offer a concrete new alternative.

True, there were visionaries in the movement. In the same year as *The Snob*, Carl Hauptmann, Gerhart's older brother, produced a remarkable work, *War: A Te Deum*. Of an older generation than most of the other Expressionists and displaying similar mystical and supernatural traits that were to colour his brother's later work, Hauptmann worked on a vast apocalyptic canvas that included such characters as 'the European Reckoner', 'the Archangel in Armour', 'the wounded of various nationalities', and 'creatures variously crippled and vilely clad'. The power of the imagination is undeniable but staging the whole would have taxed the most imaginative of designers while, with lines such as,

> The new dawn has come, O Lord. Out of the goodness of our rich, good heart let your great love for this poor lovely earth spill over into the blood of this sweet boy...

the piece would surely have been something of a trial for both actors and audience.

More viable theatrically, more thoroughly Expressionist and probably more influential was Reinhard Goering's *Naval Encounter* (1916). By then, the Great War was underway and this piece at least has its foundations in experience rather than pure imagination. Set inside the gun turret of a vast battleship, the play features nameless characters – reminiscent of Büchner and to be echoed later by writers like Kaiser – and the 'Telegram style' of dialogue that was the hall-mark of many Expressionist plays and poems. There are simply seven sailors, differentiated in the text by numbers who, when they don their gas masks during the battle, become faceless as well as nameless. (This scene has a more famous echo in the middle act of Sean O'Casey's *The Silver Tassie* in the production designed by Augustus John where the same impersonality, though this time of soldiers, was expressed by the use of gasmasks.)

The threat of rebellion in the shape of mutiny is overwhelmed by the onset of the battle. However, this is not a simple exhortation to do one's patriotic duty in wartime but rather an expression of man's freedom to choose his destiny, a definite anticipatory echo of Existentialism. The Fifth Sailor, the nearest we have to a protagonist in the play, utters these dying words:

> We are not dead yet, no need for unseemly haste...the action continues, do you hear? Don't close your eyes yet. I made a good gunner, eh? I'd have made a good mutineer, too. But firing the gun came easier. Eh? Must just have come easier.[11]

The end of the war did not see the end of the movement. If anything, it gained momentum and effect. B.J. Kenworthy summarised the position thus:

> What the Expressionist generation rebelled against was at bottom a view of life that denied man free will, for the messianic or revolutionary postures that are the essence of German Expressionism at the end of the war, together with its hortatory vehemence, must be mere gestures in the void unless free will is postulated. The reassertion of free will, then, is the metaphysical basis of the Expressionist revolt.[12]

It was not all so austere and sombre. Iwan Goll, the bilingual Alsatian poet and playwright, created *Methusalem* with more than a touch of Pere Ubu in him and, in the Prologue, expounded 'Alogic', reminiscent of Jarry's 'Pataphysics'.

> Alogic is today the most intellectual form of humour and therefore the best weapon against the empty clichés which dominate all our lives. Almost invariably the average man opens his mouth only to set his tongue, not his brain, in motion. What is the point of talking so much and taking it all so seriously?...Dramatic alogic must ridicule all our banalities of language...At the same time alogic will serve to demonstrate the multi-hued spectrum of the human brain, which can think one thing and say another and leap with mercurial speed from one idea to another without the slightest ostensible logical connection.
>
> But to avoid being a moaner, a pacifist and Salvation Army type, the author must perform a few somersaults, that you all may become as little children again. For what is he after: to present you with dolls, to teach you to play, and then to scatter the sawdust from the broken dolls to the four winds again...
>
> Drama should be without beginning, without end, like everything else here on earth. But...the drama stops because you have tired, grown old in a single hour, and because truth, the most potent poison for the human heart, may only be swallowed in very small doses.[13]

By now we are far from Chekhov's 'unconditional and honest truth' and immersed in a totally subjective vision of the world. The fact that Georg Grosz designed the first production in 1922 comes as no surprise when one reads the description of our hero and heroine:

Methusalem, *the* original bourgeois...his face is dark red, fat, bald head, tiny eyes, clean shaven. Across his belly stretches a solid copper watch chain, as thick as a small hawser, with a miniature safe as a charm on it...Amalia Methusalem, the essence of bourgeois house-wifery, wearing a rich dress...much diamond and pearl jewelry round her neck and on her hands; fat, bulging breasts; and over it all, a filthy kitchen apron.

The opening exchanges between Methusalem and his wife are banal in the extreme, inevitably prompting comparisons with Ionesco's *Bald Prima Donna*, written some thirty years later:

METHUSALEM	(*asleep – awakes with a start*): Nothing new. The world's getting so old.
AMALIA:	Life is hard.
METHUSALEM:	It's much of a muchness.
AMALIA:	No juicy little murder in the paper?
METHUSALEM:	Seven and six.
AMALIA:	Spaghetti?
METHUSALEM:	No, vegetable oil.
AMALIA:	If only you could get celluloid umbrellas!
METHUSALEM:	Is it goulash tonight?
AMALIA:	Miserable spring; the carrots are so dear!

There, encapsulated in the first few lines of the play are all the most popular topics of conversation – weather, money, food and sex, and an implicit lack of communication!

The play broke much new ground; Methusalem's dreams were presented by film sequences back-projected onto a window on stage, while the daughter is courted by a student, played by three different actors in identical masks bearing the labels, 'Ego', 'Id' and 'Superego', all of whom converse with each other about the motives behind the wooing.

Methusalem has a 'joke-box' which tells him dubious jokes – a precursor of television, perhaps – and the living-room full of stuffed animals comes alive to discuss their owner, predating *Cats* by some sixty years! The inspired madness is continued in the shape of Felix, Methusalem's son. He enters and exits by means of a lift and is the thoroughly modern mechanical man: 'For a mouth he wears a copper megaphone, for a nose he has a telephone receiver, for eyes two gold coins, for a forehead and hat a typewriter and on top antennae which light up every time he speaks.'[14]

The revolutionary Student who leads the mob against Methusalem demands equality but it is the equality of a 'Wonderland' world:

No man shall have a jam tart more than his brother!

Initially, the threat of revolution terrifies Methusalem because he believes that he will lose his beloved money, but eventually he simply opens his safe which he happens to keep filled with armed policemen who shoot down the mob. The final stage directions of the act sum up Methusalem's attitude towards the mob and one cannot help feeling that Goll's sympathies are not entirely opposed to his monster:

> While things are quietening down, two gold-braided lackeys bring in a lavishly-carved commode, help Methusalem to unbutton his trousers, pull them down and seat him on the afore-mentioned stool. The mob is completely mastered. The policemen stand stiff and respectful. Methusalem smiles and farts. Curtain.[15]

Eventually, Methusalem is killed but he manages to rise from the dead, interested only in his factory and his food.

There is no doubt that the comedy is childish and heavy-handed at times, but equally, there is a definite feeling of delight in the creation of this monster, more than a hint of Absurdist humour, something most welcome when compared with the intensity of the work of some of Goll's fellow playwrights.

Georg Kaiser (1878-1945), one of the finest, most prolific and most succesful of this generation of German playwrights, could possibly have benefited from some of Goll's levity. The intensity of his outlook was displayed in his life as well as in his work. When arrested for selling 'objets d'art' taken from a villa that he was renting for himself, his wife and family, he faced the court with the following, sincerely felt argument:

> I hold myself to be an extravagantly exceptional case. The law does not apply to me...He who has created much is 'a priori' exempt from punishment. The obligation I have towards myself is higher than my obligation to the law...The idea that everybody is equal before the law is nonsensical. I am not everybody. I am great, therefore I am permitted to break the law...My arrest is not a personal disaster, it is a national disaster. The flags should have been at half-mast![16]

The fallibility of Kaiser's argument was proven by the fact that he was found guilty, sent to prison and his family confined to the poorhouse for a while. But, while the general opinion of his talents may not have been as high as his own, it is universally held that his play *Von Morgen Bis Mitternachts* (*From Morn to Midnight*) is one of the most influential works of Expressionism. Ashley Dukes' translation introduced the movement into America and eventually Britain, while Kaiser's *Gas Trilogy* (*Coral, Gas I, Gas II*) encapsulates most of the aspects of an Expressionist play, from the father/son conflict through the corruption of riches, the need to destroy the old, attempts at social equality to the Apocalypse of war and universal destruction.

From Morn to Midnight was written in 1912 though not performed until 1917. It is the story of the fall of 'the Bank Cashier' – here again the characters have generic rather than proper names – who misunderstands the appeal from a mysterious beautiful woman from Tuscany and absconds from the bank with sixty thousand marks, intending to help her. In the scene in the lady's hotel, the misunderstanding is revealed and, far from running away with an exotic foreigner, the little man is left with considerable wealth and no obvious aim. Seated in the bare branches of a tree set in a snow-covered field, he reviews his fate and makes an ultra-modern decision:

> I must pay! I must spend! Where are the goods I can buy for cash on the nail? For the whole sixty thousand! And the whole buyer thrown in, flesh and bone, body and soul. (*crying out*) Deal with me! Sell to me! I have the money, you have the goods; bring them together!!

This leads to a vision of his death, an event that he tries to postpone;

> I see stretching ahead of me a host of calls to pay before this evening. It's impossible that you should be the first. The last you may be, but even then, only the last resort.

He returns to his family, providing Kaiser with a chance to offer his version of bourgeois banality, with the wife worrying about grilling the chops, the daughter playing the piano and the mother finally dying because the cashier breaks a lifelong routine and leaves without eating his meal.

At a professional bicycle race, he offers all his money as prizes, the prospect of which produces 'ecstasy' among the crowd. It appears that he has been able to buy the crowd's emotions, something worthwhile, but when they fall silent at the entrance of the local prince, the Cashier withdraws his offer because Man's natural emotions, albeit avaricious, have been suppressed by an unnatural servility.

He rejects the food and sex on offer in the cabaret, leaving the waiter with the bill, and in the final scene in the Salvation Army Hall, even the hope and promise of salvation is shown to be false as the penitents fight and grovel over the money he throws; the Salvation Army Girl, apparently immune to such temptations, finally betrays him with the words: 'There he is! I've shown him to you! I've earned the reward!', which in the light of the final tableau is an obvious allusion to Judas.

The Cashier eventually resorts to the all-too-familiar Expressionist ending of suicide, with the blatant symbolism of the last scene: 'He has fallen back with arms outstretched against the cross on the back wall. His husky gasp is like an 'Ecce', his heavy sigh like a 'Homo'. One second later all the lamps explode with a loud retort.'[17] Complete with the allusion to crucifixion and the last words of Christ, this is the ultimate in 'Stationendramen'.

The last scene of Kaiser's *Gas II* is even more pessimistic; the Gas factory, having worked for generations of the Millionaire's family, is finally converted to producing poison gas, a gas which is released at the end, destroying all before it. As Kenworthy writes:

> This is...an ending...that gains in significance when its essential
> symbolism is considered...The Gas factory stands...as a symbol of
> the whole complex of modern industrial society, the explosion and
> the ever-present threat of its recurrence for the wars of mass de-
> struction which seem to be inherent in an age of mass production.
> Every element is fitted into the pattern: the workers, harnessed to
> their machines and an easy prey to the demagogue; the technicians
> with their destructively fertile invention; the capitalist, the militar-
> ist and the pacifist; and in the background the impersonal force of
> the state, pitted against just such another state. And Kaiser sees no
> end to this social development but the universal graveyard of man's
> hopes, in the ultimate self-destruction of civilization.[18]

There is no doubting the power of the vision or the writing, but it would take
the most determined Pangloss to discover any remnants of the optimism and
idealism that instigated the movement with the original quest for the Expressionist 'New Man'.

The idealism died but the style remained; it is this style that was to have
most effect, in Germany, the rest of Europe and, ultimately, in America. It
was also the prevailing style of the early works of Brecht, for while such pieces
as *In the Jungle of the Cities* were juvenile in their nihilistic content, their
structure owed much to the earlier Expressionism. Eventually Brecht was to
reject the movement:

> Expressionism signifies crude exaggeration. In cases where it does
> not deal in allegory...it deals with proclamation or overstatement
> of Spirit, of Ideals...consequently it remains a movement that re-
> mains on the surface and external, rather than a revelation: that is,
> instead of filling the body with spirit, they sell the (most colourful)
> skin for the body and instead of showing the...soul on the body, they
> make the soul into the body, thus crudely exaggerating it.

This, however, is the judgement of the mature man, a man who was to become
one of the most influential dramatic theorists of the century as well as a
playwright of genius; it does not remove the fact that he owed an invaluable
debt to this earlier school nor that his first considerable work, *Baal* (1919),
contained much that can only be described as Expressionistic.

Baal is worth closer examination because of its obvious genealogy. The
eponymous hero, like Woyzeck, is an outsider, but this time an outsider of
his own making, an amoral poet, like Wedekind. In the opening scene, when
Baal's poetry is praised by a bourgeois audience, Brecht employs the same
stock caricature techniques that Büchner, Sternheim, Goll and Kaiser had
already pioneered, while Baal's anti-social, amoral approach to life in general and to sex in particular is motivated by exactly the same 'earth-spirit'
that had destroyed Wedekind's Lulu. Had Brecht been judged, like Büchner, only on his first three plays (*Drums in the Night, Baal* and *In the Jungle*

of the Cities), it is doubtful whether his impression upon world theatre would have had much significance at all. However, these crude, derivative pieces were simply the early experiments of one of the most influential playwrights of the century, a man who not only wrote some half a dozen great plays but also, in the creation of his company, the Berliner Ensemble, and in the presentation of his theories on the content and production of such plays, caused an impact whose effect is still being felt throughout the world.

If Brecht were to be fairly judged, then the synthesis of the theory in practice, namely his productions of his own plays, are the only suitable evidence; however, this is no longer possible, for even though the Berliner Ensemble may still have such productions in their repertoire, Brecht died over thirty years ago and some transformation must inevitably have happened, either a deterioration or, perhaps worse still, an enshrinement. And yet, much continues to be written about his plays and his theories; for the serious non-German-speaking student, the works of John Willet are probably the best source of further information on the subject. However, a basic explanation of two of the terms most bandied about in enthusiastic but possibly uncertain discussion of 'Brechtian theatre' may be of help: 'Epic Theatre' and 'Alienation' – in German the 'Verfremdungseffekt', or, for the true aficionado, the 'V-effekt'.

For an Anglophone, the very mention of 'epic' implies size and spectacle, more often than not evoking some Hollywood Bible-busting movie such as 'The Ten Commandments' or 'Ben Hur'. As regards Brecht's theatre, this is a misconception. He himself admits that it is impossible to define his concept of 'epic' theatre easily but he does state that: 'the essential point of the epic theatre is perhaps that it appeals less to the feelings than to the spectator's reason'. Essentially, 'epic' describes the structure of a play that is not strictly 'tied to time', where the action has a fluidity which is not restricted by the so-called Aristotelian unities of time, place and action. There can be no doubting that the cinema was to benefit from and probably encourage this style because cross-cutting, fading and 'montage' techniques that were to develop in the film industry were not only impressive and desirable in the eyes of the stage director but, given the breadth of a film's distribution, far more likely to have a wider impact than any one play or theatrical movement. It is possibly here, with the adoption of 'epic' structure by the cinema, that the confusion over the meaning arose.

Like most good theories, Brecht's 'epic' concept was not established until after it had been developed in practice; the theory is simply a rationalisation of practical achievements that are discovered 'to be good' and worthy of taking further. A diagram of the relationship of 'epic' to the ordinary, 'dramatic' form of theatre is offered by Brecht in his *Schriften zum Theater* (*Writings on the Theatre*), a plan that simplifies matters still further:

DRAMATIC FORM OF THEATRE	EPIC FORM OF THEATRE
Plot	Narrative
Implicates the spectator in a stage situation and wears down his power of action. The human being is taken for granted. He is unalterable.	Turns the spectator into an observer but arouses his power of action. The human being is the object of the inquiry. He is alterable and able to alter.
Eyes on the finish. One scene makes another. Growth.	Eyes on the course. Each scene for itself. 'Montage'.

There is of course a danger of what Peter Brook calls 'Deadly Theatre' if such theories are pursued religiously without an awareness of what will or will not work in the theatre, but Brecht obviously possessed this awareness; in fact, he was even prepared to prescribe what should happen in the auditorium as well as on stage. He knew what sort of an audience he did *not* want: 'they stare rather than see, just as they listen rather than hear. They look at the stage as if in a trance... Seeing and hearing are activities and can be pleasant ones, but these people seem relieved of any activity, like men to whom something is being done.' In other words, Brecht's anathema audience is being entertained passively. In order to avoid this, he proposed that sensual stimuli were to be given to the audience. Not, it is true, like some of the developments of the Sixties and Seventies when plays like Peter Handke's *Offending the Audience* gave a whole new meaning to audience alienation and entertainments like Ken Campbell's Road Show never for a moment allowed the audience to forget that they were an integral part of the process. Instead, back-projections or banners declaiming scene titles were used – in some of Brecht's earlier plays, actors shouted out the contents of subsequent scenes like newspaper sellers; music was essential, making songs a regular interruption to the 'growth', and musicians were often visible on stage. The famous 'Brechtian' half-curtains were introduced for scene changing, so that only the bottom half of the stage was hidden, lights were left on so that the process could be watched and Brecht had visions of a theatre audience like a boxing crowd, on cheap, hard seats under blazing lights, free to chat, smoke and shout, thus actively participating in the event. Anything that would stop the audience's passive empathy and stimulate its active thought was considered a valid 'alienation' effect.

The translation of 'Verfremdung' to 'alienation' is unfortunate because it implies an element of hostility; 'distancing' is more accurate. Brecht also demanded this of his actors; they should not become totally immersed in a character, as the Method School was to demand, but should maintain distance from the character so that the audience is always aware that this is an actor. An interesting improvisation exercise that Brecht used in rehearsal to gain this distance was to ask his actor to deliver a monologue as reported speech, starting with: 'He says that –'. It is practical detail such as this that helps one to understand better the much-vaunted expression, 'alienation effect'.

With this in mind, an examination or re-examination of the plays themselves bears further fruit. It is fair to say that works like *The Good Person of Setzuan, The Caucasian Chalk Circle, The Life of Galileo, The Threepenny Opera* and, most especially, *Mother Courage and her Children* are among the finest plays written this century in any language, but it is also worth remembering that Büchner and *Woyzeck,* Wedekind and *Lulu*, Goll and *Methusalem* and Kaiser and his little Bank Cashier did much to pave the way for their inception.

Ten plays for further consideration

1. Georg Büchner, *Woyzeck*
2. Georg Büchner, *Danton's Death*
3. Frank Wedekind, *Earth Spirit*
4. Carl Sternheim, *The Snob*
5. Reinhard Goering, *Naval Encounter*
6. Iwan Goll, *Methusalem*
7. Georg Kaiser, *From Morn to Midnight*
8. Georg Kaiser, *Gas II*
9. Bertolt Brecht, *Baal*
10. Bertolt Brecht, *Mother Courage and her Children*

Notes

1. Max Spalter, *Brecht's Tradition*, pp. 80-1
2. ibid., pp. 98-9
3. Büchner, *Woyzeck*
4. ibid.
5. ibid.
6. Frank Wedekind, *The Lulu Plays*, p. 10
7. ibid., pp. 9-10

8. Elisabeth Boa, *The Sexual Circus*, p. 227

9. R.S. Furness, *Expressionism*

10. J.M. Ritchie, *German Expressionist Drama*, p. 15

11. R. Goering, *Naval Encounter* in Ritchie, *Seven Expressionist Plays*, p. 110

12. B.J. Kenworthy, intro. to Georg Kaiser, *Gas I, II and III*, in ibid.

13. Iwan Goll, Preface to *Methusalem* in ibid., pp. 79-80

14. ibid., stage directions, p. 90

15. ibid., p. 92

16. quoted in Benson, *German Expressionist Drama*, p. 96

17. Kaiser, *From Morn to Midnight* stage directions

18. B.J. Kenworthy, *Georg Kaiser*, p. 62

3: FRENCH LESSONS

Despite the considerable efforts to 'decentralise' the theatre in France since the Second World War and without any attempt to belittle the major achievements of such directors as Roger Planchon in Villeurbanne and Ariane Mnouchkine with the Théâtre du Soleil, in the minds of most people theatrical France means Paris, just as Britain means London and America means New York. For much of this century, Paris was synonymous with all that was new and exciting in the world of the Arts, from Picasso to the Ballet Russe, Cocteau to Henry Miller, Hemingway and the Fitzgeralds, Sartre, Gide and Genet, Symbolism, Surrealism, Cubism and Existentialism as well as the most notoriously 'naughty' nightlife that any tourist could imagine (if not actually find).

At the turn of the century, it had housed Antoine's 'Théâtre Libre', the example for many other little theatres experimenting with a naturalistic form of theatre while, almost at the same time (1896), witnessing the monstrous incursion of Alfred Jarry's Pere Ubu onto the stage and into the history books, as yet another Parisian first night caused riots and controversial, partisan debate.

From the opening line, 'Merde', the story of the lazy, devious and murderous Ubu unfolded, not only as an uproarious parody of *Macbeth*, but also with a definite element of anarchic originality with Ubu, egged on by Mere Ubu, slaughtering his way to the throne of a mythical Poland. In a sequence of plays – *Ubu Roi, Ubu Enchainé, Ubu Cocu* and *Ubu sur la Butte,* this manifestation of all that is rude, crude, adolescent and rebellious rampages through his world with the panache of a Punch and the violence of a Tom and Jerry cartoon. He is anti-social, anti-heroic, anti-establishment and totally egocentric, a spoiled baby which has had its morals doctored at birth. It is hardly surprising that anyone possessing an ounce of nonconformity and a feeling for the theatrical should fall for Ubu. Peter Brook's productions of a composite text in the mid-70s at his Bouffes du Nord theatre, coupled with Jean-Louis Barrault's *Jarry sur la Butte* in 1970, proved that Jarry could still be enormously successful, some seventy years after the original manifestation. Jarry died at the age of 34 in 1907, a victim of his own excesses, another in the line of *monstres sacrés* who died too young that leads up to Joe Orton and beyond. His legacy however remains in the person of Ubu.

At the same time, there was a move towards Symbolism, a movement epitomised by the work of Maeterlinck and the precious *Axel* of Villiers de l'Isle Adam, but this was more of an intellectual curio than a practical force in the theatre. Similarly, there existed a developing 'avant-garde' where perhaps the most lasting theatrical work was the poet, Guillaume Apollinaire's *Les Mammelles de Tirésias (The Breasts of Tiresias)*, but most theatre-goers were bourgeois or aristocratic and happy to bask in reflections of 'la Belle Epoque'. It took the work of innovative directors, rather than revolutionary playwrights, to shake this complacency.

Jacques Copeau (1879-1949), like Shaw, started his involvement with the theatre as a critic and became incensed by the diet of adulterous comedies, bedroom farces and pieces that relied entirely on scenic spectacle rather than intellectual content for their appeal. As he did not judge his contemporary playwrights to have any great merit, he proposed a return to the classics, to Shakespeare and Molière, and in 1913 formed the Théâtre du Vieux-Colombier on the left bank on the Seine, away from the fashionable theatre-land, propounding a style of playing that was to be developed in a school attached to the theatre:

> The training given at the school was based on a quasi-religious search for truth through a mystical trinity of qualities: *le Beau, le Bien et le Vrai*. Emphasis was laid on cultivating the complete man, not just the technical faculties, and on training actors to work for the group rather than for themselves. Discipline was harsh, control of their body a major priority. The early stages of training relied solely on physical exercise and cultivation of expressive faculties of the body, with an absolute ban on using words.[1]

While Copeau did not realise all his ambitions, his school and company had an enormous effect on both French and European theatre. A group of his students, after he had left them, became 'La Compagnie des Quinze' who, working with the playwright Andre Obey, displayed a whole new 'vocabulary' of stage movement, including *Commedia dell'Arte*-style pantomime, music and tumbling. Sir Michael Redgrave writes in his autobiography of their visit to London as 'a revelation', while one of their number, Michel Saint-Denis, left the company to live in London, founded the London Theatre Studio where Copeau's ideas were taught, and eventually helped to revive the Old Vic and establish its school as well as others in France, the United States and Canada.

Among Copeau's other disciples were Louis Jouvet and Charles Dullin, two actors who were to become directors of their own theatres and, with Gaston Baty and Georges and Ludmilla Pitoeff, established a quartet of theatres known as the 'Cartel'. This confederation was formed initially as a reaction to destructive or pointless criticism, with each company promoting the work of the other to try to avoid the power of the Press. Eventually, they agreed on a common, constructive policy which has been summarised thus:

'respect for the text, simplicity and truthfulness in staging, the search for poetic impact rather than spectacular effect. Their attitude towards the public was similar. They asked for intelligent participation, offered lectures and other supplementary events, and insisted on starting punctually.'[2]

This last element may appear peculiar to today's reader but there was a tendency not to start the performance until about half an hour after the advertised time, in order to allow tardy theatre-goers plenty of time to finish their dinner and arrive in comfort. When Dullin started on time and critics arrived late, to discover the play under way and the doors closed, there was considerable outcry in the Press.

Of the four 'Cartel' directors – the Pitoeffs worked as a team – Jouvet has proved to be the most influential. One of his early successes after leaving Copeau's company was with Jules Romains' satire *Knock ou le triomphe de la médecine* (1923), a success that he was to repeat on many occasions. However, it was in his work with Jean Giraudoux (1882-1944) that he was to make the greatest impact. In this close collaboration of playwright with creative stage director, Jouvet and Giraudoux were to get nearest to one of Copeau's ambitions whereby the writing and directing of the piece would develop together. Much in Giraudoux's scripts would be changed in rehearsal, so that the finished product was an evolved, developing entity, rather than a simple transference of the sacrosanct manuscript to the stage; the result was pieces like *Intermezzo, L'Impromptu de Paris, Amphitryon 38* and, most famous, *La Guerre de Troie N'Aura Pas Lieu* (1935), to be translated by Christopher Fry as *Tiger at the Gates*. This happy working relationship, of course, is nothing new; Shakespeare, after all, was a jobbing hack, working for a specific company of actors, while Molière probably came closest to Copeau's ideal of actor/author/director. As Guicharnaud has written:

> Giraudoux's theatre was one of collaboration – a rather different notion to the more fashionable one of participation, but not foreign to it, simply more active. Like reformers such as Jouvet and the Cartel, he wanted his audience to be ready for action...Like the reformers, he wrote neither for the real public nor for an ideal public but for the potential in the real public.[3]

In plays like *Amphitryon, La Guerre de Troie* and *Sodome et Gomorrhe*, Giraudoux followed the example of Cocteau by setting his work within a legend or myth in order to have readily recognisable parameters within which he could then manipulate the material to his own ends, an example that both Sartre and Anouilh were to follow later. The plays are famous for their stylish writing, wit and theatricality, although much credit for this latter element has been attributed to Jouvet, who not only directed the pieces but also played in many.

The most controversial and eventually the widest-spread influence to come out of this fertile era of quest and reassessment was a student of Dullin's, a failed surrealist, occasional actor, idiosyncratic director, and visionary theoretician, Antonin Artaud (1896-1949). When one looks at movements and schools that have pervaded the world of theatre this century, Artaud's 'Theatre of Cruelty' – an unfortunate, misleading label – demands attention, although it is possible to argue that much of the initial attraction is caused by the label rather than the content of the theory.

One of the finest directors of the second half of the century, one of the most influential writers on, and ardent researchers into, the practice and potential of the theatre, Peter Brook, has acknowledged his debt to Artaud with a season in 1964 devoted to his work which culminated in the remarkable *Marat/Sade*; Jean-Louis Barrault looked on him as a formative influence; Roger Blin, the director of the first production of *Waiting for Godot*, saw Artaud as being as influential as Beckett whom he described as 'one of the two most important people in my life. He and Artaud divide my sentiments between them'. Julian Beck and Judith Molina's 'Living Theatre', the anarchic, nomadic company that originated in 1948 in New York and then took to travelling the world, a company that was instrumental in breaking both new ground and old taboos in the Sixties, used many of Artaud's ideas as axioms in their work, whilst in Poland the work of Jerzy Grotowski and his Teatr Laboratorium owes a similar allegiance.

And yet, this same Antonin Artaud was a long-term drug addict who spent the last eight years of his life in a variety of asylums, certified insane. When at liberty, he was capable of the most anti-social behaviour. Barrault, a great friend, relates two such examples; once, having been invited to dinner at the house of 'une bourgeoise fortunée', Artaud stripped to the waist during the meal and finished by beating his hostess on the head with his dessert spoon, shouting – 'Madame, you're getting on my nerves!' On another occasion, he ended a fund-raising dinner for his aborted project *La Conquête de Mexique* by addressing the potential 'angels' in words which, roughly translated, went: 'If I've agreed to piss about with you lot, it's just so you can give back to the theatre and to the people a bit of that money you've squeezed out of the poor!',[4] a statement which Barrault modifies with: 'Enfin, quelque chose de cette veine'. Who then, was this enigma and what, in fact, did he write that was to impress the theatre world so much?

He was born in Marseille in 1896; a long history of childhood illnesses and mental problems led to drug addiction from an early age. It has been suggested that this addiction had taken grip by the time that he was nineteen, 'bump-started', as it were, by a dangerous mix of tranquillisers for his psychological problems and opium for his headaches. Given such 'inspiration', it is not surprising that his writings are a mixture of insights and incomprehensible passages. However, they can be viewed as a definite manifesto for change and do suggest, albeit often impracticably, some radical alternatives. In his essay translated as 'No More Masterpieces', there is a cry familar to all revolutionaries, an echo of Victor Hugo's 'Il n'y a ni règles ni modèles'. The message may not be particularly remarkable, but the language which he employs is:

> We must finally do away with the idea of masterpieces reserved for a so-called élite but incomprehensible to the masses, since the mind has no red-light districts like those used for illicit sexual relations.[5]

His targets, too, are surprising:

> Shakespeare himself is responsible for this aberration and decline, this isolationist concept of theatre, holding that a stage performance ought not to affect the public, or that a projected image should not cause a shock to the anatomy, leaving an indelible impression on it.[6]

Like other megalomaniacs, Artaud neither brooks opposition nor offers logical support for his arguments; he simply states.

This idiosyncratic use of language is most evident in his choice of title for his alternative to the status quo. He chose to call it the 'Theatre of Cruelty', but appeared to be applying 'Alice In Wonderland' logic to his semantics where a word or phrase takes on whatever meaning the author likes. '...philosophically speaking, what is cruelty? From a mental viewpoint, cruelty means strictness, diligence, unrelenting decisiveness, irreversible and absolute determination'.[7]

> With this mania we all have today for belittling everything, as soon as I said 'cruelty' everyone took it to mean 'blood'. But a *Theatre of Cruelty* means theatre that is difficult and cruel for myself first of all. And on a performing level, it has nothing to do with the cruelty we practise on one another, hacking at each other's bodies, carving up our individual anatomies, or like ancient Assyrian Emperors, posting sackfulls of human ears, noses or neatly dissected nostrils, but the far more terrible, essential cruelty objects can practise upon us. We are not free and the sky can still fall on our heads. And above all else, theatre is made to teach us.

He seems to be confusing cruelty with discipline while displaying at the same time an obsession with more general cruelty that has nothing to do with the theatre. This confusion is not surprising when one discovers some of his other obsessions:

> He asked his friends not to make love. 'There is no longer anything pure in sexuality. It has become a dirty thing, like the function of eating in certain periods...Each time a man and woman make love, I feel it...Each time a child is born, it takes blood from my heart...'
> He was convinced that there had been gatherings of Mexicans, Tibetan lamas and rabbis to weaken him by masturbating collectively. He wanted to retaliate by leading a party of fifty friends,

armed with machine guns, to Tibet.[8]

However, in spite of these confusions, he claimed a definite cathartic value for his new kind of theatre:

> Whatever conflicts may obsess the mentality of the times, I defy any spectator infused with the blood of violent scenes...once outside the theatre, I defy him to indulge in thoughts of war, riot or motiveless murder.

Ignoring the use or misuse of the epithet 'cruel', there are definite positive theories proposed in his two manifestoes, ideas which may, in retrospect, appear self-evident but which have influenced people like Brook, Beck and Jerome Savary who have adopted, adapted and improved them.

> We have lost the idea of theatre. And in as much as theatre restricts itself to probing the intimacy of a few puppets, thereby transforming the audience into Peeping Toms, one understands why the élite have turned away from it or why the masses go to the cinema, music-hall and circus to find violent gratification whose intention does not disappoint them...Practically speaking, we want to bring back the idea of total theatre...this division between analytical theatre and a world of movement seems stupid to us. One cannot separate body and mind, nor the senses from the intellect...words mean little to the mind; expanded areas and objects speak out...spatial, thundering images replete with sound also speak...[9]

The rejection of a theatre of words had been inspired by a visit to a troupe of Balinese dancers where their language of gesture so excited him that he was ready to reject the word-orientated theatre for one that used other physical attributes instead. This idea of a 'total theatre' is a very attractive one, one that has been adopted by many disciples and improved practically, but equally, it is not so far from the ideas that had formed the basis of Copeau's training in his school. It is also interesting to note that the same remedies were resorted to in experimental French theatre after the 'events' of May 1968.

In the essays entitled 'An Affective Athleticism' and 'Seraphim's Theatre', Artaud offered a remarkable succession of pronouncements about his ideal training of the actor; while the exact meanings of some are difficult to grasp: 'The soul can be physiologically summarised as a maze of vibrations'[10] or 'rehearsed, cultivated breathing...was not made merely to prepare us for a declaration of adulterous love',[11] there is no doubt that his theories on the inter-relationship between the body, breathing, the voice and those emotions to be portrayed on stage have proved inspirational to many (even though, given his allusive style of writing, they may need to have been translated by others such as Brook). There is, however, nothing obscure about his postscript to the 'Affective Athleticism' essay:

In Europe no one knows how to scream any more, particularly actors in a trance no longer know how to cry out, since they do nothing but talk, having forgotten they have a body on stage, they have also lost the use of their throats. Abnormally shrunk, these throats are no longer organs but monstrous, talking abstractions. French actors now only know how to talk.[12]

Some of Artaud's suggestions are impossible, but his Copeau/Dullin-inspired demands that: 'the old duality between author and producer will disappear, to be replaced by a kind of single Creator'[13] have indeed been realised by Peter Brook and his International Centre for Theatre Research and directors like Mike Leigh with his devised and improvised plays.

And yet, the ideology was in continual conflict with the character of the man. When Barrault, possibly the most gifted director of his day, suggested that they collaborate on a piece, Artaud replied: 'In a production staged by me, *I do not want* there to be so much as the bat of an eyelid which does not belong to me...in fact, I do not believe in collaboration...because I no longer believe in human purity. Highly though I esteem you, I think you are fallible.' He was equally emphatic about the content of his show, insisting that it should contain:

> Shouts, groans, apparitions, surprise, dramatic moments of all kinds...we intend to do away with stage and auditorium, replacing them by a kind of single, undivided locale...disregarding the text, we intend to stage:
> 1. An adaptation of a Shakespearean work.
> 2. A very free poetic play by Leon-Paul Fargue.
> 3. An excerpt from *The Zohar*, the story of Rabbi Simeon.
> 4. The story of Bluebeard.
> 5. The Fall of Jerusalem, according to the Bible.
> 6. One of the Marquis de Sade's tales.
> 7. One or more Romantic melodramas.
> 8. Büchner's *Woyzeck*.
> 9. Elizabethan theatre works stripped of the lines, retaining only their period machinery, situations, character and plot.[14]

The zest, mania even, for exciting theatre is everywhere in Artaud's writing and yet the element of imbalance always topples the theories towards the impracticable. His more practical, possibly saner disciples took the inspiration and the stimulus and abandoned the idiosyncratic excesses, the most obvious example of which is the very name, Theatre of Cruelty.

Surprisingly, the Second World War and the German Occupation of Paris proved to be a fertile forcing ground for several major playwriting talents as well as providing impetus for the regions; some influential people moved out of Paris into the unoccupied zone while those living and working in the provinces were obliged to stay there, eventually fulfilling the demands of the new, optimistic young audience that would be coming for the first time to a liberated French theatre.

Among the major theatrical events during the Occupation were Sartre's move into playwriting, Anouilh's version of the Antigone story and Jean-Louis Barrault's production of Paul Claudel's *Le Soulier de Satin*. Claudel (1868-1955) was an unlikely collaborator for the physical young actor/director. Deeply religious but rejected by the church for training in the priesthood, Claudel had joined the diplomatic corps and concentrated on his poetry. His plays, written in verse, were infused with Catholicism, with *L'Annonce Faite à Marie* (*The Tidings Delivered to Mary*) being the first to be performed in 1912, even though it had its origins in a piece written twenty years previously. *Le Soulier de Satin (The Satin Slipper)* was written in 1924; set in the Spanish Golden Age, when Catholicism was opposing the Counter-Reformation, it was originally considered unstageable because of its length. However, Barrault chose it for production in 1943 at the Comedie-Française and persuaded the seventy-five year old poet to work with him, cutting and re-writing pieces to suit the production. The war-time austerity taxed the designer, whose inventiveness was, if anything, stimulated by the limitations, while Barrault, pupil of Dullin and self-confessed adherent to Artaud's theories of non-verbal theatre, found the text of this 'wordy' playwright exceptional.

> ...Claudel's verse style is entirely original...unlike anything before it in the French literary tradition, being based on the rhythm of the breath group, not on the number of feet in a line or the elegant balance of paradox. It builds its effects by slow accumulation, not by sudden sally, and it has an extraordinary physical effect on the listener. Barrault regards the actor's body as an instrument and Claudel's verse as a kind of body music; Barrault discovered that it had to be spoken with the whole body, not just with the articulatory and respiratory organs, and that movement, position, attitude were as vital to the proper rendering of each line as accent and intonation.[15]

The success of this production and of its 1958 revival opened directors' eyes to the merit of Claudel, who has now been re-assessed as one of the century's more significant playwrights.

While Barrault can be credited with the realisation of Claudel's genius, it was Charles Dullin who performed a similar service for Jean-Paul Sartre (1905-80). Prior to the war, this author of Existential philosophy had confined his writing to essays and fiction. However, the theatre was seen to be an effective medium for both philosophy and propaganda and in his dramatic parable, *Les Mouches* (*The Flies*) (1943), Sartre attempted a piece for the theatre which, despite the over-long monologues in the second half, succeeded as a positive anti-Occupation play.

It is a re-working of the Electra story; on 'the Day of the Dead', with the city in mourning, Orestes returns to Argos, a city wallowing in the oppressive foreign rule of Aegisthus, who had murdered Orestes' father and married his mother, Clytemnestra. Orestes meets his sister, Electra, and decides to remain in Argos to avenge his father's death. After the murder of the tyrant and of Clytemnestra, Electra cannot face the responsibility of her actions, as embodied by the Fates (the 'flies' of the title); Orestes can and does accept the responsibility – a gesture of Existential freedom – and leaves the city, prepared to face whatever the Fates may have in store for him, thereby freeing the city of their retribution as well as their foreign tyrant.

The parallels with occupied Paris are obvious, particularly when it is discovered that 'les mouches' was also contemporary Parisian slang for 'informers'. The popular view of the play saw Orestes as patriotic liberator, but the extent of the Existential justification for action in the second half, something that overbalances it as a piece of effective theatre, shows that Sartre was more interested in personal moral philsosophy than in simplistic political propaganda.

This view is supported by his next play, the famous, perhaps even infamous *Huis Clos* (translated variously as *In Camera* and *No Exit*). Set in hell with the infernal triangle of the sadist, the lesbian and the nymphomaniac and the moral that 'hell is other people', it not only proves that Sartre's interest lay in people rather than politics but it also demonstrated how quickly he learned, for it is an infinitely better play than *Les Mouches*, albeit a smaller, 'chamber' work.

After the war, Sartre continued interspersing his philosophical treatises, such as *L'Etre et le Néant* and novels like the monumental *Le Fer dans l'Ame* with plays. *Les Mains Sales (Dirty Hands)* (1948) which considers involvement in action rather than words, where the motives for the young Hugo shooting his mentor could have been either political, and hence acceptable to the Party, or personal and reprehensible, and *Les Séquestrés d'Altona*, (*The Prisoners of Altona* is an unsatisfactory translation) (1959) are among the most successful; however, it must be said that on a number of occasions, the man of ideas overcame the man of the theatre and the balance of the pieces was tilted away from effective theatre towards political and philosophical details.

The opposite is true of the author of the other major play about the Occupation, Anouilh's *Antigone*. Jean Anouilh (1910-87), like Samuel Beckett, shunned personal publicity. Fortunately for him, his plays are more accessible than Beckett's and so he has been spared the plague of requests for enlightenment. His one concession to autobiography has been brief;

I have no biography, and am very happy with it so...I was born on 23 June 1910 in Bordeaux...a year and a half at the Law Faculty in

Paris, two years in an advertising agency where I learned to be exact and ingenious which for me was a substitute for the study of literature. After *L'Hermine* (*The Ermine*, 1932) I decided to earn my living solely by the theatre and a little film work. It was folly, but I did well in making that decision. I got by without journalism, and I have on my conscience in the cinema one or two comic sketches, and some forgotten and unsigned lyrics. The rest is my life...and I shall keep the details to myself.[16]

However, this quiet Bordelais produced in some fifty years many different plays, including comedies, tragedies and farces as well as combinations of the three. He labelled them *pièces roses, pièces noires, pièces brillantes, pièces grinçantes, pièces costumées, pièces baroques* and *pièces secrètes*. Being such a prolific and successful writer, he has – especially in the light of subsequent writers – been criticised for his very accessibility, as if this implies a lack of depth or commitment. It is a sad reflection on some literary critics that such inferences are made, simply because a writer manages to entertain rather than baffle or bore his audience. While he may not have worried himself with quite the same abstractions, one has only to look at such pieces as his *Antigone*, written during the war, and *Pauvre Bitos*, written as a result of the war, to discover a very real awareness of human complexity.

Antigone is, in fact, a successful realisation of what Sartre was trying to do with *Les Mouches*. There is the similar classical setting with its obvious allegorical allusions to occupied France; there is the similar apparently criminal act (in Orestes' case it was the murder of the tyrant, in Antigone's it is the forbidden burial of her brother); there is the same conscious decision of the protagonist to accept responsibility for that action, though in Antigone's case it leads to death, and while Sartre's work floundered in a welter of words, Anouilh managed to create a great play, one of the last tragedies to be written before the atomic bomb eliminated the potential for tragic stature by its indiscriminate destructive power.

The story-line is simple, borrowed from Sophocles: Antigone disobeys the instructions of Creon, the ruler, by choosing to perform a ritual burial of her brother, Polyneices who had been killed with his brother, Eteocles, in an abortive revolt. The authorities allow the burial of one with full honours while insisting that the other be left to rot. By the symbolic scattering of earth on the remains, Antigone would free her brother's soul but would thereby condemn herself to death. Even when told that the bodies were so badly disfigured that neither was recognisable and that it is uncertain who has been buried and who abandoned, she still insists on doing her duty, forcing Creon to condemn her to death. He accepts the responsibility, whereupon his son, who was engaged to Antigone, commits suicide with her.

When the play appeared during the war, it was initially viewed as pro-Nazi, promoting Creon, but soon the character of Antigone was recognised as symbolic of the Resistance and the whole piece taken as an attack on the occupying powers. However, the ambiguity of the content is testimony to Anouilh's skill, while the delightful mixture of anachronism in both the language and the detail, the eminently 'actable' minor parts like the Guard, the Nurse and the Chorus – a part chosen by Laurence Olivier in the British production – and the blend of emotion, comedy and tragedy make the play worthy of examination by any student of the theatre. Harold Hobson saves his most eulogistic style for it;

> *Antigone* does not owe its immortality to the fact that...it was at one particular point in history...a document of high social significance, but to the other and more important fact that it is a living, breathing play, instinct with the spirit of bitterness and regret, of poetry and disgust, of horror at the contrast between what life could be and what life is that makes Anouilh the most deeply seering as well as the greatest of modern French dramatists: indeed one of the very greatest dramatists in the whole of European history. No other French dramatist passes through such torments as Anouilh: no other dramatist has so poignant a vision of such soaring heights...[17]

And yet he was able to write gentle comedies like *L'Invitation au Chateau* (called, by Christopher Fry, in what must be one of the finest but freest pieces of translation – *Ring Round the Moon*) which again taxed the superlatives of the critics: 'a perfectly faceted jewel of theatricality' (O'Connor);[18] 'a delightful theatrical fantasy, full of wit, charm and comic invention' (McIntyre);[19] while Peter Brook, the play's first director in London described Anouilh as: 'A poet, but not a poet of words: he is a poet of words-acted, of scenes-set, of players performing.'[20]

In *L'Invitation*, Anouilh employs the classic comic device of identical twins with its subsequent potential for mistaken identities, but he uses it to examine the two conflicting elements in man's character and creates a theatrical 'tour de force'.

> Mankind has from time immemorial transposed reality into comic and conventionalized terms. He has created in the theatre an alternative, timeless world in which he can laugh at his own absurdity and ineffectualness and in which things turn out all right in the end...The vision of life may be bleak but the antidote lies to it in the comic form of the play. This is...the real significance of *L'Invitation au Chateau*...the Theatre, by helping us to laugh at ourselves, offers the possibility of some reconciliation with the harsh realities of life and a chance for a respite from them which gives us the courage to go on.[21]

Anouilh regularly claimed that he was not a political or philosophical figure, stating that he could not take himself sufficiently seriously: 'la critique sociale ne m'intéresse pas. Il faut moquer l'homme, cela suffit.' (Social criticism does not interest me; it's enough to make fun of mankind.)[22] While his comic style may be more accessible than that of Ionesco or Beckett, his claim that: 'thanks to Molière, the real French theatre is the one where we laugh, like men at war...at our misery and horror'[23] is little more than a paraphrase of Ionesco's: 'Even when we see corpses, we have to respond by laughing.' It was this comic element in what was to be called 'the Theatre of the Absurd' that was not immediately obvious when it first appeared after the war.

As was so often the case, Paris had become the refuge for many exiled writers, amongst whom were the Irishman, Samuel Beckett, the Rumanian Eugene Ionesco and the Armenian Russian, Arthur Adamov. The other author whose work would come to be categorised with that of the exiles was in his own way an outsider, for Jean Genet, whose play *Les Bonnes* (*The Maids*) (1947) predates any dramatic work by the other three, had set himself beyond 'normal' society by his novels in praise of his criminal and homosexual youth. Eventually, Martin Esslin was to group the work of these authors under the title of 'the Theatre of the Absurd' but this label has been seen to be less and less suitable, with Peter Hall offering instead 'the Theatre of Despair' as a more suitable epithet.

Kenneth Tynan, for one, in *Tynan on Theatre* could not accept Esslin's thesis:

> Tracing the forebears of the Absurd, Mr Esslin leads us back to the mime plays of antiquity; to the Commedia dell'Arte; to Edward Lear and Lewis Carroll; to Jarry, Strindberg and the young Rimbaud-impregnated Brecht...to the Surrealists and Antoin Artaud's 'Theatre of Cruelty'; to Kafka and Joyce.
>
> All this is helpful and credible. But when Mr Esslin ropes in Shakespeare, Goethe and Ibsen as harbingers of the Absurd, one begins to feel that the whole history of dramatic literature has been nothing but a prelude to the glorious emergence of Beckett and Ionesco.[24]

Excessive proselytising of an emergent faith is nothing new but is perhaps necessary in this case when the 'new theatre' appeared to be so difficult.

Now that Genet's plays are performed internationally, Ionesco's *The Bald Prima Donna* has been running for over twenty years in the same Paris theatre and Beckett's *Waiting for Godot* has received the ultimate accolade of becoming a set text for English schools, it is difficult to remember the bewilderment and incomprehension with which they were greeted by many of their first audiences. The main reason for this is because they did away with the reassuring conventions of character and plot, without which the audiences were as uncertain of the intended direction of the pieces as were the people portrayed in them. Once this new convention, that nothing was necessarily as expected, had been accepted, audiences were prepared to react to whatever it was they saw and heard. Ionesco had thought that the anti-logic of his *The Bald Prima Donna* was tragic, but once he and the actors discovered that the audience found it funny, he accepted this discovery and developed 'tragic farce', a description that can also be applied to Beckett's *Waiting for Godot* (1953).

It is arguable that no other single play has set up reverberations equivalent to those produced by *Waiting for Godot*. The images of the two tramps in the wasteland, waiting beneath a tree, of Lucky tied to Pozzo and of the boy with his messages have taken their places alongside the blinded Oedipus, Lear on the heath, Malvolio in the yellow garters, Tartuffe and his handkerchief, Faust in his study, Peer Gynt and the Button Moulder, and the sound of the felling of an orchard of cherry trees in a pan-European, if not world-wide theatrical consciousness.

Beckett (1906-89) would not or could not tell his actors what he meant by *Godot* and took delight in the confused and contradictory theories that abounded, theories that have generated a whole industry of critical speculation. This in its way is one aspect of the play's importance in that it generated so much thought and discussion, thereby bringing with it a seriousness of approach to the theatre which, in Britain at least, had not beeen particularly prevalent in the first half of the century.

The two most popular explanations, both apparently stemming from Beckett, are that: 'it suggested itself to him by the slang word for 'boot' – *Godillot, godasse,* because feet' – and boots – 'play such a prominent role in the play'[25] (and it is entertaining to wonder if such a suggestion prompted the predilection for the name 'Boot' that Tom Stoppard displays in a number of his plays), while the other tale is that, during the Tour de France, a crowd of fans was standing by the road after all the other cyclists had passed; when Beckett asked what they were doing, they replied: 'We're waiting for Godot', apparently the oldest and slowest of the competitors.

Whatever the 'meaning', there is considerable danger that the intense search for enlightenment will disguise the fact that the piece was intended as a comedy and, when played correctly, is very funny. The success of the veteran comedian, Max Wall, in a revival highlighted this element, although the choice of Bert Lahr, best known as the Cowardly Lion in the film of *The Wizard of Oz*, for the American premiere was less successful.

The comic element was obvious from the start to Roger Blin, the director and original Pozzo of the first production. Blin, a student of Dullin and colleague of Artaud and Barrault, had intended to play Vladimir and Estragon as circus clowns but Beckett had the idea of Chaplin and Keaton's type of comedy in mind and so the image of the little tramps took over. This, rather than any deep socio-economic comment, is the reason for dressing the two main characters as down-and-outs. Unfortunately, some directors got hold of the wrong end of the stick and played the piece as some sort of reflection on the Depression, rather than a clowning double act.

Deirdre Bair, in her masterly biography of Beckett, explains the origins of this type of dialogue:

> Beckett and Suzanne [Suzanne Descheveaux-Dumesnil, Beckett's long-time companion and eventual wife] had a relationship which many of their friends described as being like two Irish 'butties', trading vaudeville one-liners in the best music hall tradition. ['You should have been a poet', Vladimir says.' I was. Isn't that obvious?' Estragon replies] It would seem that Beckett took ordinary conversations between himself and Suzanne and incorporated them in *Godot*. Friends were astonished at how like their ordinary conversations the play's dialogue seemed. It was as if Beckett had transported wholesale the teasing, whining, loving, caring and sometimes bitter conversations his friends occasionally overheard.[26]

Equally, the search for a meaning to Vladimir's carrot – the sort of exercise that has taxed some over-zealous academics – becomes pointless in the light of Beckett's period of flight while fighting with the Resistance, when he was reduced to eating raw turnips from a field.

If *Godot* was open to all sorts of interpretations, then *Fin de Partie* (1957) (*Endgame*, the term taken from chess) inspired even more and fanciful theories. Hamm, who cannot see and is confined to a wheelchair is waited upon by Clov, who cannot sit down. They live in a blank room, with two windows, high up. In the corner, in dustbins, are Nell and Nagg, Hamm's parents.

It was possibly this relegation of the parents to the dustbin that outraged many early audiences but Beckett has a very practical reason for the image that has become indelibly associated with his plays. Initially he had considered having them going on and off in wheelchairs but this would have been confusing, given Hamm's situation, and would clutter up the wings. 'It is simply a question of logistics', Beckett is reported to have told Jean Martin, the original Clov. 'I put them there so they can pop their heads up and down as needed and nothing else was called for.'

One of the other, few pronouncements that Beckett made about the play was: 'There are no accidents in *Fin de Partie*. Everything is based on analogy', a statement that has generated the most wonderful speculation.

> Much has been found in *Fin de Partie*. King Lear, Hamlet, Noah in his ark; even Beckett and Suzanne in Roussillon, or Beckett in Ireland. The stage with its windows high up on the back wall has been interpreted as the interior of a human skull, also as a bomb shelter containing the last remaining human beings on earth. Hamm has been called Joyce and Beckett's father, Clov, Beckett the disciple and Beckett the son. The possibilities have been explored by critics and scholars who find in *Fin de Partie* endless opportunities for the brilliant workings of their own minds.[27]

Two quotations from the text of the play help to put it all into some perspective;

> HAMM: Breath held and then...(*he breathes out*) Then babble, babble, words like the solitary child who turns himself into children, two, three so as to be together and whisper together in the dark. (*pause*) Moment upon moment, pattering down like the millet grains of... (*he hesitates*) that old Greek and all life long you wait for that to mount up to a life.

– while an earlier conversation may be Beckett's joke:

> HAMM: Clov!
> CLOV: (*impatiently*) What is it!?
> HAMM: We're not beginning to...to...mean something?
> CLOV: Mean something? You and I? Mean something? (*brief laugh*) Ah, that's a good one!'

Only slightly more seriously, he said: 'My work is a matter of fundamental sounds...made as fully as possible and I accept responsibility for nothing else. If people want to have headaches among the overtones, let them. And provide their own aspirins...!'

If Beckett is secretive about himself to the point of paranoia, Eugene Ionesco (b. 1912) is quite the opposite. He is more than prepared to publicise himself and his work but, when discussing its 'message', has favoured Nabokov's rejoinder that he is a writer not a postman. To a certain extent, this is coy, because elsewhere he has explained the motivating force behind his work: 'I imagine that the world was created as a joke that God is playing on man. And what is the answer to that? Even when we see corpses, we have to respond by laughing.'[28]

Amazement at the content of his English language course textbook was the starting point for *The Bald Prima Donna*, where the 'tragedy of language' was to be displayed. Instead, this 'tragedy' provoked laughter and, eventually, for Le Théâtre de la Huchette, a production that ran for more than ten thousand performances, although, like *The Mousetrap*, there has been a considerable element of self-perpetuation in the run. Extravagant claims are made about the play; the actor, Nicolas Bataille has said:

> Of course, nonsense already existed with Lewis Carroll, but that was literature, not theatre, and Ionesco brought nonsense to the realist theatre and at the time it was like an explosion. I say explosion because it is a happier word than bomb, but it was a bomb in the realist bourgeois theatre of this century.[29]

In the light of the work of Jarry, Apollinaire and Goll, not to mention W.S. Gilbert and the English pantomime, this claim is somewhat extravagant, but perhaps it is true to say that the reverberations of this explosion were felt further afield than previous ones.

Apart from *The Bald Prima Donna*, Ionesco's most successful plays have been *The Lesson* (1951), *The Chairs* (1952), *Tueur sans Gages* (1959 – unsatisfactorily translated as *The Killer*, omitting the 'sans gages', 'without wages', which implies unpaid or amateur, as if for pleasure), and perhaps most famous of all, *Rhinoceros*, the terrifying world in which everyone with the exception of the 'hero', Berenger, turns into a rhinoceros. Again the interpretations have been legion with the rhinoceroses standing for conformity, the Nazis or, as Ionesco says:

> They staged it in Germany and the Germans said: 'That's us.' In Argentina they said: 'It's the Peronists'. In Spain they said: 'It's the Communists'. In the Eastern bloc they said: 'It's the Americans' and so on. But despite the different interpretations one fact remains: mass movement, conformity, man's incapacity, his difficulty in living alone, in resisting alone. In someone who resists there is an inner strength which is more real than the outside world but which is difficult for him to understand.[30]

The final words of Ionesco's final play, *Journeys Among the Dead*, are: 'I don't know'; in Beckett's *Breath*, actors and words are eliminated entirely and the whole reduced to a baby's cry, an inhalation, an exhalation and a death rattle. While it appears that Sir Peter Hall may be correct in describing it as a theatre of despair, there is at least one positive element: there may be an attempt to 'strip away the significance from human action, strip away the meaning', but the very act of creation, of producing the play, both on paper and on stage, of making people laugh at the tragedy, the absurdity or even the ludicrous nature of their existence is a positive, life-enhancing one. Life may be 'absurd' or even desperate but one of the things that combats the absurdity and the despair is the aspiration towards, and the actual achievement of, such works.

And a chief figure in the realisation of the work of many of the so-called 'Absurd' writers, as well as other major playwrights, brings us back to the influence of the directors on the history of French theatre this century.

Jean-Louis Barrault (b. 1910) synthesised the major influences of the first third of the century – Copeau, Dullin, Artaud and the mime, Decroux – and developed them in definitive productions of all the major French dramatists of the second third, reaching an international peak with his own celebration of life in *Rabelais* in 1968. He continues to be the 'grand seigneur' of French theatre, with his wife, Madeleine Renaud, as the indisputable 'grande dame'.

In his autobiographical jottings: *Souvenirs pour Demain* (*Memories for Tomorrow*) he is refreshingly modest when he says that his motto has always been: 'Se passionner pour tout et ne tenir à rien' ('To be fascinated by everything and to hold on to nothing'). He admitted his debt to Artaud but, like

Peter Brook, realised that he had to interpret the pronouncements himself: 'C'est ainsi qu'Artaud me passait une clef. A moi d'en trouver la surrure.' ('That's how Artaud gave me a key. It was up to me to find the lock'.)[31]

There is a catholicity about Barrault's choice of work which proves that he really does 'Se passioner pour tout', from Claudel's *Le Soulier de Satin* to Gide's adaptation of Kafka's *The Trial*, from Aeschylus to Shakespeare and Molière, from Lope de Vega to Brendan Behan, including the premieres of Beckett's *Oh, Les Beaux Jours (Oh, Happy Days)*, Genet's *Les Paravents (The Screens)* and Ionesco's *Rhinoceros*.

Prior to *Rabelais*, most people outside France would only have come across Barrault on film, most especially as 'Baptiste' the mime in Carne's *Les Enfants du Paradis* which not only demonstrated Barrault's exceptional physical control but also provided some sort of insight into the world of the theatre in nineteenth-century France. He continued playing in pantomime (a slightly less bastardised version than that which survived in England and nothing like the travesty that bears the name today) by keeping it in the repertoire of the company which he established with his wife in 1946. The company was a great adventure for them as they were both, Madeleine in particular, abandoning secure jobs in the established theatre in order to attempt to realise the sort of production style that Barrault envisaged. It is a mark of the attraction that the new company held when one sees that Honegger composed some of the music and Pierre Boulez and Maurice Jarre were involved in its performance.

The company was installed first at the Marigny and moved in 1959 to the Odéon where they stayed until they were literally driven from it in the student riots of May 1968; Barrault was sacked as a result of this debâcle, a brush with authority that was to encourage the creation of *Rabelais*. In 1972 they moved to the converted Quai d'Orsay, playing for a while in a circus tent within the station and realising, albeit briefly, Artaud's ideal theatre – 'Abandoning the architecture of present-day theatres, we will rent some kind of barn or hangar rebuilt along lines culminating in the architecture of some churches, holy places, or certain Tibetan temples'.[32]

In 1981 by which time he was over seventy, Barrault moved his company into the Théâtre du Rond Point, an erstwhile skating rink.

Barrault has been a most successful interpreter of other people's work but it was in a piece of his own concoction, his tribute to Rabelais, that he displayed both his delight in 'total theatre' and his *joie de vivre*. His paean to the sixteenth-century monk, surely a progenitor of the Absurd if ever there was one, in *Souvenirs Pour Demain* echoes the style of the original and shares its exuberance:

He is at one and the same time local, French and universal, everything I'd like to be...He's a tree. His roots suck up earth and dung.

> His trunk is as stiff as a phallus...His foliage reaches the sky and 'touches' God...he is a complete man...Rabelais is my oxygen. It is he, without my knowing it, who assured the continuity of my personal career. In my unconscious pursuit of a Father that made me choose the Dullins and the Claudels of this world, it was fated that some day, I should demand to be adopted by Rabelais.[33]

The piece that evolved was very physical, very sexy and very successful. It played in Paris, in Britain and then on tour in the United States, where it reached the University of Berkely in California just after the killing of students during the anti-war demonstrations at Kent State. There was a danger of riots but the authorities permitted the performance to go ahead. Four thousand squeezed into an auditorium intended for two and a half thousand. As Barrault says, it was: 'A unique moment for the victory of *l'esprit*, of the supremacy of human intelligence; the human heart took off like a rocket.' The script for *Rabelais* does not read well but it must be remembered that it was intended as the basis for a piece of theatre which was not to have the Word as its most important aspect.

The search for a 'New Theatre' that was to free the stage from what was seen as the restrictive, even lethal dominance of wordy pieces, manifested itself in several ways. The work of those directors who gave rise to, and eventually rationalised, Artaud's theories was one aspect of this search; the so-called 'Theatre of the Absurd' was another. Both, as embodied by Barrault and his younger colleagues such as Planchon, Mnouchkine, Savary and – since his move to Paris – Peter Brook, proclaim the fact that the twentieth century has been the most exciting period in French theatre since the heyday of Corneille, Racine and Molière in the latter half of the seventeenth; indeed, there are those for whom the Alexandrine hexameter lies dead on a school desk, who would claim supremacy for this present age over that past.

Ten plays for further consideration

1. Paul Claudel, *Le Soulier de Satin*
2. Jules Romains, *Knock*
3. Jean Giraudoux, *La Guerre de Troie n'aura pas lieu*
4. Jean Anouilh, *Antigone*
5. Jean Anouilh, *L'Invitation au Chateau* (*Ring Round the Moon*)
6. Jean Genet, *Les Bonnes* (*The Maids*)
7. Eugene Ionesco, *La Cantatrice Chauve* (*The Bald Prima Donna*)
8. Samuel Beckett, *En Attendant Godot* (*Waiting for Godot*)
9. Arthur Adamov, *Professeur Taranne*
10. Jean-Louis Barrault, *Rabelais*

Notes

1. David Bradby, *Modern French Drama from 1940 to 1980*
2. ibid., p. 3
3. T. Guicharnaud, *Modern French Theatre From Giraudoux to Genet*, p. 35
4. Jean-Louis Barrault, *Souvenirs pour Demain*, p. 103
5. Antonin Artaud, *Theatre and Its Double*, p. 55
6. ibid., p. 57
7. ibid., p. 60
8. R. Hayman, *Artaud and After*
9. Artaud, *Theatre and Its Double*, p. 64
10. ibid., p. 90
11. ibid., p. 92
12. ibid., p. 95
13. ibid., p. 72
14. ibid., pp. 76-8
15. Bradby, op. cit., p. 25
16. H.G. McIntyre, *The Theatre of Jean Anouilh*
17. Harold Hobson, *French Theatre since 1830*, p. 205
18. Gary O'Connor, *French Theatre Today*, p. 77
19. McIntyre, op. cit., p. 60
20. O'Connor, op. cit., p. 77
21. McIntyre, op. cit., p. 64
22. Extract from *Le Figaro*, quoted in McIntyre, op. cit., p. 136
23. ibid., p. 137
24. Kenneth Tynan, *Tynan on Theatre*, p. 190
25. Deirdre Bair, *Samuel Beckett: a biography*, p. 382
26. ibid., p. 385
27. ibid., p. 467
28. Eugene Ionesco, *The Joke's On Us*, BBC 2, 17 February 1989
29. ibid.
30. ibid.
31. Jean Louis Barrault, *Souvenirs pour Demain*, p. 106
32. Artaud, op. cit., p. 74
33. Barrault, intro. to *Rabelais*, pp. 15-16

4: LATIN MASTERS

The histories of the Italian and Spanish theatre display two distinct parallels in the twentieth century; firstly, they both produced men of genius in the early years who considerably overshadowed their contemporaries and secondly, they both suffered under fascist governments, which severely restricted the opportunities, if not actually blighting the atmosphere, for creative work. While plays of the highest calibre were being written despite the Franco regime in Spain, opportunities for production were limited; in Italy little of international note has appeared between the death of Ugo Betti in 1953 and the emergence of Dario Fo in the early seventies.

Italy's greatest legacy to world theatre has doubtlessly been the *Commedia dell'Arte* but, as with the Spanish Golden Age of Calderon and Lope de Vega, the era of Corneille, Racine and Molière in France and, to a certain extent, Shakespeare and his contemporaries in Britain, there is a danger that these achievements of the past are looked upon as insuperable and therefore not worth the effort of surpassing.

Luigi Pirandello (1867-1936) established himself as a novelist and writer of short stories and it was not until he was nearly fifty that he turned to the theatre; when at last he did, he started with dialect plays and a number of pieces which caused him to be 'pigeon-holed' with the *teatro del grottesco* authors; however, with his *Sei Personaggoi in Cerca D'Autore* (*Six Characters in Search of an Author*) (1921), he produced one of the most innovative and stimulating plays of the century, setting him beside his hero, Ibsen, his contemporary Shaw, his opposite, Brecht, and the man claimed by many to be his direct descendant, Beckett, as a universal theatrical influence. Walter Starkie, one of Pirandello's doughtiest champions, sees him as *the* father of modern drama:

> In those days the theatre slumbered on amid well-defined problems of social and moral order...nowadays, all is chaos...the modern mind might be compared to the inextricable maze...to Pirandello belongs the credit of having more than any Italian writer explored this maze...Through his instrumentality the ideas of the Grotesque theatre together with those of the Futurists have extended their influences over Europe, and even over the whole theatrical world, and we have witnessed in every country the death of the bourgeois, well-made play with its vestiges of Romanticism and the rise of a new

criticial drama which was to be an expression of the modern active mentality.[1]

Starkie's espousal of Pirandello's cause is excessively partisan, particularly when we compare the Italian work with what was going on in Germany. Starkie describes the Futurist, D'Annunzio's work as 'a ceaseless battle between decadent self-indulgence and a vigorous desire for action'[2] while '...mechanical puppetization is characteristic of all the productions of the Grotesque school' and 'in the Grotesque dramatists we saw the tendency to treat human beings as puppets or else cogwheels in an immense engine-driven world';[3] this could equally apply to Ernst Toller's *Masse Mench* or Georg Kaiser's *Gas*, to Fritz Lang's film *Metropolis* or, more popularly, the most widely seen of all such attacks, Charlie Chaplin's *Modern Times*. The lesson from all this is simply that the need for change was being felt throughout Europe, with each culture reacting in a different, though comparable way.

The *teatro del grottesco* with which Pirandello was initially aligned was simply a label attached, often by the writers themselves, to plays which attempted a move away from naturalism: 'by the development of ironic, parodistic and grotesque situations'.[4]

The most widely performed piece to which this label was given was Luigi Chiarelli's *La Maschera ed il Volto* (*The Mask and the Face*) (1916) which rather crudely grafts the popular dichotomy about the differences between appearances and reality onto what is initially a sexist comedy of adultery. During a languorous evening of high-society indulgence, flirting, drinking and gambling, Savina – Paolo's wife – is discovered almost 'in flagrante delicto' after an assignation with Luciano, Paolo's friend and lawyer. Paolo insists that she go away, never to return, with which she complies, whereupon Paolo claims to all that he has killed her by throwing her off the veranda into the lake! What is remarkable to modern eyes and ears is that this is treated as being morally acceptable, that the woman should be treated as a chattel by her husband who is free to dispose of her as he likes; with the aid of Luciano, Paolo is declared innocent of any crime. There are great celebrations during the course of which a body is discovered in the lake. Paolo, inexplicably, identifies it as that of Savina and a large and lavish funeral is arranged. During the funeral, the real Savina returns, Paolo discovers how much he loves her and the play ends with the two of them watching the cortège in which the supposed body of Savina is being taken away for burial.

Although concepts of reality, identity and the falsity of social conventions are aired, the lasting reaction to the piece nowadays would be one of distaste. This, however, is the sort of theatre that Pirandello was entering.

Pirandello was born in Sicily in 1867. While some writers choose to be reticent about their lives and the ignorance of such details is no hindrance to an appreciation of their work, an awareness of the drama, not to say tragedy, of Pirandello's life adds considerably to an understanding of the themes that continually surface in his work.

A few years after the birth of their third child, his wife, Antonietta, suffered a complete mental breakdown. The family business – his wife was the daughter of his father's partner – had been a Sicilian sulphur mine and when this was destroyed by floods, Pirandello's financial independence went with it. He was forced to earn a living teaching, while at the same time coping with his wife's gradual mental deterioration. He struggled to look after her for sixteen years but eventually she had to be committed and spent the last forty years of her life in an asylum. As John Linstrum has written: 'She was convinced that her husband was unfaithful, and she created her own image that was far from reality. Pirandello was condemned to live with this constant picture of this other man presented to himself...'[5]

Here, in his own family life, we see the themes that were to surface in two of his major plays; in *Six Characters*, they are reality and illusion, the author's responsibility as creator, and family life; in *Henry IV* (1922), they are madness, illusion and performance. And pervading all his work, perhaps inevitably, is a powerful misogyny. Silvia in *Il Giuoco delle Parti* (*The Rules of the Game*) (1918), the step-daughter and the leading actress in *Six Characters*, Mathilda and to some extent Frieda in *Henry IV* are all dangerous, destructive women who, if not always intentionally, tend to bring about the tragedy.

Six Characters in Search of an Author must vie with *The Bald Prima Donna*, *Waiting for Godot* and *Look Back In Anger* for the most memorable title of a play written this century. It is rarely performed and best known by report; on examination, it is easy to see why. At first sight, it is brilliant, a *coup de théâtre* of genius, namely bringing characters, creations of the playwright, on stage to mingle with 'real' people.

Into a rehearsal of a play by Pirandello, interrupting the Producer, cast and crew, come a family of six 'characters', fugitives from an unwilling author's mind. As Pirandello himself says in his stage-direction:

> The most effective idea is to use masks for the CHARACTERS... this is the way to bring out the deep significance of the play. The CHARACTERS should not appear as ghosts, but as created realities, timeless creations of the imagination, and so more real and consistent than the changeable realities of the ACTORS. The masks are designed to give the impression of figures constructed by art, each one fixed forever in its own fundamental emotion; that is, Remorse for the FATHER, Revenge for the STEPDAUGHTER, Scorn for the SON, Sorrow for the MOTHER...

The debt to the set-character masks of the *Commedia dell'Arte* is obvious but Pirandello's mixing of types with actors is ingenious indeed. Throughout the piece, the Characters are trying to tell their story to the Producer so that the Actors can realise it. The best way for them to tell their story is to play it out, for the actors to copy. The main scene in the story takes place when the Father, ignorant of the existence of the Stepdaughter, meets her in a dressmaker's-cum-brothel; it is only the fortuitous arrival of the Mother that stops the seduction by the Father of the Stepdaughter. When the Actors try to play the same scene, relying on technique and trickery, it all becomes ludicrously false. The play concludes with the deaths of the Young Brother and the Little Sister, performed in a stylised manner and yet supposed to be real, for the piece ends with only the four surviving Characters on stage until the Stepdaughter runs out through the audience, laughing hysterically. The final stage direction is: 'We can still hear her manic laughter out in the foyer and beyond.'

Throughout the play, the theme of the impossibility of communication reappears, along with those of time, space, reality and permanence. The Father says: 'But isn't that the cause of all the trouble? Words! We all have a world of things inside ourselves and each one of us has his private world. How can we understand each other if the words I use have the sense and value that I expect them to have, but whoever is listening to me inevitably thinks that those same words have a different sense and value, because of the private world he has inside of himself too!'[6] This philosophical nicety, carried by the Father to the extreme of paranoia, is expressed further: 'This is the real drama for me; the belief that we all, you see, think of ourselves as one single person: but it's not true: each of us is several different people, and all these people live inside us. With one person we seem like this and with another we seem very different. But we always have the illusion of being the same person for everybody...but it's not true!'[7]

This theme, realised in such a brilliant image as the Characters, is perfectly valid, but the very act of staging the play destroys the concept, because human actors have to adopt the roles of the timeless Characters. Beings from the same level of reality have to play both the Actors and the Characters and the clear distinction that Pirandello can establish in his own mind and to a lesser extent on paper becomes irreparably confused, in spite of the use of masks. The masterpiece has to remain a cerebral exercise for, when the climax of the death of the children is reached on stage, the refinement of the idea is reduced by the very act of realisation. Because of the nature of the Characters, it is not possible for the audience to rely upon any suspension of disbelief and *Six Characters* remains a spectacular display of intellectual pyrotechnics, rather than a solid, effective masterpiece.

In *Enrico IV* (*Henry IV*) (1922), Pirandello came nearer to creating this masterpiece, although it has to be said that it has been faulted on grounds of excessive verbosity, perhaps a legacy of the novelist. In this play the false world is more easily established and maintained. The nameless twentieth-century hero who, as a result of an accident, believes himself to be the

Emperor Henry IV of Germany, is maintained in this illusory world by servants and friends. Unbeknown to the others he regains his sanity but does not let on, and so *pretends* to be both insane and someone else. At the end, he kills Belcredi, the man who had caused the initial accident and, even though he has revealed his sanity, he has to revert to a pretence of madness in order to protect himself from the legal responsibility for the killing.

The remarkable convolutions of the plot are more satisfactory here because they are, at least, feasible and there is a definite tragic stature in Henry's final lines:

> HENRY IV [*he has remained on stage, eyes wide, appalled at the force of his own acting, which has so suddenly made him commit a crime.*]
> Yes…no choice now…[*He calls them round him, as if for protection.*]
> Here together…here together…and for always!

Pirandello has written of his theatre and his world: 'I see, as it were, a labyrinth where our soul wanders through countless, conflicting paths, without ever finding a way out. In this labyrinth I see a two-headed Hermes which with one face laughs and with the other weeps; it laughs with one face at the other face's weeping.'[8] His own experience of life provided him with this philosophy, one that was to appeal greatly to the writers of the Absurd. However, his claim – 'One of the novelties that I have given to modern drama consists in converting the intellect into passion' – is wrong and should be completely transposed; like Beckett, he has imposed his intellect upon the pain and passions of his own life, using this intellectual rigour to fashion out of the suffering of the years of his wife's insanity, works which by their very creation impose order upon disorder and madness.

Pirandello's plays have been so popular and their ideas have had so much influence throughout both Europe and America that it is not surprising that contemporaries and successors tend to pale in comparison, although it must be remembered that Mussolini came to power in 1922 and that the following twenty years can hardly have been conducive to the liberal creative spirit.

Ugo Betti (1892-1953) was the remarkable combination of poet, playwright and High Court judge and it is hardly surprising that his work dealt with the fallibility of human justice and the nature of guilt. In *L'Aiuola Bruciata* (*The Burnt Flower-Bed*) written 1951-2 and performed in 1955 at the Arts Theatre, London, Betti combined his obsession with 'men's fatal disregard or defiance of God' (Henry Reed) with a political topic, reminiscent of Sartre's *Les Mains Sales*.

The play deals with responsibility for actions, be they the collective actions of a government or the existential responsibility of an individual. Giovanni and his wife Luisa have retired from public life to a house high in the mountains; they are having great difficulty overcoming the grief and guilt experienced by the fact that they may have unwittingly been responsible for the apparently accidental death of their son, an obsession that is sending Luisa mad. Tomaso, a figure from the Government of which Giovanni was once leader, visits in an attempt to coax him back to public life. This is a trap, because the motive behind it is to sacrifice Giovanni in order to induce a war. Eventually, Giovanni forces his wife to face the truth that their son's death was suicide:

> ...don't you see what's happening? Children are refusing to live. There's nothing more to do about it, everything's wrong and rotten within! The marrow in the bone is revolting against itself, the stones are turning into toads!...

Faced with such a bleak outlook, Giovanni is prepared to let himself be killed. However, Rosa, a young girl, sacrifices herself by drawing the fire intended for Giovanni and the piece ends on a note of muted optimism.

Betti's advocates regard him as a finer dramatic artist than Pirandello, claiming that Pirandello's major work was his body of short stories and that his drama, influential as it was, was more effective theoretically than theatrically. This does seem to be making too great a claim for Betti; there is no doubt that he is a very capable craftsman, one whose work has been ignored for too long, particularly in Britain, but while he may be in the 'Italian First Division', Pirandello has to be considered as the member of a European 'Super-League'.

After the death of Betti in 1953 the leading figure in the Italian theatre was Eduardo de Filippo (1900-1985). The de Filippo family was born and bred in the world of the theatre and in 1932, Eduardo, his sister Titina and brother Peppino formed their own company which lasted until the end of the war. When Peppino left to work alone, Eduardo and his sister formed 'Il Teatro di Eduardo', the company for which de Filippo was to write some forty plays, all couched in the dialect of Naples and all providing 'meaty' roles for himself and his sister. In Britain, the best-known of these have been *Filumena Maturano (Filumena)* (1946) and *Sabato, Domenica e Lunedì (Saturday, Sunday, Monday)* (1959) which was performed in an adaptation by Keith Waterhouse and Willis Hall at the National Theatre in 1973, with a cast that included Frank Finlay and Joan Plowright, with Laurence Olivier as the irascible old grandfather and former hatter, forever stretching people's hats on his last. This play is a fine example of de Filippo's style, filled as it is with three well-defined but squabbling generations of a Neapolitan family, their friends and neighbours. It deals with the deteriorating relationship between the husband and wife who have no time to talk to each other because of their obligations to business and family respectively, and centres upon the preparations for and the eating of the 'ragù' or Sunday lunch. Rosa's preparation of the Sunday joint anticipates the sort of detail that Arnold

Wesker was to include in his play *The Kitchen*, while the skill with which de Filippo depicts and delineates the various characters with all their whims, frailties, individual quirks and mannerisms displays not only acute observation but also a masterly handling of comic situations; it implies and demands considerable 'ensemble' playing, both from the company that originated it and from one that might choose to attempt it.

However it was not until the early seventies when Dario Fo (b. 1926) burst on to the collective theatre-going consciousness with his superb one-man 'epic', *Mistero Buffo* and followed it with the plays *Morte Accidentale di un Anarchico* (*Accidental Death of an Anarchist*) (1970), *Non si Paga! Non si Paga!* (*Can't Pay, Won't Pay*) (1974) and *Clacson, Trombette e Pernacchi* (*Trumpets and Raspberries*) (1981), that a figure of anything like international status appeared to threaten Pirandello's mythic position.

Anyone who has seen Fo perform will be aware that he is a great comic actor; he has the ability to infect an audience with laughter, using mime, clowning and an orchestral vocal range, a one-man 'total theatre'. However, when one realises that the targets for his humour in *Mistero Buffo* are organised religion, exploitative Capitalism and the conservative, if not actually fascist, government of Italy, then the clowning takes on a new significance, a significance that is emphasised in the plays.

Dario Fo started as a story-teller-cum-cabaret performer and, with his wife, Franca Rame, ran a company that specialised in comedy and satire. However, the events of 1968 were as momentous for Fo in Italy as they were for Jean-Louis Barrault in France, inspiring a new direction in his career. The Fos abandoned 'bourgeois' theatres and with a short-lived new company, Nuova Scena, attempted to take theatre to a new working-class audience in factories and working-men's clubs, even playing in tents and the open air. Unfortunately, they found the Communist Party to include elements as intransigent as some of the institutions that they were attacking in their stage-shows and so a further split occurred, resulting in another new company, La Commune. This was the group that first produced *Can't Pay, Won't Pay* and the remarkable *Accidental Death*.

Accidental Death is based on the true story of an anarchist who, while in police custody, was supposed to have committed suicide by jumping out of an upper window. There were so many suspicious non-sequiturs and blatant contradictions in the various eye-witness reports that it was obvious that the man had been killed by the police and the affair hushed up. Using some of the actual testimonies and featuring his own character, 'the Lunatic', who acts as a comic catalyst, Fo creates a hilarious farce which not only entertains the audience but employs the greatest educative method – comedy – to make a very serious criticism of a legal and political system.

His plays were greeted with two distinctly differing attitudes: the eulogistic and the reserved:

If an Italian theatre exists, it should be produced exactly like this...If there were a hundred plays like this a year, one could say that the Italian theatre was alive. Probably ninety-nine of these plays could be discarded...In compensation, however, we would have the delight of feeling that inside the enormous, semi-paralysed, gaudy but bloodless body of Italian theatre, hot and surging blood has started to flow again. Since there are unfortunately only two or three plays like this a year instead of a hundred, they end up being regarded with suspicion, from the viewpoint of orderliness and definement of museum theatre.[9]

This sort of view is balanced by a more conservative Zeffirelli;

Fo is a very great actor, director and clown, the last great clown of our time. I don't judge Fo's work from a political point of view; to me it's enough that his work is good, which it is, on an artistic level.

It may seem that this sort of reaction to politics in theatre is the correct view, that polemics can, more often than not, overbalance the piece and detract from the theatrical effect, a criticism that can be applied to Fo's *Trumpets and Raspberries* and which has to be laid at Brecht's door on occasions. However, when one discovers that Franca Rame, Fo's wife, was abducted at gunpoint in March 1973 by a group of Right-wing sympathisers, thrown in the back of van, beaten up, raped, burned with cigarettes, slashed with razors and then abandoned in a park because of their dislike of the political content of La Commune's performances – an experience that, with Fo, she was able to synthesise into the one-woman show, *Female Parts,* then the political necessity rather than the theatrical luxury of such work becomes apparent. The remarkable thing, in the light of this event, was the return of the Fos to a broader audience for, as Ms Rame wrote: 'I realised that in turning our backs on the so-called bourgeois theatre, we were refusing a portion of spectators who would never have come to a stadium or under a tent but still had the right to be entertained, to laugh and at the same time to see certain problems dealt with.'[10]

It may well prove that Fo's work is ephemeral; in the case of *Mistero Buffo* this is inevitable; but others have performed his plays elsewhere and while differing political climates may cause the effect of the satire to diminish, there is no doubting his remarkable theatrical expertise.

The effects of a fascist rule are also indelibly evident in the history of Spain in the twentieth century and, as with every other aspect of life, the theatre did not escape this malignancy. In fact, Frederico Garcia Lorca (1898-1936) was murdered by the Falangists at the beginning of the Civil War, thereby depriving Spain of its greatest poet and playwright this century.

Being first and foremost a poet, Garcia Lorca displayed strong lyrical and figurative elements in his plays; indeed, in a piece like *Dona Rosita la soltera, o el lenguaje de las flores* (*Dona Rosita the Spinster or the Language of Flowers*) (1935) it is possible to argue that the essential image, of the girl Rosita who waits twenty years in vain for her lover to return, only to blossom and fade like the roses in her uncle's garden, is too obvious to maintain an entire play, no matter how effective the verse.

Some of his early plays were written simply for the amusement of his family and friends, for his own puppet theatre at home, although when one learns that he had the assistance of his friend, the composer, Manuel de Falla, in setting these early works to music, one realises that they must have been amateur dramatics of some merit!

Lorca experimented with rustic farces, such as *La zapatera prodigiosa* (*The Prodigious Shoemaker's Wife*) (1926), which dealt with the age-old theme of the old husband taking a young wife. The old shoemaker was not happy with his new bride and so left home; in order to make ends meet, the wife turned the home into a bar and the neighbours automatically assumed the worst about the 'goings-on' there. The shoemaker returns in disguise as a ballad singer, discovers that not only was his wife faithful, but also devoted to him, and so the outcome is happy. Lorca dealt with a similar theme in *El amor de don Perlimpin con Belisa en su jardin* (*The Love of Don Perlimpin with Belisa in his Garden*) (1928) but this time expressing quite the opposite view of the fidelity of young wives.

However, it was with his three peasant tragedies, *Bodas de Sangre* (*Blood Wedding*) (1933), *Yerma* (1934) and *La casa de Bernada Alba* (*The House of Bernada Alba*) (1936), that Lorca displayed his ever-increasing mastery of tragic theatre; the calibre of this last piece, completed in the year of his murder, leaves one speculating sadly about what might have been. The development from the sparse verse and brutal exposition of *Blood Wedding*, where the tragedy appears to be not so much inevitable as obvious, to the terrible inexorability of the obsession that drives Bernarda Alba is remarkable when one considers that only three years separate the two pieces.

The first play, in the style of the Gypsy Ballad, depends for much of its effect on the poetry; the story itself is as elemental as that of his earlier farces: a man runs off with the bride during the wedding and so the groom is honour-bound to hunt the fugitives down and the two men kill each other in a final fight. It is the telling of the tale that is all important and because of the verse, Lorca's work – more than that of most other playwrights – is bound to lose in translation; what may be powerful and effective in the original can appear florid and even banal in translation. *Blood Wedding* uses song a great deal, as well as the personification of such elemental figures as the Moon and Death. To an English audience, unaccustomed, despite the efforts of Fry and Eliot, to contemporary verse drama, the speech of the Moon, prior to the death of Leonardo and the bridegroom, can be hard to credit:

I'm cold! My ashes
Of somnolent metals
Seek the fire's crest
On mountains and streets.
But the snow carries me
Upon its mottled back
And pools soak me
In their water, hard and cold
But this night there will be
Red blood for my cheeks
And for the reeds that cluster
At the wide feet of the wind
…Oh let me enter a breast
Where I may get warm!
A heart for me!
Warm!That will spurt
Over the mountains of my chest…

The symbolism above may be difficult for a foreign audience to accept nowadays but there is no doubting the emptiness and pain at the end of the piece when the bride and the mother are left to grieve over the deaths of the two men:

MOTHER: Neighbours: with a knife
With a little knife
On their appointed day, between two and three,
These two men killed each other for love.
With a knife,
With a tiny knife
That barely fits the hand
But that slides in clean
Through the astonished flesh
And stops at the place
Where trembles, enmeshed
The dark root of a scream.

Even in translation, the images of 'the astonished flesh' and 'the dark root of a scream' have immense power; that said, though, it has to be admitted that the recent flamenco ballet version, inspired by the play and expressing the essence rather than the actual words, has infinitely more effect than a simple translation.

The same, though, cannot be said of *The House of Bernarda Alba*; even in translation, this is one of the great tragedies, one of the last in a tradition that goes back for thousands of years but which, arguably, can no longer be followed. Although this is not the place for debating the thesis that the creation of the atomic bomb brought about the death of tragedy, with the potential for arbitrary and universal destruction eliminating that element of control of one's destiny that was essential to tragedy, it must be said that *Bernarda Alba* would have been a worthy member of the chorus for the swansong.

Whereas the deaths of the bridegroom and Leonardo were sad, there is an atmosphere of inevitability that pervades *Bernarda Alba* right from the start, from the gathering of the women of the town, all clad in black, to mourn the death of the husband, to the hounding of Adela to self-destruction at the end. The situation is fraught and unnatural, for it is a house full of women, and only women. There is Bernarda Alba, her five spinster daughters, her senile mother and two female servants. There is an inevitable difficulty in differentiating between the daughters who are all of much the same age, though it is really only Angustias, the eldest, and Adela, the youngest, that feature strongly; they are the rivals for the attentions of Pepe el Romano, the play's symbol of masculinity who, like everything else male, remains off-stage throughout, to be imagined by the audience and ogled by the women.

The atmosphere of stifling emotion is heightened by the insistence upon the heat and by the fact that they are in mourning. The grandmother, Maria Josepha, is physically locked away because of her senility while the others are confined by invisible but equally restrictive codes. Bernarda represses her daughters with a fury that verges upon the manic: 'None of them has ever had a beau and they've never needed one! They get along very well!', and there is nothing that Poncia the servant – a character reminiscent of Juliet's Nurse – can do to change her mistress' mind.

As the daughters must be married in order of age, men are forbidden to all but the eldest – Bernarda permits Angustias to speak with Pepe from her balcony – and, inevitably, men are the thing the women talk about the most. Martirio, (an apt name if ever there was one), says: 'It's better never to look at a man. I've been afraid of them since I was a little girl... One time I stood in my nightgown at the window until daybreak because he [Enrique] let me know...that he was going to come, and he didn't. It was all just talk. Then he married someone else who had more money than I.'

Even the senile grandmother is still obsessed with men and marriage: 'I don't want to see these single women, longing for marriage, turning their hearts to dust; and I want to go to my home town. Bernarda, I want a man to get married to and be happy with.' And this from a character who is specified as being eighty.

This obsession with sex and the effect that repression has on the women is shown to have perverted Bernarda when, in the second act, Poncia tells of a girl who has had an illegitimate child:

PONCIA: And to hide her shame she killed it and hid it under the rocks, but the dogs, with more heart than most Christians, dug it out and as though directed by the hand of God, left it at her door. Now they want to kill her.

This incenses Bernarda until she cries: 'Yes, let them all come with olive whips and hoe handles – let them come and kill her...finish her before the guards come. Hot coals in the place where she sinned!' and the scene ends with Martirio and Barnarda egging each other on to greater heights of hysteria while Adela, sympathetic because she fears a similar fate – 'holding her belly' – screams 'No, no!'

The inevitability of the tragedy that unfolds after Adela has made love to Pepe in the stables is terrible to see. The women try to shoot Pepe like some vermin while Adela, believing him to be dead, hangs herself. And it is the absence of repentance and understanding in the remaining women that heightens the tragedy as, led by Bernarda, they are forced to present a respectable face to the world:

> BERNARDA: ...Cut her down. My daughter died a virgin. Take her to another room and dress her as though she were a virgin. No-one will say anything about this! She died a virgin. Tell them so that at dawn the bells will ring twice.
>
> MARTIRIO: A thousand times happy she who had him.
>
> BERNARDA: And I want no weeping. Death must be looked at face to face. Silence! [*To one daughter*] Be still, I said! [*To another*] Tears when you are alone! We'll drown ourselves in a sea of mourning. She, the youngest daughter of Bernarda Alba, died a virgin! Did you hear me? Silence, I said. Silence.

This terrible attitude, preferring death and virginity to life and sexual fulfilment, takes on even greater power when one remembers that a society that could breed a Bernarda also instigated the murder of her creator.

Garcia Lorca was killed in 1936 at the outset of the Civil War, a war that brought about the dictatorship of General Franco, a restrictive regime that lasted until his death in 1975. One of the many suppressive effects that this government had upon the cultural life of Spain was a censorship that would have been positively comic if it had been the invention of a George Orwell in a *1984* or an *Animal Farm* but which, being real, was responsible for the strictures put upon tentative playwrights and for the ignorance in other countries of the work produced under these restrictions. The system is so remarkable that it is worth quoting in full a description of the critical climate:

> Gabriel Arias Salgado, the first Minister of Information, whose background included fourteen years spent in training to become a Jesuit priest, displayed a loyalty to Franco that bordered on servility. Arias was paternalistic and puritanical in his approach to what Spaniards could safely read or hear and later claimed in all seriousness that his censorship had saved 80,000 souls from Hell. During his

thirteen years of administration, theatrical censorship consisted of circulating scripts to readers – usually government employees or priests – for approval or disapproval. These well-meaning but biased, unsophisticated readers capriciously forbade works or blue-pencilled words and entire scenes deemed detrimental to the prevailing political, social or moral order. It was not until after Arias' successor, Manuel Fraga Iribarne, took office that norms were formalised and a board of supposedly knowledgeable readers established. The guiding philosophy behind theatrical censorship in effect from 1963 until after Franco's death was to forbid all works or parts thereof that: 1) offended in any way the fundamental principles of the new Spanish state; 2) ran counter to the beliefs, practices and morality of the Catholic Church; 3) portrayed negatively any representative of church, state or army. Numerous specific prohibitions also forbade: colloquial expressions (swear words); images that might offend conjugal love or provoke low passion; scenes that denied one's obligation to defend the homeland; the undignified presentation of political ideologies; the falsification of facts, personalities or historical events; works that encouraged a hatred between the classes; any pornographic or blasphemous works; any work offensive to the most elementary standards of good taste. The definition of the terms used (e.g. blasphemous, falsification, pornography, good taste) was left to the discretion of the censor involved.[11]

In the light of such restrictions, it is amazing that anything even vaguely effective was produced and hardly surprising that what was written tended to be either allegorical in an attempt to circumvent the censorship, historical or else a realistic 'slice of life', leaving the audience to draw whatever conclusions they could from the observations.

The use of allegory has a long and strong tradition in the Spanish theatre, a tradition in which the works of the seventeenth-century playwright, Calderon, arguably Spain's greatest, feature strongly. *La vida es sueno* (*Life is a dream*) and *El gran teatro del mundo* (*The great theatre of the world*) not only provided examples for Spanish authors but also, in the 1920s, for Hugo von Hofmannsthal, the Austrian playwright and librettist.

The allegorical use of a building in *La vida es sueno* is repeated in José Ruibal's *El hombre y la mosca* (*The Man and the Fly*) where, instead of Calderon's tower, the structure is a dome within which the Man and his Double exist, keeping what is left of the world at bay outside.

The stage directions at the opening leave one in no doubt as to the allegorical content:

The Man and his Double live in an enormous crystal dome...It is constructed of glass panels decorated with battle scenes, trophies of hunting, fishing and war...The dome rests on a base of skulls...The Man is very old, his face weathered and tough. The Double, seventy years younger, is physically identical to the Man but his pallid face reflects the fact that he has been nurtured in a greenhouse.

At the end of the piece, the Double destroys the dome while trying to kill an enormous fly on the outside.

The play sets up many echoes, apart from that of Calderon; the interdependent relationship between the Man and the Double is reminiscent of Beckett, be it Pozzo and Lucky, Vladimir and Estragon or, given the restricted space, Hamm and Clov. The Double inevitably reminds one of the German predilection for the 'doppelganger' which appears both in Kaiser's *Gas* and Werfel's *Spiegelmensch*, while the use of the fly as the symbol of retribution comes straight from Sartre's *Les Mouches*.

Appreciation of the satire in Antonio Martinez Ballesteros' play, *The Best of All Possible Worlds*, does not demand such literary allusions; apart from its obvious reference to Voltaire's *Candide* in the title, the comedy is robust, even blatant, employing stage violence that is as physical as that of any Molière farce or Chaplin 'short'; it is not surprising that the piece was banned, for the 'allegory' is hardly subtle.

The play features a character called 'John Poor', another entitled 'Mr Chameleon' who starts off as a revolutionary being atrociously beaten and ends as secretary to the Minister of Repression, continuously feeding himself and only occasionaly finding time for arbitrary yet important decisions; there is a General White and a General Black who spend their whole time contradicting each other; the Dictator dictates the news reports that are to be issued about himself, and a pair of comic jailers indulge in cartoon-style violence, eventually breaking John's leg. However, for all its comic-strip simplicity, the play has a definite power and the juxtapositions in the final scene are very effective, with John, battered and alone in his cell, condemned to twelve years imprisonment, despite the Dictator's admission of his innocence, his wife alone and in tears at home, while the Dictator is seen with the neighbouring tyrant at a public ceremony of mutual presentation of such ludicrous awards as: 'The Medal of Good Will in Observation of Social and Political Problems' and 'The Promoter of Football and Other Sports'.

However, allegorical satire was not the only style being used in the sixties and seventies. A fine example of social realism, reminiscent of Wesker and early Tennessee Williams, is Lauro Olmo's *The Shirt*. It deals with the problems of unemployment and of emigration enforced by poverty. While those are the bare essentials of description, they do not do justice to what is a panoramic portrait of the teeming life of a Spanish back street and tenement. In scenes that bear comparison with O'Casey's depiction of Dublin or the New Orleans of Williams' *A Streetcar Named Desire*, Olmo depicts a world which, in spite of its poverty, is a vibrant and often funny community.

Set on the street corner, centred on Paco's bar to one side and the shack that is home for Juan, Lola, the grandmother, Lolita and Agustinello on the other, the play manages to entertain as well as educate without reverting to the maudlin and melodramatic elements that characterised a British handling of a similar theme, *Love on the Dole*.

Realised alongside the family we see Mr Paco, the aging lecher of a barkeeper, Uncle Maravillas, a sad, drunken old balloon seller, the tragic young couple from the neighbouring flats, Ricardo and Maria, their neighbour, Miss Balabina, three 'lads', Lolo, Luis and Sebas, and a street-wise delinquent, Nacho, whose heart, if not of gold, is certainly gilt.

Permeating the presentation of this little society is the central dilemma, whether Lola should leave her husband and family and emigrate to Germany to take a job as a maid. This is highlighted by 'the tale of the shirt' as Lola tries hard to find a shirt good enough for Juan to wear to make a suitable impression when going for job interviews.

But it is the background detail that makes the whole thing so effective and which displays Olmo's mastery of his medium. The grandmother cooks and bathes, Lola washes, irons and mends the precious shirt, Paco entices people into his bar, Maria and the young drunk, Ricardo, act out their little tragedy almost as a side-show to the rest, Uncle Maravillas' wife dies, Lolo wins the pools and enventually Lola does leave for Germany. There may be echoes of Williams and Wesker, de Filippo and Gorki in the situation but the whole is integrated by Olmo to produce a peculiar and touching tribute to the Spanish character, in spite of all the social difficulties.

Antonio Buerjo Vallejo's *The Basement Window* does not depend upon its 'Spanishness' for effect, although the crowded train journey in the distant past that proves axiomatic to the drama must have occurred during the Civil War. *The Basement Window* has been described as 'the most successful play of contemporary Spain's major playwright'[12] and it is the universality of the theme that helps to justify the claim.

The action is presented by two characters, simply called He and She. It is set some time in the future, as the case-history of a piece of research and experiment. They explain that they have the technology to see back into the past and examine 'the infinite importance of the individual'. In the process of this review, a dramatic story is revealed, of how a child starved to death because her brother, Vincente, had, in a time of general privation and social chaos – the Civil War, we presume – gone off in a train, with the family's food and water, abandoning the girl, her little brother and her parents. Eventually, the family is reunited but the girl has died.

The father at the time of the play, some thirty years after the trauma, is suffering from what appears to be senile dementia. The mother jovially tries to keep the family together, regularly providing sweet rolls for Vincente whenever he visits. Mario, the younger son, still lives with his parents. Eventually, the truth about the death of the sister emerges and the Father kills Vincente with the scissors that he uses in his continual, apparently demented pastime of cutting out figures from pictures, photographs and postcards of the past. Mario and the girl abandoned by Vincente when pregnant with his child eventually commit themselves to a very tentative but very touching relationship and Mario's final words – 'Perhaps, some day, Encarna, they... they, yes...some day they...' imply that in spite of the classic form of tragic retribution visited upon Vincente, there is hope, a hope that is underlined by the fact that He and She are attempting this examination of 'the infinite importance of the individual'.

Since the death of Franco and the restoration of democracy, there has been a relaxation of censorship and a considerable growth in Spanish theatre, particulary in the regions, where Barcelona has shown itself to be a cultural powerhouse.

However, one of the positive aspects of the censorship of scripted plays was the development of companies whose work, as if dictated by the writings of Artaud, is based on non-verbal theatre, a 'total' theatrical style that exploits mime, music, acrobatics, light shows, and even fireworks in their creation of dramatic events. The work of such companies as Els Comediants, whose shows *Demonis* and *The Night* were a 'hit' in the 1989 Edinburgh Festival, have had considerable effect throughout the world.

Founded in 1971, Els Comediants developed a style of presenting myths and legends that is founded in circus, puppetry and 'popular' entertainment, particularly the medieval Catholic processions, morality plays and their 'antidote', carnival. The actors of Els Comediants declare that: 'We wanted to bring to the theatre a sensation rather than an idea; to send out an electric current rather than a message'[13] and, in their outdoor 'Happenings', this is exactly what they achieve.

This move away from scripted theatre – indeed, away from actual theatres at all – towards vast, communal events is not confined to Spain. Its twentieth-century roots can be seen in The Living Theatre and there are other, more recent companies throughout Europe who believe that the way to bring theatre to the people is to revert to procession and spectacle, the masks and movement of the medieval carnival and to abandon the rigid, repetitive restriction of a sequence of performances in one place or theatre.

Such radical examination of the essence of theatre can only be productive and the burgeoning of the reputation of Els Comediants and other such practitioners reflects the healthy state to which the Spanish Theatre is being restored after the restriction of Franco.

Ten plays for further consideration

1. Luigi Chiarelli, *The Mask and the Face*
2. Luigi Pirandello, *Six Characters in Search of an Author*
3. Luigi Pirandello, *Henry IV*
4. Ugo Betti, *The Burnt Flower-Bed*
5. Eduardo de Filippo, *Saturday, Sunday, Monday*
6. Dario Fo, *Accidental Death of An Anarchist*
7. Garcia Lorca, *Blood Wedding*
8. José Ruibal, *The Man and the Fly*
9. Lauro Olmo, *The Shirt*
10. Antonio Buerjo Vallejo, *The Basement Window*

Notes

1. Walter Starkie, *Luigi Pirandello*, p. 31
2. ibid., p. 3
3. ibid., p. 3
4. Laura Richards, 'Teatro del grottesco' in *Cambridge Guide to World Theatre*, pp. 949-50
5. John Linstrum, intro. to *Three Plays by Pirandello*, p. ix
6. Luigi Pirandello, *Six Characters in Search of an Author*, p. 85
7. ibid., p. 92
8. Starkie, op. cit.
9. Review by Dacia Maraina of *Ordine per D.10.000.000.000* trans. as *Orders for Mammon's Sake,* quoted in Tony Mitchell, *Dario Fo: People's Court Jester*
10. ibid., p. 83
11. Patricia O'Connor, Introduction to *Five Plays of Protest from the Franco Era*, p. 7
12. ibid., p. 17
13. Programme Note to *Demonis*

5: IRISH INFUSIONS

For such a comparatively small nation, it is remarkable how many playwrights have come from Ireland in order to rejuvenate not only the English but also the European and the world stage. The Restoration Comedy would be far less influential if Farquhar, Goldsmith and Sheridan had never been; Britain, Ireland, France and America would have missed the greatest nineteenth-century entertainer if Dion Boucicault had stuck to civil engineering; the 1890s would have been deprived both of a champion and a whipping boy if Oscar O'Flahertie Wills Wilde had remained in Dublin. There would have been no competitor – or, in his own eyes, equal – to Shakespeare for the title of Greatest Playwright in the English language without George Bernard Shaw, and the drama might still be confined by French windows to the drawing-room comedies of Coward if it had not been for the explosion provided by the enigmatic comedies and the agonised universalities of Samuel Beckett. True, few plays actually written in the Irish language have either travelled or lasted (Brendan Behan's *An Giall* which became *The Hostage* in the hands of Joan Littlewood's Theatre Workshop being the only obvious exception) but Wilde, Synge, Shaw, O'Casey, Beckett and Behan have left indelible and invaluable contributions to the stage while, more recently, Hugh Leonard, Stewart Parker and perhaps most significantly, Brian Friel have continued this tradition of widely influential theatre.

Dion Boucicault was squarely set within the nineteenth century, having been born in Dublin in 1820 and died in New York in 1890; at the early age of twenty-one he wrote *London Assurance*, a play that was not only reminiscent of Sheridan's depictions of the London 'Beau Monde' (here in the shape of Sir Harcourt Courtly) and of Goldsmith's *She Stoops To Conquer* but also provided a definite link between the work of these Irishmen and that of Wilde.

Although Wilde (1854-1900) died before the twentieth century was under way, no review of its theatre would be complete without at least a mention of *The Importance of Being Earnest*. Sir Tyrone Guthrie, one of the most accomplished directors in the British theatre in this century, has said that: '*The Importance of Being Earnest*, though it's full of nonsense, is also full of a great deal of profound and utterly charming sense. It is the greatest play of all time by an Irish dramatist.'[1] While this claim may be open to debate, especially by Shavians or the supporters of *Waiting for Godot*, there is no doubt that *The Importance* has worked its way into the subconscious of more than one culture, so that such lines as 'A handbag!', especially when uttered with the swoop of an Edith Evans, or: 'The truth is rarely pure and never simple', have become among the most quoted lines in English literature, even when their source has been uncertain.

It is the quality of the wit and of the language that makes the play so successful. As Christopher Fitz-Simon says:

> ...the form of expression conditions the character, and the seemingly inconsequential flow of dialogue – arranged as duets, trios, quartets and full ensembles – imposes the dramatic structure. Interestingly, none of the stage musicals made from this play has been very successful; its structure may be that of operetta, in a sense, but Wilde's sentences are all-important – they cannot be chopped up as libretto, or subsumed by a score.[2]

And it is not surprising that no composer or librettist could improve on the balance of lines such as:

> The amount of women in London who flirt with their own husbands is perfectly scandalous. It looks so bad. It is simply washing one's clean linen in public.

or:

> To lose one parent, Mr Worthing, may be regarded as a misfortune; to lose both looks like carelessness.

and:

> I never travel without my diary. One should always have something sensational to read on the train.

while Wilde's definition of fiction: 'The good end happily, and the bad unhappily. That's what fiction means' has inspired the following homage from Tom Stoppard in his definition of tragedy from *Rosencrantz and Guildenstern are Dead*: 'The bad end unhappily, the good unluckily. That is what tragedy means.'

In fact, *The Importance of Being Earnest* has come to suffer a fate similar to *Hamlet* in that the enjoyment of any production tends to be marred by members of the audience joining in with all the famous lines.

However, it is not only as the author of comedies like *Lady Windermere's Fan*, *A Woman of No Importance* and the eternal *Importance* that Wilde influenced the theatre of the twentieth century. He, like many of his fellow Irishmen, left his homeland but it was not only to London that he went, for Wilde was as desirous of success in Paris as he was in London. In *Salome*, written primarily in French in the hope that either the Comédie Française or Sarah Bernhardt would take it up, he created a work which some of his critics have hailed as a masterpiece although until recently it remained almost unknown.

Alan Bird, in his *Plays of Oscar Wilde*[3] has said: '...the literary and artistic originality of *Salome* was never to be surpassed by him in the remaining years of his career as a dramatist.' Even though Mr Bird is given to hyperbolic claims for much of Wilde's work, it is interesting to examine *Salome* to see if the grounds for such a claim are there. And the answer is, for the modern reader at least, probably not, even though Steven Berkoff's highly-acclaimed production for Dublin's Gate Theatre, seen at the 1989 Edinburgh Festival and again at the National Theatre, proved that, in the hands of a director of genius, all things are possible.

Even remembering that the original was written in French and rather basic French at that, it is difficult to imagine how any actress could cope with these words of Salome to Jokannan: 'Neither the floods nor the great waters can quench my passion. I was a princess and thou didst scorn me. I was a virgin and thou didst take my virginity from me. I was chaste and thou didst fill my veins with fire...' while a sample from Herod's promises to Salome shows that an audience expecting the wit of the later plays would be considerably disappointed:

> I have amethysts of two kinds: one that is black like wine and one that is red, like wine that has been coloured with water. I have topazes yellow as are the eyes of tigers, and topazes that are pink as are the eyes of a wood-pigeon, and green topazes that are the eyes of cats. I have opals that burn always with a flame that is cold as ice, opals that make sad men's minds, and are afraid of the shadows. I have onyxes like the eyeballs of a dead woman...

However, while it may take a Berkoff to make this sort of language work on the 'straight' stage, it is very much the stuff that opera is made of. As Bird says: 'There is a general rule that anything that is too silly, too indecent or too shocking to be spoken may be safely sung without offence to anyone'[4] and that is exactly what Richard Strauss did with Wilde's banned play. His *Salome* was first performed after Wilde's death, in December 1905, and while some dismissed it as 'monstrous', others hailed it as a masterpiece, since when it has become something of a favourite with the more daring of the prima donnas, for, as well as singing the part, they have to perform an acceptable dance of the seven veils.

Along with Strauss' opera, Wilde's piece also inspired Aubrey Beardsley's illustrations for the original and it is they, rather than the play, which are best known today. It remains to be seen whether Berkoff's production can greatly influence that balance.

Despite Wilde's aspirations, *Salome* is perhaps best left to the opera house and poster shop; Wilde's immortality is assured by the incomparable

Importance of Being Earnest. Coupled with the extraordinary wit is the ability to criticise as he amuses. As Christopher Fitz-Simon says:

> In satirically exposing the *mores* of the English upper classes, and in making fun of the Englishman's serious regard for his own social institutions, Wilde followed the lead set by the earlier playwrights of the Irish school. As an outsider – in more senses than one – he is able to view the English national foibles with a fresh eye; and, like Goldsmith and Sheridan before him, he makes use of that most sacred of all English institutions – the language – to far better advantage than many Englishmen.[5]

It is this ability to juggle with the English language in a remarkable way that sets the Irish writers apart from many of their British counterparts; one of the greatest virtuosi was George Bernard Shaw (1856-1950). He did not turn to writing for the stage until he was in his late thirties but when he did, it was with great success and considerable controversy.

Shaw had been a critic of music, books and the stage before he took to writing for the latter and had been a major force behind the introduction and championing of the works of Ibsen in England (see chap. 1). When he finally decided to use the stage as a pulpit for the propagation of his developing social, economic and philosophical views, it was with the same verve and volume that had characterised his critical works. As he himself says in his Preface to *Back To Methuselah*, his vast 'Metabiological pentateuch':

> The fashionable theatre prescribed one serious subject: clandestine adultery: the dullest of all subjects for a serious author...I tried slum-landlordism, doctrinaire free-love (pseudo-Ibsenism), prostitution, militarism, marriage, history, current politics, natural Christianity, national and individual character, paradoxes of conventional society, husband-hunting, questions of conscience, professional delusions and impostures, all worked into a series of comedies of manners in the classic fashion...But this, though it occupied me and established me professionally, did not constitute me as an iconographer of the religion of my time, and thus fulfill my natural function as an artist.

It is not possible to examine the remarkable breadth of Shaw's works here, but the above quotation not only gives an idea of that breadth but also of the high opinion in which he held himself and his role as creative artist.

Early in his career in the theatre, he used his plays as weapons against injustices, with *Widowers' Houses* (1892) being his attack on 'slum landlordism' and *Mrs Warren's Profession* opposing 'prostitution'. The subject of the latter caused Shaw, like Wilde, to fall foul of the Lord Chamberlain, and although *Mrs Warren's Profession* was written in 1894 and given a brief private premiere in 1902, it was not allowed a major public performance in England until 1925. In a later Preface to the play, Shaw wrote that it was written...to draw attention to the truth that prostitution is caused, not by female depravity and male licentiousness, but simply by underpaying, undervaluing, and overworking women so shamefully that the poorest of them are forced to resort to prostitution to keep body and soul together. Indeed all attractive unpropertied women lose money by being infallibly virtuous or contract marriages that are not more or less venal.

As well as reiterating his political opinions, Shaw used these Prefaces to voice his views on the theatre, and in the same Preface we see him offering arguments that are not only strongly felt but also powerfully expressed: 'The voluptuous sentimentality of Gounod's *Faust* and Bizet's *Carmen* has captured the common playgoer; and there is, flatly, no future now for any drama without music except the drama of thought.' And again:

In trying to produce the sensuous effect of opera, the fashionable drama has become so flaccid in its sentimentality, and the intellect of its frequenters so atrophied by disuse, that the reintroduction of problem, with its remorseless logic and iron framework of fact, inevitably produces at first an overwhelming impression of coldness and inhuman rationalism. But this will soon pass away.

However, no matter how articulate the arguments presented in the Prefaces may be, it is not these that set Shaw in the vanguard of all playwrights; it is, of course, with the plays themselves that Shaw, like Brecht after him, transcends the politics and transforms the theories to create pieces that will live long after the issues that inspired them have been forgotten.

It is not possible to examine all of Shaw's twenty-four plays here; every Shavian will have his favourite but if one briefly looks at *Man and Superman* (1901-3) as an example of Shaw as both entertainer and educator, it becomes obvious why he is ranked with Shakespeare in the pantheon of British playwrights.

The plot is an ingenious reversal of a stock comedy, with the heroine 'Ann Whitefield' chasing the hero 'John Tanner' and inveigling him into marriage. It has remarkable elements, notably the *Don Juan In Hell* dream in Act III and a string of amusing and eminently 'playable' characters from the sensible Violet, the 'fey' Octavius and the 'New Man', the practical chauffeur, Henry Straker, to the more exotic Medoza and Shaw's own version of a stage Irishman, Mr Malone Snr. ('English rule drove me and mine out of Ireland. Well, you can keep Ireland. Me and me like are coming back to buy England; and we'll buy the best of it.' Act I)

However, it is the battle between Tanner and Ann, the 'Life Force', that provides the meat of the play and the greater part of the comedy. Shaw provides Tanner with splendidly furious parries to the subtle attacks of Ann: 'No man is a match for a woman, except with a poker and a pair of hobnailed boots. Not always even then,' and: 'She can't bully me as she bullies women; so she habitually and unscrupulously uses her personal fascination to make men give her what she wants. That makes her almost something for which I know no polite name.'

In the end, Tanner succumbs to the Life Force and Ann 'gets her man' with the wonderfully dismissive line, that could so easily have been addressed to her creator: 'Never mind her, dear. Go on talking!'

Talk is what Shaw's characters are about; and it is the talk, the 'crack', that characterises the work of all these major Irish playwrights.

When W.B. Yeats met J.M. Synge (1871-1909) in Paris where Synge was pursuing his musical and literary studies, he told him: '…Go to the Aran Islands. Live there as if you were one of the people themselves; express a life that has never found expression.'⁶ Synge himself, in his Preface to *The Playboy of the Western World* (1907) has written, famously:

> When I was writing *The Shadow of the Glen*, some years ago, I got more aid than any learning could have given me from a chink in the floor of the old Wicklow house where I was staying, that let me hear what was being said by the servant girls in the kitchen. This matter, I think, is of importance, for in countries where the imagination of the people and the language they use, is rich and living, it is possible for a writer to be rich and copious in his words, and at the same time to give the reality, which is the root of all poetry, in a comprehensive and natural form.

Synge claims that Ibsen and Zola are ineffectual because they are 'joyless', that city life is joyless too and that it is the language of the people of the country that will provide the source of the theatrical renaissance that he, along with Yeats and Lady Augusta Gregory, so much desired in their own Irish National Theatre. In his preface to *The Playboy of the Western World*, he writes:

> On the one stage one must have reality, and one must have joy; and that is why the intellectual modern drama has failed, and people have grown sick of the false joy of the musical comedy that has been given them in place of the rich joy found only in what is superb and wild in reality. In a good play, every speech should be as fully flavoured as a nut or apple, and such speeches cannot be written by anyone who works among people who have shut their lips upon poetry. In Ireland, for a few years more, we have a popular imagination that is fiery and magnificent and tender, so that those of us who wish to write start with a chance that is not given to writers in places where the spring-time of local life has been forgotten, and the harvest is a memory only and the straw has been turned to bricks.

Of course, to call language such as this 'natural' is somewhat self-deprecatory and to claim that there is much 'joy' in Synge's powerful little tragedy

Riders to the Sea (1904) is stretching the credibility of his audience. But Synge did practise what he preached in *The Playboy of the Western World* and Yeats and Lady Gregory had, in Synge, the playwright of genius who would provide their dream of a national theatre with the impetus that was to bring it to fruition, in the creation of the Abbey Theatre.

In *The Playboy of the Western World*, Synge creates a series of characters that have become favourites with actors and audiences alike, although it would be unjust to attribute the originality of their creation to Synge alone. Quite rightly, he admits his debt to the Irish plays of Dion Boucicault, where in *The Colleen Bawn*, *Arrah na Pogue* and, most particularly, *The Shaughraun*, Boucicault created characters for himself to play, Miles, Shaun and Conn, that are the immediate progenitors of Synge's 'Christy Mahon'. It may well be that, in the small Western Irish communities where Synge had studied and the play takes place, there are individuals such as Michael James, Pegeen's father; Widow Quinn the neighbour; Shawn Keogh the ineffectual suitor; the drunken 'locals' Philly Cullen, Jimmy Farrel and Old Mahon, Synge's own *deus ex machina*, but they had all already appeared, perhaps more broadly caricatured but already there, on the stages of Ireland, America and London wherever Boucicault had toured.

Synge's play centres on the relationship between Pegeen Mike and Christy Mahon and it is here that Synge differs from his earlier benefactor. Boucicault's 'bog Irish' are comic and he did not allow them the role of hero and heroine, lover and beloved. Boucicault's protagonists were upper-class, Anglo-Irish if not English, and the 'shaughrauns' mere comic relief. With Pegeen Mike and Christy, the 'heroism' and the love element were firmly entrenched in the peasant class.

Michael O'hAodha sets the scene:

> Christy Mahon is neither a buffoon nor a fool but a gamey fellow with a touch of the poet in him...one day he lashes out, as even a poet will, and strikes his father with a loy, leaves him for dead and runs away. He arrives in a wild part of the West, where outlaws are still admired, and finds himself a hero, not because he is a murderer but because, if he is to live at all, he must vaingloriously tell a 'gallous story' about his dirty deed.[7]

It is interesting to note here how Christy, like many of O'Casey's rebels, Boucicault's poachers and Behan's various pimps and tarts, is attractive because of his very illegal status.

O'hAodha is somewhat biased in favour of Christy, for anyone who will kill his father three times must have something of the simpleton, if not the buffoon, in him and to ascribe the poetry to Christy rather than Synge seems unfair on the author. True, Christy has his fair share of the poetry:

And it's yourself will send me off, to have a horny-fingered hangman hitching his bloody slip-knots at the butt of my ear.

and:

> Up to the day I killed my father, there wasn't a person in Ireland
> knew the kind I was, and I there drinking, waking, eating, sleeping,
> a quiet, simple poor fellow with no man giving me heed.

However, Pegeen demonstrates the same rhythm and loquaciousness:

> And I thinking you should have been living the like of a king of Nor-
> way or the eastern world.

and:

> And to think it's me is talking sweetly, Christy Mahon, and I the
> fright of seven townlands for my biting tongue.

So it is the sureness of Synge's ear that should be praised, rather than the
poetry of any one of his creations.

In *Riders to the Sea*, Synge displays the same foreign magic in the language:

> It's hard set we'll be surely the day you're drowned with the rest.
> What way will I live and the girls with me, and I an old woman look-
> ing for the grave?

While even a simple question set in Synge's version of the Aran-islanders'
English: 'Will she see it was crying I was?' has a peculiar and original beauty.

The premiere of *The Playboy of the Western World* created a furore in
Dublin in January 1907. As O'hAodha writes:

> The acrimonious disputes carried on in the newspapers and maga-
> zines for over a decade, an argument which has not yet quite
> subsided, is the eternal dispute between the artist and the mob-
> mind. In those days, Synge was seen as a bogey-man, a drop-out, a
> subversive, a degenerate who defamed the Irish people.[8]

The main objection was from the righteous, or perhaps self-righteous, who
criticised it in the words of the *Freeman's Journal* as being 'a libel upon Irish
peasant men, and worse still upon Irish peasant girlhood', while another ma-
gazine described it as 'the vile and inhuman story told in the foullest language
we have ever listened to from a public platform'. It is interesting to note here
the similarities between the objections to this play and *Ghosts* on its first appearance in London and, while there may well have been much narrow-
mindedness and bigotry in the objections to both, a comparison of the two
attacks not only reflect, on the state of mind of the audience but also on the
nature of the fare that they were used to. To us, the objections seem laugh-
able, but obviously the evolution of the theatre from the nineteenth to the
twentieth century was more revolutionary than perhaps it may appear at this

distance. That said, though, one of the more unbiased observers of the actual riot, Ben Iden Payne, has written:

> The night before I had been present at the opening performance of
> *The Playboy of the Western World* and had seen the audience...after
> a long, simmering period of sporadic exclamations of opposition,
> boil over into a howling chorus of execration...And I remember
> thinking that the audience, incomprehensible as their opposition to
> *The Playboy* was to my English understanding, must be peculiarly
> vital or it could not have expressed its prejudice so violently...[9]

When the Abbey Theatre went on tour to the United States with the play, reactions were similar, with expatriates irate that their idealised memories of the 'auld place' should be so foully besmirched. However, a young Eugene O'Neill was both impressed and influenced by a later performance of *Riders to the Sea* by the Abbey on tour and it was this that first prompted him to start writing for the Provincetown Players.

The Playboy of the Western World stands comparison with any other work of this century and for that, and his contribution towards the establishment of the Abbey Theatre, Synge has earned himself a lasting position in the history of Irish theatre. The tragedy, or at least the shame, was that he died at the comparatively early age of thirty-eight, surely at the height of his powers. His was not one of those self-destructive, self-publicising talents that were to surface in other Celtic poets later in the century; while it is possible to argue that his contemporary, Wilde, had burned himself out perfecting the performance of his own persona and after *The Importance*, the trial and *The Ballad of Reading Jail*, there was nothing left for him to do but die, in Synge's case, this was not so. He was never strong, a swelling in the neck grew, two operations failed and he died in March 1909. But the impetus was there, the Abbey existed and Irish theatre was 'on its way'.

In his preface to *The Tinker's Wedding*, Synge wrote:

> The drama is made serious...by the degree in which it gives nourishment, not easy to define, on which our imaginations live...Of the things which nourish the imagination, humour is one of the most needful, and it is dangerous to limit or destroy it...where a country loses its humour, as some towns in Ireland are doing, there will be a morbidity of mind...

However, in spite of the evidence of a certain 'morbidity' as displayed by the *Playboy* riots, there was in Dublin, in the supposedly 'joyless and pallid words' of the cities, a poet whose stature was equal to Synge's, a playwright who was to do for the Dublin tenement dwellers what Synge had done for the peasants of the West.

Sean O'Casey was born in Dublin in 1880. Although from a Protestant, lower middle-class background, he chose to associate with the Catholic working-classes; these were the background and models for his first three plays which are also his best-known and, arguably, his best pieces of work. He experienced the transport strike of 1913 firsthand, became Secretary of the Irish Citizen Army which took part in the 1916 Easter Rising and was a witness to, rather than participant in, the War of Independence, the Civil War and the bitter conflict between the IRA and the notorious 'Black and Tans'. If anyone can be said to have benefited from the experience of those terrible times, O'Casey may be that man.

The three 'tenement' plays, *The Shadow of a Gunman* (1923), *Juno and the Paycock* (1924) and *The Plough and the Stars* (1926) are all described by O'Casey as tragedies, but to expect them to have the atmosphere of a *Hamlet, Le Cid* or even Synge's *Riders to the Sea* would be quite wrong. All three plays have their comic elements, all have their battling, indomitable wives and mothers, their insignificant men, their drunken buffoons, their blusterers and braggards in the Boucicault vein, as well as their tragic figures, all of whom, significantly, are women. While only three years separate them, it is interesting to plot the development of O'Casey's craftsmanship through the three pieces.

The Shadow of a Gunman is a slight piece in comparison with the two later plays. It was first staged in 1923 and concerns Donal Davoren, an ineffectual poet whom, because he is continually and apparently pointlessly indoors all the while, his fellow-occupants of the tenement house take to be a gunman on the run. As this is a romantic notion, one that attracts the pretty Minnie Powell (she is described by O'Casey as having a 'well-shaped figure – a rare thing in a city girl'), Davoren does nothing to disabuse his neighbours. He is accorded a mythic quality similar to that of Christy Mahon, feared by the men and admired by the women. Unfortunately, the rumour reaches the ears of the Black and Tans, who raid the place. During a previous scene, a bag of bombs have been left, unknown to Davoren, by a member of the IRA who is killed. Donal, his room-mate Seamus and Minnie discover the bombs. Their reactions sum up their characters:

> DAVOREN: Bombs, bombs, bombs; my God! in the bag on the table there; we're done, we're done!
>
> SEAMUS: Hail, Mary, full of grace – pray for us miserable sinners – Holy St Anthony, do you hear them batterin' at the door – now an' at the hour of our death – say an act of contrition, Donal – there's the glass gone!
>
> MINNIE: I'll take them to my room; maybe they won't search it; if they do aself, they won' harm a girl. Goodbye...Donal.
> (*She glances lovingly at Donal, who is only semi-conscious, as she rushes out the room*)

Minnie is arrested and killed trying to escape while the men are left, Donal bemoaning his lot and Seamus blaming Fate.

While the play obviously deals with serious topics, it is a slight piece when compared with *Juno and the Paycock* and, more especially, *The Plough and the Stars*. Technically simple, *The Shadow of a Gunman* is set in one scene, in two acts. In *Juno and the Paycock*, although the setting remains the same, O'Casey handles a greater time span and three acts, while in *The Plough and the Stars*, he spreads the action across four acts and four separate settings.

There is considerable debate concerning the respective merits of the two later plays; some critics feel that it is the former, with the roguish layabout, 'Captain' Boyle and his motto: 'Th' whole worl's in a terrible state o'chassis', with 'Joxer' Daly and his universal compliment: – 'darlin' ('A cup o'tay's a darlin' thing, a daaarlin' thing') and, of course, the long-suffering Mrs Boyle, the 'Juno' of the title, that is the greater play and it is true that it is performed in Britain more often than is *The Plough and the Stars*. The reasons for this are several.

Firstly, as has been said above, there is only the one setting, compared to the four of the later play, and managements have to take such things into consideration. Secondly, there is no role in *The Plough and the Stars* to equal that of the 'Captain'. Here is a rascal to match any of Molière's obsessives, though while Argan may be a chronic hypochondriac and Harpagon a miser, it is the Captain's idleness that O'Casey has offered up for criticism through ridicule. In fact, in the second act, when the family believes that it has been left a small fortune, the behaviour of both Boyle and 'Juno' is reminiscent of M. Jourdain in *Le Bourgeois Gentilhomme*, albeit set down a class or two. And the quality of the comedy lives up to such comparisons.

The double act of the 'butties', Joxer and Boyle, is one to equal Belch and Aguecheek and one in the light of which Beckett's Vladimir and Estragon, despite their foreign names, display their obvious Irish antecedents. The routines are worthy of the circus or music hall:

(*A thundering knock is heard at the street door*)

BOYLE: There's a terrible tatheraraa – that's a stranger – that's nobody belongin' to the house.

(*Another loud knock*)

JOXER: (*sticking his head in at the door*) Did ye hear them tatherarahs?

BOYLE: Well, Joxer, I'm not deaf.

JOHNNY: Who's that at the door…?

BOYLE: How the hell do I know who 'tis? Joxer, stick your head out o' the window an' see.

JOXER: An' mebbe get a bullet in the kisser? Ah, none o' them thricks for Joxer! It's betther to be a coward than a corpse![10]

Joxer's last line there could be a motto for both himself and Boyle. However, in spite of the comedy, O'Casey more than leavens his piece with drama that does indeed verge upon tragedy.

Mary, the Boyle's daughter, is abandoned, pregnant, by the so-called bearer of glad tidings, Bentham (an event and character that smack of classic melodrama). Johnny, the son, is a more original creation in that he has been crippled during the 'Troubles', having been shot in the hip and, later, lost an arm. He lurks in the backroom, terrified of visitors and, at the end, is taken away to be executed by the Irregulars for betraying a comrade. 'Juno', the mother, suffers with and for her children, all the while lacking any true support from the comic, yet degenerate 'Captain'.

Juno's final words, before abandoning the tenement and accompanying her daughter God knows where, set a fine balance to the previous comedy:

Blessed Virgin, where were you when me darlin' son was riddled with bullets, when me darlin' son was riddled with bullets? Sacred Heart o' Jesus, take away our hearts o' stone and give us hearts o' flesh! Take away this murdherin' hate, and give us Thine own eternal love!

And yet, O'Casey does not allow 'Juno' the last words, because the two clowns enter after all the others have gone, 'both of them very drunk'[11] and it is to Boyle and Joxer, the one collapsed on the bed and the other subsided to the floor, that the final words are given: 'I'm telling you...Joxer...th'whole worl's...in a terr...ible state o'...chassis!'

True the words may be but, by giving them to the drunken Boyle, O'Casey avoids obvious sermonising and establishes a nice moral uncertainty, the sort of dogma-free position that is to be explored further, both in his own later play and also, more thoroughly though perhaps obliquely, by Beckett, and lauded by Behan in his rumbustious tribute, *The Hostage*.

With *The Plough and the Stars*, a title taken from the name of the Irish Volunteers' banner, O'Casey reached a pinnacle of achievement. As O'hAodha says:

The juxtaposition of tragedy and comedy, of prayer and mockery, often in the same scene, must have come as a shock to those early audiences who were unaccustomed to the genius of O'Casey who could handle the stuff of melodrama with ironic detachment. Even more so than in *Juno and the Paycock*...there is a perfect equilibrium between the comic and tragic elements...[12]

The play is set in and around a Dublin tenement, prior to and during the

Easter Week rising of 1916. There are no obvious heroes and, in spite of the appearances of the British soldiers whose job it is to clear away the resistance manifested in the rising, no real villains. Every character has its strengths and its weaknesses and those that are touched with tragedy at the end have also been lit by comedy earlier in the play. The young and slightly silly Nora – an intentional echo of Ibsen – loses her husband, her child and her reason; Bessie Burgess, whose son is fighting for the British in France and yet who always has a helping hand for the sick, is killed by accident right at the end, even though she is the only one left to care for the mad Nora; the men are either weak, drunken or fanatical and, with the deaths of Jack and Lieutenant Langon, death is seen as anything but noble.

Captain Brennan brings the news of Jack's death to an attic where the coffin for the corpse of one child, the consumptive Mollser, also contains the body of Nora's still-born baby:

> He took it like a man. His last whisper was to 'Tell Nora to be brave; that I'm ready to meet my God, an' that I'm proud to die for Ireland.' An' when our General heard it he said that 'Commandant Clitheroe's end was a gleam of glory. Mrs Clitheroe's grief will be a joy when she realises that she had a hero for a husband.'[13]

Nora's subsequent appearance, Ophelia-like, belies all this.

> *Nora appears at door, left. She is clad only in her nightdress; her hair, uncared for for some days, is hanging in disorder over her shoulders. Her pale face looks paler still because of a vivid red spot on the tip of each cheek. Her eyes are glimmering with the light of incipient insanity...* [14]

However, the drama of the piece is heightened by its comedy, for example, in the earlier scenes, particularly in the pub where the prostitute Rosie bemoans her lot because:

> They're all in a holy mood. Th'solemn-lookin' dials on th'whole o' them an' they marchin' to th' meetin'. You'd think they were the glorious company of th'saints, an' th' noble army of martyrs thrampin' through th' sthreets of paradise. They're all thinkin' of higher things than a girl's garthers... [15]

The seriousness of the situation is continually being lightened by O'Casey's comic skill. Fluther Good, a carpenter, advises his neighbours:

> There's no reason to bring religion into it. I think we ought to have as great a regard for religion as we can, so as to keep it out of as many things as possible.[16]

While 'the Young Covey', Clitheroe's cousin, gives an explanation of biology that would delight any Darwinian:

There's nothin' complicated in it. There's no fear o' the Church tellin' you that mollycewels is a stickin' together of millions of atoms o'sodium, carbon, potassium o' iodide, etcetera, that, accordin' to th' way they're mixed, make a flower, a fish, a star that you see shinin' in th' sky, or a man with a big brain like me, or a man with a little brain like you![17]

His grasp of evolution is demonstrated further when commenting on Fluther;

When I hear some men talkin' I'm inclined to disbelieve that th' world's eight-hundred million years old, for it's not long since th'fathers o' some o' them crawled out o' th' sheltherin' slime o' the sea![18]

In the apparent tradition of all great Irish plays, *The Plough and the Stars* invoked its own riots at the Abbey. On the fourth night, following rumours that the play was immoral, the performance was interrupted by a group of protesters, an event described by O'Casey in his idiosyncratic autobiography *Inishfallen, Fare Thee Well*:

The high, hysterical, distorted voices of women kept squealing that Irish girls were noted over the whole world for their modesty, and that Ireland's name was holy; that the Republican flag had never seen the inside of a public house; that the slander on the Irish race would mean an end of the Abbey Theatre and that Ireland was Ireland through joys and through tears...

A stand-up fight between the actors and protesters ensued, during which Yeats appeared on stage, berating the audience throughout the rumpus. Eventually, the play continued to great acclaim, although O'Casey was shaken and upset: 'He was bewildered and felt sick rather than hilarious. Slandered the people! He had slandered his class no more than Chekhov had slandered his. Did these bawling fools think that their shouting would make him docile. He would leave them to their green hills of holy Ireland!'[19]

However, it was not this event that brought about the exile; it was the rejection by Yeats and Lady Gregory of his next play *The Silver Tassie* that was to do this. The critics and the audience might oppose him but when his supposed supporters and erstwhile champions did so, it was time for him to go. O'Casey moved to London, where *The Silver Tassie* received a highly effective production at the hands of C.B. Cochran in 1929, with a stage design by Augustus John.

Opinion is mixed about his later work. His wife, Eileen Reynolds, believes that such pieces as *The Star Turns Red* (1940) and *Red Roses for Me* (1943) are among his best and are the ones that should be revived, an opinion supported by Hugh Hunt in his book on the Abbey Theatre. Whatever their merits, though, O'Casey's reputation as a great dramatist would have been established by the Tenement Trilogy alone. One comes to them for the first time with delight and returns to them with pleasure. On reading or hearing Synge's work, one wonders if people could ever have spoken such poetry 'for real'; O'Casey's creations remove all doubt.

And then Brendan Behan (1923-1964) reinforces this view. With his autobiographical novel, *Borstal Boy*, the prison play, *The Quare Fellow* and, most especially, *The Hostage*, Behan shows himself to be a direct descendant of O'Casey, Synge and Boucicault.

Based on his own experiences as a 'soldier' in the IRA, when he went to England as a sixteen-year old with the intention of running a one-man bombing campaign against the British and was duly arrested and jailed, *Borstal Boy* (1958) was not only successful as a book but also when dramatised by Frank McMahon. It may appear incredible that a boy, albeit an IRA sympathiser, should take it upon himself to oppose Britain single-handed, but Behan came from a remarkable family. His father, Stephen, was a republican prisoner at the time of Brendan's birth in 1923. This extraordinary painter and decorator, someone who in any other country would have been looked down upon as 'working-class' and hence, in the 1920s and 1930s, as one of 'The Poor', had been educated by the Jesuits and himself oversaw the 'extracurricular' education of his family. As Colbert Kearney describes in *The Writings of Brendan Behan*:

> Undoubtedly, Stephen Behan was most content when ensconced in a snug bar...but his income could not sustain this pleasure seven nights a week. When confined to his home, he educated his children...The curriculum of the little academy included Lever, Shaw, Yeats, Synge, O'Casey, Pepys, Dickens, Galsworthy, Zola, Maupassant and Dostoyevsky, as well as Boccaccio...and Marcus Aurelius who bored even the precocious Brendan.[20]

Behan's political and revolutionary zeal came from his Granny Furlong. Faced with a decline in the activities of the official IRA, she took it upon herself to continue the struggle: 'In the summer of 1939, at the age of seventy-seven, she...travelled to Birmingham with her daughters to conduct their own campaign; an explosion in the house where they were staying led to their arrest.'[21] With such a pedigree, perhaps Behan's achievements are less remarkable.

In *The Quare Fellow*, rejected by the Abbey but first staged in 1954 by Alan Simpson in Dublin's tiny Pike Theatre, Behan drew on his experiences in Mountjoy Prison on the eve of an execution.'The Quare Fellow' is inmates' slang for the condemned man, a character never seen in the play and never named except by euphemism; it would appear that such a subject might be bleak and fruitless but, for someone weaned on a diet of Synge and O'Casey, it is not surprising that Behan produces a work that is both comic and suitably grim, but never gratuitously so. We learn unpalatable details about capital punishment:

You forget the times the fellow gets caught and has to be kicked off
the edge of the trap hole. You never heard the warders below swinging on his legs the better to break his neck, or jumping on his back
when the drop was too short.

Yet there are still characters like Dunlavin who are recognisable sons of Captain Boyle and Fluther Good. In an attempt to steal some meths to drink,
Dunlavin confuses which of his legs is supposed to be 'bad' but tops it all with
the classic riposte:

It's only the mercy of God I'm not a centipede, sir, with the weather
that's in it.

The subject is dealt with comically, through jokes, parody and repartee but
at the end, when 'the quare fellow' is hanged, there is no escaping the reality
of the event:

*The hour strikes. The WARDERS cross themselves and put on their caps.
From the PRISONERS comes a ferocious howling.*

As Kearney says:

Far from being thematically unsubtle or structurally unsound, it is
dramatically extremely effective and a deeply moving play. The per-
sistence of the theme in Behan's mind and the strange structure of
the play – the unnamed victim, the imagined agony, the drunken ca-
maraderie of Death the Entertainer and the hysterical climax –
suggest that the dramatist was attempting to exorcise some horrible
recurring nightmare of his own, the twisting of another rope, another neck.[22]

A further example of Behan's natural theatrical skill coupled with his
sympathy for his fellow man and distaste for the futility of war is *The Hostage*; it is a sad reflection of the state of affairs in Northern Ireland today that
the play is not often performed because of the sensitivity of the subject matter. A British soldier is kidnapped in the North and held as a hostage against
the execution of a terrorist in jail in Belfast. Nowadays, as the 'tit-for-tat' killings go apparently unabated, it would be either a very brave or a very
insensitive management that would attempt the play.

The basic skeleton is comparatively slight, in that the prisoner *is* indeed
hanged and the hostage shot, albeit by mistake. The strength of the piece, as
with all of the Irish plays examined so far, is the warmth, the sympathy and
the comedy of the characterisations. The hostage, Leslie, is held in a Dublin
house, owned by 'Monsewer', a 'cracked' Anglo-Irish gentleman who has
taken to wearing the kilt and playing bagpipes. The house is run by Patrick,
a victim of the rising, where he lost a leg; in order that it make any sort of
money, the place is run as a brothel. Patrick, like 'Captain' Boyle, is full of
his past exploits:

Frank Wedekind as the ringmaster in his own production of 'Erdgeist': the author as puppeteer and the actor as clown. (*Institut für Theater, Film und Fernsehwissenschaft, Köln*)

The original stage production of Zola's 'L'Assommoir' in Paris (1900) pursued naturalistic effect almost to excess. (*British Library*)

Despite Eugene O'Neill's Expressionistic leanings the Provincetown Players' 1917 production of 'In the Zone' employed a set as wooden as the acting! (*Mander and Mitchenson Theatre Collection*)

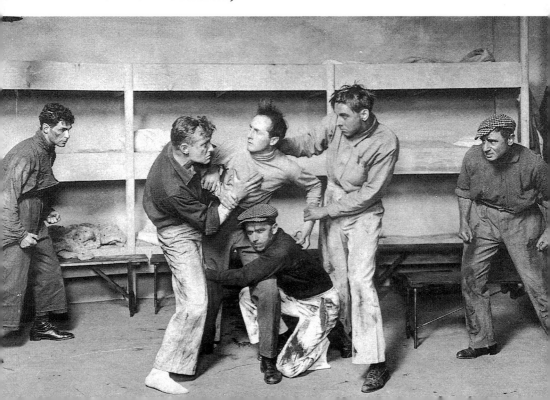

This 1938 production of Olive Schreiner's 'The Story of an African Farm', like many productions of the 1930s, attempted to break away from established modes of theatrical presentation by removing obtrusive walls so that the audience watched several scenes at the same time. (*Mander and Mitchenson Theatre Collection*)

In stark contrast to earlier set designs this 1971 Royal Court production of 'The Lovers of Viorne' by Marguerite Duras illustrated the dramatic potential of the bare stage. (*Mander and Mitchenson Theatre Collection*)

In Samuel Beckett's 'Happy Days' a woman sits up to her waist in sand. Sets in absurdist and non-naturalistic theatre often deny the audience the security of a recognisable, familiar situation. (*Derek Balmer*)

The white face make-up of the 'commedia dell'arte' clown has been adopted as a popular mask in many modern productions. Here it is used in a production of Voltaire's 'Candide', directed by the author.

Roger Blin in Samuel Beckett's 'Endgame'.

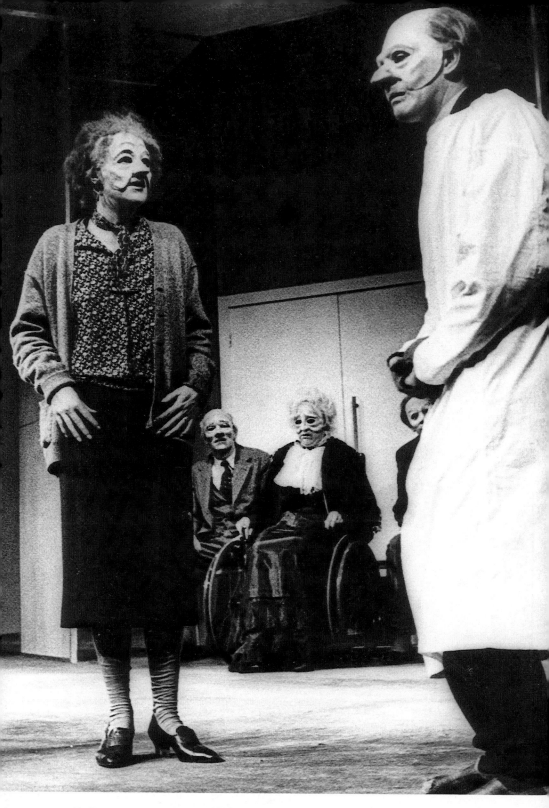

In John Arden's 'The Happy Haven' masks were originally introduced to help young actors play the geriatric inmates of an old peoples' home. (*Mander and Mitchenson Theatre Collection*)

In 'The Silver Tassie' O'Casey exhibited the typically Expressionist tendency to break down traditional notions of human identity and character by using gas-masks to conceal the actors' faces. (*Fergus Bourke*)

The striking charisma of Dario Fo, shown here directing 'Mistero Buffo'. (*La Comune*)

For three days non-stop the battle raged with terrible ferocity. Ourselves and the West-Limerick Brigade. Lewis machine guns, Thomson sub-machine guns, mortars, grenades, revolvers and rifles, the town blazing and the dead on the road.

However, Kate, a 'Juno-esque' character and the 'madame' of the house, cuts him down to size:

You told me before that only one man was killed. The West Meath County surveyor who wasn't bothering anybody but was measuring the roads.

Leslie falls for Teresa, the 'skivvy', whereupon the whole household, a mixture of whores of every sex, their customers, comic IRA volunteers, do-gooders, old soldiers and even a resident pianist, essential for the songs that interlard the action, come to realise that the 'enemy', in the shape of their own Hostage, is nothing to be frightened of. When theories and ideals take on flesh and become human, it is the humanity that triumphs over the polemics. The death of Leslie comes as a suitably dramatic shock but his resurrection, one of the elements included by Joan Littlewood during rehearsals for the Theatre Workshop production at Stratford East, brings the emotion into focus as Leslie faces the audience and sings, with the rest of the cast:

The bells of Hell go ting-a-ling-a-ling
For you but not for me.
Oh, Death, where is thy sting-a-ling-a-ling,
Or grave thy victory.

This World War One song used by Theatre Workshop in one of their other great successes, *Oh, What A Lovely War!*, is an example of the 'Theatricalisation' by Joan Littlewood of *An Giall*, the Irish language original, a process approved of by Behan:

She has the same views on the theatre as I have, which is that the music hall is the thing to aim at for to amuse people and any time they get bored, divert them with a song or dance. I've always thought T.S. Eliot wasn't far wrong when he said that the main problem of the dramatist today was to keep his audience amused; and that while they were laughing their heads off, you could be up to any bloody thing behind their backs; and it was what you were doing behind their bloody backs that made your play great.[23]

Of course, there are purists who quite rightly will criticise this approach, probably the same scholars who sat solemnly and earnestly in front of *Waiting for Godot* not believing that such an 'avant-garde' play could possibly be funny. Of course, it is possible to emphasise the religious, the sombre, the hallowed element of 'The Drama', but to do so ignores one of the essentials of the two-way relationship in a theatre, namely the audience.

Of the more recent Irish playwrights, the most stimulating has been Brian Friel. This sweeping generalisation, of course, is subjective and excludes Samuel Beckett, who has assumed a universal pedigree, with his Irish background, his use of French as the language of his original works, and the subsequent English translations that have brought his plays to a world-wide audience. *Godot, Endgame, Oh, Happy Days!* and the rest of that remarkable body of work were written in French in a gesture of enormous bravery, to escape the very facility with the language that characterises the Irish drama. This, and the universal influence of his work, puts him beyond the confines of this chapter.

Brian Friel was born in 1929 in Omagh and many of his plays have dealt with his adopted home, Londonderry, sometimes under the fictional garb of Ballybeg. Early pieces, such as *Philadelphia, Here I Come!* (1964) and its thematic sequel, *The Loves of Cass Maguire*, were presented by the Abbey but as 'the Troubles', often centered on Derry, escalated, Friel and Stephen Rea, along with Seamus Heaney, Seamus Deane and Tom Paulin, established 'Field Day', a theatre company based in Derry, where many of Friel's later works have received their 'premiere'.

Friel has the same delight in language, the same compassionate humour and, ultimately, the same pessimistic – or perhaps 'realistic' – view of the state of Ireland as his predecessors. In *The Freedom of the City* (1973), three innocent demonstrators are shot by the army in Derry. This subject, like capital punishment or the Easter Rising, is deadly serious, and yet Friel presents the three protagonists as victims of Fate as much as oppression and, in Skinner and Lilly at least, has created characters in the tradition of O'Casey and Behan.

However, it was with *Translations* (1980) that he reached an apotheosis, not only of his own work, but of much of Irish theatre. The reason for this universality of relevance is that the play deals with 'The English Language' and its imposition onto the Irish.

It is set again in his beloved 'Ballybeg' but in the 1830s, in a setting very similar to Boucicault's *The Shaughraun*. The situation is one of the great pieces of recent theatrical invention. The British Army is surveying the countryside, anglicising all the name places, and while the Donegal peasants cannot understand the soldiery and the army cannot understand the Irish, the whole piece is played in the same language, namely English. Hugh, an erudite 'magister', runs a hedge-school, teaching the locals at all levels, from the basics of reading and writing to the subtleties of Greek and Latin. He is helped by one son, Manus, while the other son, Owen, is employed by the army as translator. There is an archetypical sub-plot within this remarkable setting, in that one of the officers falls for one of the local girls, a relationship that is paralleled in the Boucicault in everything but the girl's class, but this lack of originality matters little when there is so much else to enjoy. Hugh, when more than a little drunk – a semi-permanent state for him – says, in English, of his own language:

> Yes, it is a rich language, Lieutenant, full of the mythologies of fantasy and hope and self-deception – a syntax opulent with tomorrows. It is our response to mud cabins and a diet of potatoes; our only method of replying to...inevitabilities.[24]

In Hugh and his sons there is summed up the dichotomy of the Irish writer, an artist who must adopt a foreign language to express himself and who, almost by way of revenge, uses that adopted tongue better than those whose it is from birth. Just as Shaw's Malone threatened to invade England and buy up all the best bits, so Wilde, Shaw, Synge, O'Casey, Behan, Friel and their compatriots have carved their imprint upon England and the rest of the world by their use of a weapon thrust upon them, but used best by them.

Ten plays for further consideration

1. Dion Boucicault, *The Shaughraun*
2. Oscar Wilde, *The Importance of Being Earnest*
3. J.M. Synge, *The Playboy of the Western World*
4. George Bernard Shaw, *Man and Superman*
5. Sean O'Casey, *Juno and the Paycock*
6. Sean O'Casey, *The Plough and the Stars*
7. Brendan Behan, *The Quare Fellow*
8. Brendan Behan, *The Hostage*
9. Brian Friel, *The Loves of Cass Maguire*
10. Brian Friel, *Translations*

Notes

1. Christopher Fitz-Simon, *The Irish Theatre*, p. 114
2. ibid., pp. 111-12
3. Alan Bird, *The Plays of Oscar Wilde*, p. 89
4. ibid., p. 77
5. Fitz-Simon, op. cit., p. 114
6. Quoted in Michael O'hAodha's *Theatre In Ireland*, pp. 40-1
7. O'hAodha, op. cit.
8. ibid., p. 51
9. Quoted in O'hAodha, op. cit., pp. 56-7

10. O'Casey, *Juno and the Paycock* (Act I)
11. ibid., stage direction
12. O'hAodha, op. cit.
13. O'Casey, *The Plough and the Stars* (Act IV)
14. ibid., stage direction, (Act IV)
15. ibid.
16. ibid.
17. ibid.
18. ibid.
19. O'Casey, *Inishfallen, Fare Thee Well*
20. Colbert Kearney, *Writings of Brendan Behan*, p. 6
21. ibid.
22. ibid.
23. *Brendan Behan's Island*, p. 17, quoted by Kearney, op. cit., p. 130
24. Brian Friel, *Translations*

6: THE FOUNDING FATHERS

Although it is tempting to view the major American playwrights in the light of the popular image of that nation, of heroic loners battling against all odds to achieve the American dream, this would, unfortunately, not be fair. True, it was necessary for 'pioneers' to establish a native theatre to set against what, prior to their efforts, had been a complete diet of 'foreign imports', but such a theatre could not be carved out single-handed with a Bowie knife, a six gun and a four-legged friend; a playwright needed a company as much as a company needed a playwright.

Although purists will rightly claim that the Red Indian medicine dances with their totems and shamans, or witch doctors, were as 'dramatic' as any of those early Dionysiac festivals that are seen as the source of all theatre, there was no tradition of a 'native' American theatre in the popular sense of the word until early in this century. Scholars are, of course, divided on whom to award the accolade of 'Father of the American Theatre'; some advocate William Vaughan Moody with his 1906 play, *The Great Divide*, but most have now accepted Eugene O'Neill in that role.

O'Neill (1888-1953) was the son of one of the most successful actors of his day, James O'Neill, whose wife, Ella, became addicted to morphine after the birth of Eugene. This is not simply gratuitous gossip but a fact that dominated the O'Neill family life and one that is superbly portrayed in O'Neill's masterpiece, *Long Day's Journey Into Night* (written 1939-41). In this remarkable play, O'Neill examines and portrays his family meticulously, not afraid of showing his father's charm and power, drunkenness and avarice, his brother Jamie's abject alcoholism, his mother's addiction to the pain-killing drug and his own suffering, both from the tuberculosis that had dogged his youth and the reliance upon alcohol that seemed to be a family weakness. The final scene where the mother comes back down into the living room after a day of morphine 'fixes' and is completely unreachable inside her evocation of the past, while the men sit impotent and isolated in their respective drunken stupors, not only demonstrates O'Neill's mastery of character depiction but also creates a scene that is both reminiscent of, and as harrowing as, the final moments of Ibsen's *Ghosts*.

James O'Neill had the potential to be one of the finest actors of his generation but had 'the good bad luck' to be a great success in the melodrama based on Dumas' *The Count of Monte Cristo*. Having come from an impoverished Irish background and – despite his success – continually fearing financial ruin, James went for the safe commercial option of continuously touring his goldmine throughout the country, rather than chancing anything more artistically demanding. While this course of action brought financial security, it had a deleterious effect upon both the family and his talent. The part made no demands upon James who tended to centre his life on the hotel bars and saloons of whatever town they were playing, thus condemning Ella to waiting in hotel rooms, initially with the children while they were young, but eventually on her own; a situation from which she escaped with her morphine. Both Eugene and his elder brother Jamie at times played parts in *Monte Cristo* but, as Eugene wrote:

> My early experiences with the theatre through my father really made me revolt against it. As a boy, I saw so much of the old, ranting artificial romantic stuff that I always had a sort of contempt for the theatre.[1]

The contempt for all that his father stood for manifested itself in the young Eugene by running away to sea, a concept which in itself is romantic and which in fact proved to be both inspirational and educational. The experiences of being an ordinary seaman in a fo'c'sle were synthesised into early plays like *East Bound for Cardiff*, *Beyond the Horizon* and one of his earliest successes, *The Hairy Ape*, while the more damaging times when he was 'beached' on the waterfronts of New York and Buenos Aires were to reappear in *The Iceman Cometh*.

The aimless wandering was stopped when he contracted tuberculosis and was confined to a succession of sanatoria (the debate over their respective merits and costs resurfacing in *Long Day's Journey into Night*). However, the enforced confinement provided him with time to continue an education which he had never appreciated or worked at as a boy. Like many of his contemporaries in Europe, he discovered the plays of Strindberg:

> It was reading his plays when I first started to write, back in the winter of 1913-14 that, above all else, first gave me the vision of what modern drama could be, and first inspired me with the urge to write for the theatre myself. If there is anything of lasting worth in my work, it is due to that original impulse from him...[2]

At the same time as O'Neill was reconsidering the theatre, there were similar moves among the artistic intelligentsia of New York. In 1915 the Washington Square Players started with a triple bill of one-act plays, including one by Maeterlinck, while a group of Greenwich Village writers and artists had, during their holidays that same summer, almost for fun, converted a fishhouse into a little theatre on the wharf of the Cape Cod village of Provincetown. One of the leading lights, Mary Heaton Vorse, wrote:

We made our own benches and our own scenery. The first performances were lighted by oil lamps. Four people in the wings held
lamps, beside them four more with buckets of ashes.

Suddenly everyone took to writing plays. The beginning of the
Provincetown Players was an organic thing like a plant growing. No
one said: 'Come on, let's found a little theatre.' We had no idea that
we were to help break through the traditions of Broadway and rev-
olutionise and humanise the theatre of America.[3]

O'Neill, who had recently finished *East Bound for Cardiff*, was near Provincetown that summer, and heard through a friend that these people were
looking for plays. George Cram Cook, the motivating force behind the group,
read the play and the rest, to quote the cliché, is history. Cook was looking
for 'A threshing floor on which a young and growing culture could find its
voice' – an admirable if somewhat pretentious aim – and felt that O'Neill was
that voice.

The young idealists set up a tiny theatre in Greenwich Village where
O'Neill's first plays were performed. Despite their amateurism and restricted resources, they attracted critical acclaim. Alexander Wallcott,
perhaps the most influential figure in the theatre, wrote of *Beyond the Horizon*: 'The play has greatness in it and marks O'Neill as one of the foremost
playwrights [and] one of the most spacious men to be both gifted and tempted
to write for the theatre in America.'

Success, however, was not what Cook was after; when first *Emperor
Jones* and then *The Hairy Ape* were transferred from their little theatre to
major houses on Broadway, commercialism got in the way of idealism and
O'Neill chose the former.

Both *Emperor Jones* and *The Hairy Ape* have been described as 'expressionistic', and influenced by the Germans. However, O'Neill was writing at
the same time as Kaiser, Werfel and the young Brecht and it is more a case
of him developing along the same lines under similar influences such as
Strindberg, than copying his contemporaries. *The Hairy Ape* (1921) is particularly interesting in its technical innovations; throughout, from the title
onwards, there is the continual equation of man with the animal, reminiscent
of Wedekind's Animal Trainer speech at the beginning of *Earth Spirit*. Yank,
the stoker, is a lost soul, totally bemused when the beautiful socialite Mil-
dred visits his stokehold; on land, he goes in search of her, is shunned by the
rich world and eventually is killed by a gorilla whom he frees from his cage.
O'Neill suggests the use of masks for the set attitudes of the rich, a ploy that
recalls Pirandello's *Six Characters*, written in the same year. His stage directions for the entrance of the society people are archetypal Expressionism:

*The women are rouged, calcimined, dyed, overdressed to the nth de-
gree. The men are in tail coats, tall hats, spats, canes etc. A procession*

of gaudy marionettes, yet with something of the relentless horror of Frankensteins in their detached, mechanical unawareness.

While it seems that O'Neill may be making the common mistake of confusing the Doctor with his monster, there is no confusing the point behind the final words of Yank who, having swapped the 'cage' of his stokehold for a real cage in the zoo and having been crushed by the very creature that he is trying to free, says:

> [*Then with sudden, passionate despair*] Christ, where do I get off at? Where do I fit in?...In de cage, huh? [*In the strident tones of a circus barker*] Ladies and gentlemen, step forward and take a slant at de one and only – [*His voice is weakening*] – one and original – Hairy Ape from de wilds of – [*He slips in a heap on the floor and dies. The monkeys set up a chattering, whimpering wail. And, perhaps, the Hairy Ape at last belongs.*]

But Expressionism was only a starting point; O'Neill wrote enormously, some thirty full-length plays including pieces like *Mourning Becomes Electra*, a trilogy in 13 acts, *The Iceman Cometh* which is twice the length of a normal play, and the project that he was working on when he died, *A Tale of Possessors Self-Possessed*, a sequence of historical plays about America, which was never realised.

He could write comedy, as in *Ah Wilderness!* (1932), the story of a young boy's introduction to 'cigareets and whisky and wild, wild women' as well as melodramatic symbolism in *Desire Under the Elms* (1924), the story of Ephraim Cabot, the old farmer with a third new wife, Abbie, who falls for Cabot's youngest son, Eben. The retribution, where Abbie and Eben are arrested after she has killed their son, hoping to retain the younger man's love, is awful. The air of impending doom is there from the start, hinted at in the opening stage directions:

> *Two enormous elms are on each side of the house. They bend their trailing branches down over the roof – they appear to protect and at the same time, subdue; there is a sinister maternity in their aspect, a crushing, jealous absorption.*

Ephraim's curse on the lovers accentuates the moral and demonstrates O'Neill's ability to create an archaic dialect:

> Ye make a slick pair o' murderin' turtle-doves! Ye'd ought t'be both hung on the same limb an' left thar t'swing in the breeze an' rot – a warnin' t'old fools like me t' b'ar their lonesomeness alone – an' fur young fools like ye t'hobble their lust!

O'Neill received the Nobel Prize for literature in 1936, but had not by then written his masterworks, *The Iceman Cometh* and *Long Day's Journey into Night*. O'Neill produced the latter as a mixture of homage to his dead family and cathartic emetic, needing to put down on paper the causes for so much misery and guilt in all their lives. Initially, he decreed that the piece should not be staged until twenty-five years after his death, in order to protect his children, but after his son had committed suicide – there appears to have been an unshakeable self-destructive streak in the O'Neills – Eugene's widow, his second wife, Carlotta, decided that the reason for the proviso had disappeared and so insisted upon the publication of the masterpiece.

While there is a dated feel to some of his early work, such a criticism cannot be levelled at this later piece. Recent revivals in Britain, notably that by the National Theatre with Laurence Olivier and Constance Cummings as James and Mary Tyrone, have reinforced O'Neill's position as the founding father of native American theatre.

While O'Neill abandoned collaboration with his early mentors in the Provincetown Players after a fairly short while – the desire for money and the absence of idealism being equally strong in him – Clifford Odets (1906–1963) worked assiduously for five years with another collection of visionaries before the lure of Hollywood became too strong.

In 1931, Harold Clurman, Cheryl Crawford and Lee Strasberg founded the Group Theatre. Like the Provincetown Players before them, they had broken away from the main experimental production company, the Theatre Guild (metamorphosed from the Washington Square Players in 1919); like Copeau and Dullin in France and, eventually, Brecht in Germany they had the vision of a theatre collective with a unified style. Like the Provincetown Players ten years earlier, they intended to present new *American* plays and in Odets they found their new American playwright.

Odets, like other innovatory playwrights, had started as an actor and nowadays interest in his work is due to his instinctive feel for the theatre rather than especial political insight. In its time, *Waiting for Lefty* (1935), about the effects of the taxi drivers' strike, was a radical play but, at a distance of half a century and compared with subsequent 'agit prop' pieces, it appears remarkably naive. Yet the 'cinematic' use of short scenes and the absence of realistic settings make the play dramatically interesting; the need to be able to play it almost anywhere imposed this minimalist style, a style that is still refreshingly sparse:

> As the curtain goes up, we see a bare stage. On it are sitting six or seven men in a semi-circle. Lolling against the proscenium arch down left is a young man chewing a toothpick: a gunman.[4]

The sequence of scenes is played out in this semi-circle, with the characters stepping into the action from their seats, a development that is far more interesting than the polemical slogans that make up the dialogue. The wife, Edna, 'bawls out' her husband, Joe:

This is the subject, the exact subject! Your boss makes this the subject. I never saw him in my life, but he's putting ideas into my head a mile a minute. He's giving your kids that fancy disease called rickets. He's making a jelly-fish outa you and putting wrinkles on my face. This is the subject every inch of the way![5]

It has to be admitted that Odets is always in danger of using monologues as sermons and his plays as both moral and political tracts. In *Paradise Lost* (1935) the Gordon family is being evicted in the Depression and the curtain speech, something of an Odets speciality, leaves the audience in very little doubt of his message:

No, there's more to life than this…Everywhere now men are rising from their sleep. Men, men are understanding the bitter black total of their lives. Their whispers are now growing to shouts! They become an ocean of understanding! NO MAN FIGHTS ALONE!…I want to see that new world. I want to kiss all those future men and women. What is this talk of bankrupts, failures, hatred…they won't know what that means…the world is beautiful. No fruit tree wears a lock and key. Men will sing at their work, men will love. Ohhh, darling, the world is in its morning…and NO MAN FIGHTS ALONE![6]

Such idealism is difficult to accept, especially in what is essentially a naturalistic play; equally difficult to stomach is the basic premise to what was Odets' greatest commercial success, *Golden Boy* (1937). Joe Bonaparte, the eponymous hero, is supposed to be both a violinist of genius and a contender for a major professional boxing crown. While the symbolic dichotomy between art and the more brutal aspects of Mammon is obvious, the situation is very difficult to believe (as well as difficult to realise, because an actor who not only makes a credible boxer but who can also play the violin well must be hard to find; for this reason, probably, both the boxing and the playing occur off-stage!)

However, in the characters of Tokio the trainer, Joe's father Mr Bonaparte, Eddie Fuseli the gangster, Siggie, Anna and Lorna, the girl Joe falls for and dies with, there is a whole range of well-observed and well-portrayed characters. However, in the ending, where Joe, as *deus ex machina*, kills himself and Laura in a car crash, Odets deflects the dilemma between violin and boxing ring which would add the weight of resolution to the play.

Of course, the plays were written to be performed rather than mulled over critically. Odets' feel for the theatrical is refreshing; his sympathy with the stage is even greater than O'Neill's and coupled with a facility to create 'actable' characters. In his finest play, *Awake and Sing!* (1935), he combines these two talents and, by choosing an idealistic young man as his 'messenger', makes his preaching more acceptable.

He takes his text from Isaiah: 'Awake and sing, ye that dwell in dust' and tells the story of the Bergers, a family of immigrants living in a New York tenement; again there is the tapestry of finely-drawn, credible characters and a theatrical innovation in the use of cut-away walls and lighting which allows the set to give the impression of several rooms, a technique picked up by Arthur Miller in *Death of a Salesman*.

The bare bones of the plot are most unpromising. The grandfather, Jake, falls to his death from the roof of the building, the insurance money goes to the family and to the son, Ralph, in particular, and it is presumed that the old man jumped, self-sacrificially. What makes the piece remarkable is the warmth and humour in Odets' characters. Jake in particular is revealed as being noble and heroic rather than pathetic, while all the others are shown in a sympathetic, comic light which contrasts favourably with the colder, brasher satire of *Golden Boy*. The curtain speech is left to Ralph, a vision of optimism that has left the neurosis of *Paradise Lost* far behind.

> ...My days won't be for nothing. Let Mom have the dough. I'm twenty-two and kickin'! I'll get along. Did Jake die for us to fight about nickels? No, 'Awake and Sing' he said. Right here he stood and said it. The night he died, I saw it like a thunderbolt! I saw he was dead and I was born! I swear to God, I'm one week old! I want the whole world to hear it – fresh blood, arms, we got 'em. We're glad we're living![7]

Odets is said to have been a product of the New York of the Depression; after the struggle of surviving both that and the founding of the Group Theatre, he lost direction and impetus. However, his plays helped to promote some of the major directorial talents of the time; Harold Clurman, Lee Strasberg and Elia Kazan came to the fore in these pieces and for some five years their expertise and idealism combined with that of Odets to create plays that have been seen as the epitome of an era.

While Odets' optimism appears to be frenetic and neurotic, based on naïve political idealism rather than experience, the inherent faith in mankind that is displayed in Thornton Wilder's two major plays is unmistakably heartfelt; so much so, in fact, that the Americanism 'corny' could have been coined especially to describe it.

Thornton Wilder (1897-1975) was initially a novelist, with his 1927 piece, *The Bridge of San Luis Rey*, being the best remembered; this deals with the lives of those who died when a rope bridge collapsed, demonstrating how apparently unconnected stories are in fact interwoven, as if Fate had made the disaster inevitable.

Wilder taught at the University of Chicago and his first theatrical forays were translations of contemporary European plays; these foreign adaptations culminated in *The Matchmaker*, a version of a Nestroy comedy. Initially it was not a success but Wilder rewrote it in 1954 as *The Merchant of Yonkers* which was then used by Michael Stewart and Jerry Herman as the 'book' for the musical *Hello, Dolly*. It is interesting to note that Tom Stoppard also went to the same Nestroy play *Einen Jux will er sich machen* (*He wants to go on a spree*) for the basis of his 1981 piece for the British National Theatre, *On the Razzle.*

The work of Andre Obey and Copeau's disciples, La Compagnie des Quinze, who toured the States in the early 30s made a great impression on Wilder. Echoes of Obey's *Noah* can be seen in *The Skin of Our Teeth*, while claims have been made that the 'Stage Manager' character in *Our Town* has its origins in the omnipotent actor-manager-author figure that Obey seemed to be.

Whatever its roots, *Our Town* (1938) has proved to be one of the most frequently performed plays, both in Britain and the States, partly because of its homely content but also because the simplicity of its staging has endeared it to many amateur, college and school productions.

The premise has the simplicity of genius; the Stage Manager stands on an empty stage to tell the story of Grovers Corner, a New Hampshire town at the turn of the century. He evokes the place by means of simple token props; two step ladders make the upstairs bedroom windows of a pair of houses in which the young lovers live; a plank across two stools makes a 'Soda Fountain' counter and, the most striking ploy, empty chairs in rows represent the graveyard when the Dead watch over Emily's funeral service. The stage manager adopts a number of 'cameo' roles as well as talking directly to the audience, which, combined with the stylised staging, makes for a 'Verfremdungseffekt' that is as efficient as any of Brecht's, without the urgent element that so often characterises the original.

There is an intrinsic religious element to *Our Town*, although it is not specifically Christian or evangelical. The Stage Manager expresses it, when he says:

> I don't care what they say with their mouth – everybody knows that something is eternal. And it ain't houses, and it ain't names, and it ain't earth and it ain't even the stars...everybody knows in their bones that something is eternal, and that something has to do with human beings...There's something way down deep that's eternal in every human being...

This ingrained optimism is also essential to *The Skin of Our Teeth*, Wilder's 1942 expression of faith in the human race. All pretence of realism has gone in this telling of the story of the Antrobus family; a mixture of anachronism and anarchy, it was originally directed by Elia Kazan with a cast that included Tallulah Bankhead as Sabina the maid (shades of the Sabine women), Frederick March as Mr Antrobus, Florence Eldridge as Mrs Antrobus and a young Montgomery Clift as their son, Henry.

The first act is set in the Ice Age, in the Antrobus house; Mr Antrobus has recently invented the wheel, is working on the alphabet and developing arithmetic. Mrs Antrobus, their son Henry (who has recently changed his name from Cain), their daughter Gladys and the maid Sabina are forced to evict their beloved pets, the Dinosaur and the Mammoth, in order to find room in their house for Moses, Homer, three of the Muses and other human refugees from the Ice Age. Once realised, the symbolism may not appear very subtle but it is an appealing and refreshing idea.

The second act is set on the board walk at Atlantic City where the world is having fun and Mr Antrobus, in spite of his 'peccadilloes', is chosen as the new Noah to save the world from the deluge.

The final act is set after the World War; Henry has alienated his entire family because of his delight in killing; Mrs Antrobus and Gladys have been forced to starve in cellars while Sabina has been acting as 'camp follower' to the entire army; on his return from the war, Mr Antrobus appears to be about to lose faith finally and forever in mankind but the re-appearance of the philosophers and writers eventually restores it, with quotations from Spinoza, Plato, Aristotle and the Bible ending the play.

There is no doubt that the imagery and the message in the play are obvious, but Wilder pre-empts such criticism by having actors in the play – usually the girl playing Sabina – stepping out of character and complaining. He gets round the appearance of the philosophers with a ploy that could have been the envy of Brecht; he audaciously states that an epidemic of food-poisoning has laid low the actors who were supposed to have played these world figures and their parts will be taken by a dresser, the wardrobe mistress, an usher and a maid.

The play is continually interrupted by various accidents that are used to disguise the rather blatant philosophy but, in case any one is left in any doubt, the Adam/Noah/Everyman figure of Mr Antrobus says at the end of his precious books:

> Remember...we almost lost them once before? And when we finally did collect a few torn copies out of old cellars they ran in everyone's head like a fever. They as good as rebuilt the world...Oh, I've never forgotten for long at a time that living is a struggle. I know that every good and excellent thing in the world stands moment by moment on the razor-edge of danger and must be fought for – whether it's a field, a home or a country. All I ask is the chance to build new worlds and God has always given us that second chance, and has given us voices to guide us: and the memory of our mistakes to warn us...we've come a long ways. We've learned. We're learning. And the steps of our learning are marked here for us...

This 'cracker-barrel' philosophy may seem naïve to today's audiences but it is an expression of that trait in human nature that aspires towards creation; and the Theatre, in all its guises – be they 'absurd', 'cruel', 'grotesque', 'epic' or even simply commercial – is a manifestation of that same trait.

In his introduction to his collected plays, Arthur Miller (b. 1915) describes the way an author expresses his philosophy through his work in an essay that is an invaluable insight into the workings of a playwright's mind. He displays an outlook that is similar to that of many of his European precursors and contemporaries, elevating the thought that, despite divisive labelling, there is something universal about the theatre. This piece has been collected with Miller's other theoretical writings under the title of *The Theatre Essays of Arthur Miller* but a few extracts will give a definite impression of the thought behind plays like *Death of a Salesman, All My Sons, A View from the Bridge, The Crucible* and the under-rated early piece, *A Memory of Two Mondays*.

> The assumption – or presumption – behind these plays is that life has a meaning...
> The idea is very important to me as a dramatist, but I think it is time someone said that playwrights, including the greatest...have not been noted for the new ideas they have broached in their plays...Surely there is no known philosophy which was first announced through a play, nor an ethical idea...
> Each of these plays, in varying degrees, was begun in the belief that it is unveiling a truth already known but unrecognisable as one. My concept of the audience is of a public each member of which is carrying about what he thinks is an anxiety, or a hope or a preoccupation which is his alone and isolates him from mankind [cf. Pirandello] and in this respect at least the function of a play is to reveal him to himself so that he may touch others by virtue of the revelation of his mutuality with them. If only for this reason I regard the theater as a serious business, one that makes or should make man more human, which is to say, less alone.

Miller's characters themselves are often isolated, and his 'heroes' share various other qualities. Peculiarly, probably because it is a faculty that Miller admires and shares, they are all 'good with their hands'. Joe, the corrupt engineer in *All My Sons*, the artisans in *A Memory of Two Mondays*, John Proctor, the farmer in *The Crucible*, Eddy the longshoreman in *A View from the Bridge*, even little Willy Loman who was trying to make and mend things for his family in *Death of a Salesman*, all have this admirable trait. Similarly, they all consciously bring about their own destruction, either like Joe and Willy by active suicide, or through intransigence, like Proctor and, arguably, Eddy. When writing about Willy, Miller could be describing all four of his protagonists:

> ...I did not realise...how few would be impressed by the fact that this man is actually a very brave spirit who cannot settle for half but must pursue his dream of himself to the end.[8]

This aspect of self-destruction seems to permeate much of the drama of the first half of this century; the German Expressionists – to whom Miller acknowledges a debt – employed it often; Anouilh's *Antigone* insists on her own death; Yank in O'Neill's *Hairy Ape*, Odets' Jake in *Awake and Sing!* and Joe in *Golden Boy* also cause their own destruction, as if oblivion were preferable to continuing existence. One positive aspect of what is so often looked upon as a nihilistic movement is that at least the characters from the 'Theatre of the Absurd' stoically maintain a hold on their existences rather than squander them!

The four early major works of Miller are among the best known of American plays and so it is not necessary to expound upon them at any great length.

All My Sons is essentially about greed and cowardice; Joe Keller's factory produced a batch of fractured cylinder heads during the war, as a result of which a number of pilots were killed. His son, Larry, was also killed in the war but the mother, Kate, still hopes for his return. Chris, the surviving son, now runs the plant and invites Ann, a former neighbour, girlfriend of Larry and the daughter of Joe's partner who is still in prison for his part in the scandal, to visit.

Chris' sarcastic view of the power of Capital – and one presumes that he speaks for his author – is stated succinctly:

> This is the land of the great big dogs; you don't love a man here, you eat him! That's the principle; the only one we live by – it just happened to kill a few people this time, that's all. The world's that way, how can I take it out on him? What sense does that make? This is a zoo, a zoo![9]

The flaw in the structure of the play is that Ann has a letter from Larry, saying that he knew of his father's actions and is going to 'not come back' intentionally from his next mission – another act of ethical self-destruction – and yet she does not reveal it until the end, causing Joe to shoot himself. On reflection, this appears illogical, unlikely and contrived, but a theatre audience is not a collection of literary critics forearmed with the luxury of undisturbed perusal of the text and, practically, the piece does work.

The Crucible, set in seventeenth-century Salem with its tale of witch hunts and its comparison with the hounding of supposed Communists by Senator Joe McCarthy's investigation into 'Un-American Activities', has, quite understandably, become the darling of English and Drama teachers. It combines eminently actable roles, a hint of sex, easily-understandable allegory with a contrived 'archaic' language that is a pleasure for any aspiring 'ham' to recite:

> This is a sharp time, now, a precise time – we live no longer in the dusky afternoon when evil mixed itself with good and befuddled the world. Now, by God's grace, the shining sun is up, and them that fear not light will surely praise it![10]

A View from the Bridge was controversial, not on political but 'moral' grounds. The implications of incest and homosexuality throughout the text, coupled with the scene of Eddy kissing Rodolfo to prove to his niece that Rodolfo's protestations of love were not true, appear tame when reviewed some thirty-five years later but they caused more of an impact than the play's other theme, honour.

Death of a Salesman is rightly known as one of the great plays of the century. It portrays the little tragedy of Willy Loman who eventually chooses to kill himself in a car-crash rather than face the reality of unemployment and the disillusionment of his family. As Miller has written:

> the play grew from simple images...from images of futility...and above all, perhaps, the image of a need greater than hunger or sex or thirst, a need to leave a thumbprint somewhere on the world. A need for immortality, and by admitting it, the knowing that one has carefully inscribed one's name on a cake of ice on a hot July day.'[11]

As well as being a powerful play, *Death of a Salesman* was also technically innovative. While he readily admits his debt to the Expressionists and to Brecht, Miller's use of music, light and space to portray different time scales and define subjective memory and objective reality, the 'cut-away' walls seen in *Awake and Sing!*, and the movement between different supposed settings without changing anything more than the most rudimentary furniture made *Death of a Salesman* as interesting theatrically as it was disturbing emotionally. The stage directions establish the conventions from the start:

> *Whenever the action is in the present the actors observe the imaginary wall-lines, entering the house only through its door at the left. But in the scenes of the past these boundaries are broken, and characters enter or leave a room by stepping 'through' a wall onto the forestage.*

And it was this sort of technical innovation that was to enable another young playwright, Tennessee Williams, to realise his highly idiosyncratic visions of human nature.

Williams mingled past and present, memory and reality in his first success, the semi-autobiographical *The Glass Menagerie* (1945) and the non-representative style of stage design provided him with considerable freedom in *A Streetcar Named Desire* (1947) (see illustrations).

However, the main contribution of Thomas Lanier Williams (1911-1983) to American and, indeed, world theatre will not be considered as a technical one; what Tennessee Williams epitomised, chronicled and celebrated was the pleasure and, more particularly, the pain of sexual infatuation. A homosexual, Williams transformed his desires into those of a sequence of superbly-delineated neurotic, hypersensitive females; Amanda and Laura in *The Glass Menagerie*, Maggie the Cat in *Cat on a Hot Tin Roof* 'the Princess' in *Sweet Bird of Youth* but most especially his most famous creation, Blanche Dubois, in *A Streetcar Named Desire*. However, despite the eminent 'actability' of these roles, there is a definite danger of them being seen as a succession of 'camp' transvestite 'queens', rather than real women, a danger that the actresses who undertake them must be aware of.

The ambivalent object of fear and desire in *Streetcar* is Stanley Kowalski, the role that was to make Marlon Brando famous; Williams' men are either reflections of his own father, variations on the bestial or erotic aspects that are combined in Stanley, or of himself, the weak dreamer. The 'monster' male was typified by Big Daddy Pollitt in *Cat on a Hot Tin Roof*, (remarkably realised in the original production by the benevolent folk-singer, Burl Ives) with a definite echo in Boss Finley in *Sweet Bird of Youth*, while the attractive youth is epitomised in the character of Chance Wayne in the same play.

As with O'Neill, Williams' material source is his early life; the sexual conflicts both in himself and his plays stem from his parents. His father was a bullying travelling salesman trying to live up to all the bar-room jokes which that profession had inspired (his attempts at understanding his son's complexities stopped at his nickname for him – 'Miss Nancy'); his mother was overprotective and prudish. This combination not only produced the future playwright but also a daughter, Rose, the model for Laura in *The Glass Menagerie*. However, whereas Williams represented Laura's restricted personality by a physical lameness, in fact Rose became an emotional cripple, retreating from the reality of her home life and the rude world into a dream world of insanity, spending much of her long adult life in asylums.

After some fifteen years of highly successful creativity in which he produced *Summer and Smoke*, *The Rose Tattoo*, *Orpheus Descending*, *The Milk Train Doesn't Stop Here Any More* and *The Night of the Iguana*, an underrated and more balanced piece than most, Williams' work deteriorated as he attempted to obliterate his unhappy lifestyle with alcohol and drugs (a solution which he had already proffered in the character of Brick in *Cat*).

He has been criticised for the negative aspect of his work:

> the playwright is moving away from complexity towards a terrifyingly simple view of life. The world is corrupt, the earth is the under-kingdom and the only salvation lies in withdrawal.

Given the fate of his sister and, to a lesser extent, himself, this would not be a surprising reaction; however, as with the Absurdists, it must be said that the very act of creation lends a positive balance to the work. He himself wrote:

> Personal lyricism is the outcry of prisoner to prisoner from the cell in solitary where each is confined for the duration of his life.

While there may be an element of romanticising in this, there is no doubting the stature of his early work, with the outstanding *A Streetcar Named Desire*.

It is set in a tenement building in a poor quarter of New Orleans, in the apartment of Stanley and Stella Kowalski. He is of Polish origin, she from a supposedly 'class' Tennessee family, the Dubois. We learn about her family and background when her sister, Blanche, comes to visit. Blanche continually complains about the conditions in which Stella is living, always harping back to the genteel style of life they led on the plantation that they owned, 'Belle Reve' – and it does not take a particularly analytical mind to grasp the irony in this name. In the course of the piece, Blanche is alternately repelled and attracted by the vital Stanley. (His first entrance is carrying a bloody parcel of raw meat, another example of Williams' helpful hints to the audience.) Compared with Stanley is Mitch, his friend, still living with his mother and taken in by Blanche's tales of gentility and respectability. The climax of the piece comes when Stanley manages to discover the truth about Blanche; the tales of the plantation and school teaching are 'old hat' and Blanche had been forced to leave town after a boy she had been teaching and whom she had tried to seduce had committed suicide, with Blanche herself accused of prostitution. Stanley rapes her, convinced that this is what she 'was asking for', an act which finally completely unbalances her mental state. Williams implies no criticism or contradiction of Stanley's action and so one presumes that he condones the rape; eventually, Blanche is led away to an asylum by a Doctor and Matron, who all the while maintain that they are simply taking her to stay in a home that befits her social standing.

The creation of 'Blanche' is remarkable; for while it may be his unconscious revenge on the female sex it also demonstrates how well Williams must have been acquainted with the border lands of fantasy and madness, an area which he had begun to chart in *The Glass Menagerie*.

Both *A Streetcar Named Desire* and *Death of a Salesman* were directed by Elia Kazan under the auspices of the Theatre Guild. This organisation deserves the credit for nurturing much of the new talent that was coming up through the 20s, 30s and 40s. As well as taking on O'Neill when he had become too ambitious for the Provincetown Players, the Guild also presented America's answer to German Expressionism, Elmer Rice's *The Adding Machine*, as well as a number of Shaw world premieres.

Although its younger idealists broke away in 1931 to form the Group Theatre, a move that survived ten years as a production company, it was infinitely more influential in its off-shoot, the Actors Studio, where Lee Strasberg was to promote his version of Stanislavsky's teaching as 'The Method'. The Guild represented what was most exciting in American theatre for over thirty years and it is interesting to see that Kazan, one of the founders of the Group and of the Actors' Studio, returned to the Guild to stage Miller's and Williams' masterpieces. Eric Bentley, the doyen of drama critics has written that 'Mr Kazan's name in the program guarantees an evening of

– at the very least – brilliant theatre work at a high emotional temperature',[12] a temperature necessary for both Arthur Miller and Tennessee Williams.

It may be a simple coincidence but it appears that, with the demise of such sympathetic production organisations as the Group and the Theatre Guild as well as the quick extinction of the Federal Theatre Project and Orson Wells' and John Houseman's Mercury Theatre, there has been a comparable paucity of new writing for the theatre.

Despite the volcanic power demonstrated in his enormously successful *Who's Afraid of Virginia Woolf?*, Edward Albee (b. 1928) is essentially a miniaturist, dealing with introspective character examination, as if his characters were laboratory specimens under a miscroscope; however, it is possible to speculate that the restrictions may be imposed not so much by aesthetics as by economics, when a few actors in one set is a safer gamble than anything more expansive, or expensive.

His early 'absurdist' pieces, such as *Zoo Story* (1958) and *American Dream* (1960), display this interest in character analysis focusing, in the former, on two men, Jerry and Peter, on a park bench and on a simple all-American family, including a splendidly grotesque grandmother, in the latter. *Who's Afraid of Virginia Woolf?* (1962) continues his examination of the destructive dynamics of relationships.

In Act III of *Whose Afraid of Virginia Woolf?*, subtitled 'The Exorcism', George explains to a drunken Honey just how far he and Martha go in their in-fighting and, in doing so, provides us with a description from Albee of the depth of his sort of probings:

> We all peel labels, sweetie; and when you get through the skin, all three layers, through the muscle, slosh aside the organs...them which is still sloshable – and get down to the bone, you haven't got all the way yet. There's something inside the bone ... and that's what you gotta get at.

In *A Delicate Balance* (1966), Albee continued his intricate dissection of the family that had begun, crudely, with *American Dream*. As in *Who's Afraid of Virginia Woolf?*, the characters are regularly refuelled by alcohol, with Claire starting the day on vodka and Harry oiling his confessional propensities with whiskey at seven-thirty in the morning. Yet again, Albee's people demonstrate the pain inherent in co-existence, although with Agnes, Tobias, their daughter Julia and sister Claire, the mutual destruction is more subtle than that of George and Martha. That this lacerating honesty only occurs at night is implied by Agnes' last line: 'When daylight comes again...order comes with it', although in *A Delicate Balance* there is the extra element of the unexplained terror or 'plague' that their friends, Harry and Edna, bring to them when they insist on staying the night. This is reminiscent of an Ionesco creation, or the elliptical threats in Harold Pinter's work and echoes the 'absurd' aspect of Albee's earlier plays.

His later works demonstrate his lack of interest in mainstream, 'realistic' theatre; *Seascape* (1975) features talking sea creatures, while the main character in *The Lady from Dubuque* (1979) is the angel of death.

Although *Virginia Woolf* was an international success and a 'hit' on Broadway, Albee had his roots in 'Off-Broadway', the umbrella title for those small, experimental theatres that were the successors to the venues where the Washington Square Players and the Provincetown Players worked in the 1920s.

By the sixties, though, Off-Broadway had become as much part of the established theatre as Broadway itself and so spawned the inevitable 'Off-Off-Broadway' for true experimentation, where companies like Ellen Stewart's Café La Mama and the Bread and Puppet Theatre have had international influence. To find voices representative of American Theatre in the 1970s and 80s, it is necessary to go a long way 'off' Broadway; to California and Chicago respectively.

It has been claimed that Sam Shepard (b. 1943) was the most influential and revolutionary figure working in the theatre in the latter part of the 1960s and the 70s, although he will probably be best known as an actor for his performance in the film *Fool For Love* and as a writer for the screenplay to *Paris, Texas* (1985), a film that has taken on cult status. That he is widely known through his film work is no surprise for he is of a generation that has been raised on movies and television. The most interesting, most lucrative, most influential and most demanding work is being done on film in America and the effect of the medium can be seen in some of Shepard's work.

There is such a wide range of styles and subjects in his stage work that it is difficult to generalise about him; it is possible to claim that he is the chronicler of the 'Sex, Drugs and Rock and Roll' culture of the early 1970s with pieces like the rock-duel *Tooth of the Crime* and *Cowboy Mouth*. The character list and stage directions for the latter give an impression, both of Shepard's characters and one of his writing styles:

CHARACTERS
CAVALE: a chick who looks like a crow, dressed in raggedy black.
SLIM: a cat who looks like a coyote, dressed in scruffy red. They are both beat to shit.
LOBSTER MAN.

CAVALE *has kidnapped* SLIM *off the streets with an old .45. She wants to make him into a rock-and-roll star, but they fall in love. We find them after one too many mornings. They're both mean as snakes.* SLIM *is charging round, screaming words;* CAVALE *is rummaging through junk, yelling with a cracked throat. The lights come up on them in this state.*

Shepard also displays an interest in the mythic version of American history and culture, with Wild West figures and film stars appearing in his work (characters in *Mad Dog Blues* include Mae West, Marlene Dietrich, Jesse James, Captain Kidd, Waco Texas and John Bunyan), while in a more 'realistic' piece like *Curse of the Starving Class* he displays fierce disillusionment at the destruction of the home, family life, 'the American dream', in a way that is deliberately shocking. Some elements such as the boy, Wesley, urinating on his sister's homework, or the introduction on stage of a newly-flayed corpse of a lamb seem, at least on reading the play, to be gratuitous, but the description of the death struggles of an eagle and a cat, killing each other in mid-air, transforms the shocking into something poetic, and demonstrates a definite talent.

These plays, more than any other discussed in this chapter, are plays to be performed, not read. The words on the page are not even a guide-line to some of the pieces. As Jack Gelber writes:

> Often in our best plays there is as much happening below the lines as there is action implied in them. Dialogue is the air in the bubbles breaking sea surface from the very deep, highly condensed, poetically charged experience intended by the author.[13]

That said, however, it must be admitted that, given the esoteric nature of the content, language, characters and subject matter used by Shepard in his plays, it is difficult to imagine them having as universal an impact as those of Albee, Williams, Miller or O'Neill.

The major force of the late 1970s and 80s was discovered in Chicago, where *Sexual Perversity in Chicago* and *Duck Variations* marked the advent of David Mamet (b. 1947). The promise of this early work was reinforced by *American Buffalo* in 1977 and later by *Glengarry Glen Ross* in 1983. As in the work of Sam Shepard, the use of 'foul' language has alienated many middle-class audiences but Mamet's work is seen to be a meaningful comment on, and harsh criticism of, the state of American society dominated by competetive but corrupting capitalism. Christopher Bigsby sums up Mamet's work thus:

> ...Mamet sets out to suggest that American society, in Freudian terms, has failed to progress from the adolescent to the adult level... [but]...the irony is that the confident tone of his public pronouncements rarely invades his plays, which are painfully effective precisely because of the precision with which he reproduces the dislocations, the vacuity, the desperate strategies of those who are aware of some insufficiency in their lives but seemingly have no language with which they may fully express it, no actions which can assuage it, no sense of transcendence which may serve to neutralize it. And that failure of nerve, of language, of apprehension, of imagination is, to Mamet, as true and as fundamentally destabilizing

on a private as a public level, where the collapse of communality may edge the entire culture toward apocalypse.[14]

American theatre appears to have gone full circle from the inarticulacy of O'Neill's 'Yank' to that of Mamet's thugs, estate agents and film producers in a very short time, from origins to decadence in less than a century. There are an enormous number of aspiring performers in the States and a considerable number of writers who are being seduced by the alluring but all-devouring maw of television. The cinema has been 'alive' for just as long as the home-grown American theatre and it is difficult to contradict the claim that the best creative work done in America or, at least, by Americans in the 1970s and 80s has been done in the cinema rather than on stage. But, as creation-by-committee takes an ever greater hold on television dramas and feature films, the role of the writer has diminished until – rightly, some will argue – he is just another jobber in the team. After all, the musical, that all-American creation, has always been a team product, the commercial Broadway 'hits' tended to be amalgamated from the specialist skills of various play-doctors and even the more experimental companies such as the Living Theatre and La Mama had always worked communally, but it does appear that that rare species, the American playwright, as epitomised by O'Neill, Miller and Tennessee Williams may have become extinct almost before it had time to flourish.

Ten plays for further consideration

1. Eugene O'Neill, *The Hairy Ape*
2. Eugene O'Neill, *Long Day's Journey into Night*
3. Clifford Odets, *Awake and Sing!*
4. Thornton Wilder, *The Skin of Our Teeth*
5. Arthur Miller, *The Crucible*
6. Arthur Miller, *Death of a Salesman*
7. Tennessee Williams, *A Streetcar Named Desire*
8. Edward Albee, *Who's Afraid of Virginia Woolf?*
9. Sam Shepard, *Tooth of the Crime*
10. David Mamet, *Glengarry Glen Ross*

Notes

1. Quoted in Arthur and Barbara Gelb, *Eugene O'Neill*, p. 31
2. ibid., p. 143
3. Quoted in Howard Taubman, *The Making of the American Theatre*, p. 152

4. Odets, stage directions, *Waiting for Lefty*
5. ibid.
6. Odets, *Paradise Lost*
7. Odets, *Awake and Sing!*
8. Arthur Miller, introduction to *Death of a Salesman*
9. Arthur Miller, *All My Sons*
10. Arthur Miller, *The Crucible*
11. Arthur Miller, introduction to *Death of a Salesman*, p. 29
12. Eric Bentley, *The Dramatic Event*, p. 109
13. Jack Gerber, introduction to *Angel City* by Sam Shepard
14. C.W.E. Bigsby, *David Mamet*, pp. 130-1

7: THE MUSIC MEN

While the visionaries of the Washington Square Players, the Provincetown Players and the Theatre Guild were struggling to create a theatre that was a refreshing reaction to the safe commercial bets that Broadway producers had insisted on, a quiet revolution in that most 'commercial' of vehicles, the musical comedy, was also under way.

Always ready to follow the fashion set by *fin-de-siècle* Europe, America had adopted the operetta in an enthusiastic, truly American way; the English style of Gilbert and Sullivan proved as popular in the States as it had at home, evidence of which being that, soon after *HMS Pinafore* had opened in 1878, there were almost a hundred different productions of it running in the country. 'Opera Bouffe', such as Offenbach's *Orpheus in the Underworld* and *La Belle Hélène*, realised many an impressionable American's fantasies of what the naughty 1890s in Paris were all about, while Lehar's *The Merry Widow* continued to provide Americans with as misleading an impression of Europe as the Movie Westerns and television 'cop' shows give of America for European viewers today.

While the best operettas originated in Europe, there were American contributions to the development of musical theatre that cannot be ignored. One such which, in the light of present-day views on racism, it might be preferable to ignore was the 'Nigger Minstrel' or 'Coon' show, where white performers 'blacked up' with burned cork to perform such songs as made Stephen Foster famous, the best-known exponent of this form of entertainment being Al Jolson. To modern eyes and ears, shows such as *A Trip To Coontown* are at best patronising but, more often than not, down-right insulting. However, if one looks at a play like O'Neill's *Emperor Jones* (1920) which was hailed as a major innovation in the way it portrayed blacks on stage and yet which still emphasised ignorance and superstition while mocking the manner of speech, then perhaps these Minstrel shows were less offensive than they may now appear.

One of the major figures in the early American musical theatre of this century was George M. Cohan who combined the abilities of a song-and-dance man with that of a writer and impresario. There was a definite element of chauvinism in shows like *Little Johnny Jones* (1904) which featured 'Yankee Doodle Dandy' – a song given an even wider audience by Jimmy Cagney's film portrayal of Cohan, while his song *Over There* became such a rallying cry to America in the First World War that it earned Cohan a Congressional medal!

The early musical comedies, like revues and the new 'Follies', were essentially amalgams of set and successful pieces. What has been described as 'mindless and frivolous entertainment' was epitomised by a turn-of-the-century import *Florodora*, whose high spot was a sextet of attractive girls singing: 'Tell Me, Pretty Maiden':

> Their performances...enchanted the men, for, at the end of each number...the girls would smile and wink, usually at some man in the audience...This personal touch, an innovation in musical theater... entranced the young beaux who crowded the theater night after night to see the girls and to lavish expensive gifts upon them.[1]

So successful were they in their performances that some 70 girls appeared in the sextet during the run of 500 performances, the rest either marrying monied men or finding 'wealthy admirers'.

However, there were those working in the medium who endeavoured to impose some sort of cohesion and content upon the concoctions. Victor Herbert (1859-1924), although born in Ireland, was looked upon as American and, by the early 1900s, was producing 'home-grown' musical comedies, albeit in the European style. His *Babes in Toyland* was a Christmas 'hit' in 1903 while *Naughty Marietta* provided generations of amateur singers with a favoured victim to massacre in 'Ah, Sweet Mystery of Life'.

Rudolf Friml and Sigmund Romberg may now appear to epitomise the sort of vapid, 'formula' operetta that, eventually, the American musical would displace. Friml wrote two of the classics of the 'genre', *Rose Marie* and *The Vagabond King*, and while it may now be fashionable to disparage such work, there is no doubting that, particularly in this latter piece – a romanticised version of the life of Francois Villon, the thief-poet – Friml wrote some fine, stirring musical melodrama. Romberg's contribution included *The Student Prince* and *The Desert Song* and he voiced a conscious desire to improve upon the old format:

> I have been endeavouring to have singing, dancing, comedy and a good cohesive story in one production, and to blend all these elements into one compact presentation which will not only please the ears and eyes, but also appeal to the intelligence of the playgoer. The book must be so arranged that neither dancing, music nor comedy must appear foreign to the action of the story.[2]

Aspirations worthy of a Kern or Hammerstein.

The 'book', in musical comedy parlance, is a term that not everyone may be familiar with; while 'lyrics' and 'score' simply mean words and music, the 'book' – an amalgam of story-line, structure and script for what little dialogue was needed to patch the musical numbers together – was becoming more sophisticated as the need for a 'good book' was recognised. An expert summary of this essential element describes it as:

> ...an outline of highly compressed dramatic development that provides a working umbrella for the songs and dances ...It is a skeletal play...the sturdy frame that defines the limits of everything the show can offer to its audience. In addition to standards of literary excellence, a good book prospers in proportion to the credible opportunities it offers music, dance, design and performance to do on stage what words alone are inadequate to do: to open up the show's thought or emotion in a succession of situations and build them to a satisfying resolution through music and movement.[3]

In 1915, a move from the frothy Viennese concoctions towards something that was at least contemporary even if it was not particularly demanding was made by a trio of thirty-year olds in the tiny Princess Theatre in New York. In a sequence of six shows in four years, of which *Very Good, Eddie* (1915) and *Oh, Boy!* (1917) were the most memorable, the team of composer, Jerome Kern (1885-1945), librettist Guy Bolton (1883-1979) and lyricist P.G. Wodehouse (1881-1975) began to crack the mould. The sequence was only broken when Wodehouse decided that it had all been great fun, but that he really wanted to go back home to England and write novels.

Bolton continued as a playwright and librettist producing such pieces as *Oh, Kay* and *Lady Be Good* while Wodehouse was delighting the world with Jeeves, Bertie Wooster, Lord Emsworth, Psmith and other inhabitants of his British 'upper-crust' Never-Never Land.

While Wodehouse may have looked upon the Princess Theatre musicals as a minor part of his artistic aspirations, for Kern they had more importance; his was a serious approach to something that was apparently light-hearted, believing that the musical was an important element in contemporary American Theatre and as exciting as anything that the seers of Provincetown and Washington Square might be conceiving. As Richard Kislan wrote:

> ...Kern insisted throughout that a musical theater must be THEATER, an art form meant to be performed on stage by actors who employ the elements of dramatic literature joined by song to reveal some aspect of human life.[4]

And when in 1927 Kern teamed up with arguably the most influential man in the history of the American musical, Oscar Hammerstein II, these precepts were adhered to and the product was *Showboat*.

For the first time many of the aspirations towards an integrated musical were realised. One innovation was its origin, in that the basis of the 'book' was a novel by Edna Ferber. Whereas operas were often based on already established works from another genre – *The Barber of Seville* and *The*

Marriage of Figaro both originating in Beaumarchais' plays, for example – to use a serious novel with definite character developments and a complex and serious subject matter was definitely new for what was still called a 'musical comedy'; and when that subject matter was the treatment of the poor, exploited southern negro and the still contentious issue of mixed marriage, then it is hardly surprising that the doubters were vociferous.

Prior to *Showboat*, blacks had been depicted as simpletons, clowns or, as in O'Neill's *Emperor Jones*, superstitious savages. With the character of Joe, the slave, and his lament 'Ol' Man River', the attitude towards the portrayal of blacks – if not to blacks themselves – had changed forever for the better.

It must not be thought that *Showboat* was a total transformation; it was set, obviously, on a Show Boat – one of the steamers or paddle-boats that plied the Mississippi and Ohio rivers with entertainments ranging from Shakespeare through melodrama, circus and, of course, musical comedy – so the opportunity for the protagonists to burst into song was considerable, while the storyline of Gaylord Ravenal and Magnolia, eventually reunited by their daughter, Kim, appears as hackneyed now as anything chosen by Friml or Stromberg. The theme of opposition to inter-racial marriage, when Julie, the mulatto leading lady, and her husband, Steve, have to leave the showboat because of Julie's race, is not over-emphasised and, in retrospect, does not appear to be that remarkable; however, mixed marriages were obviously a topic that concerned Hammerstein because he was to return to it over twenty years later in *South Pacific* with the ill-fated relationship between Lieutenant Cable and Bloody Mary's daughter, Liat.

For a less condescending view of black Americans, employing jazz, a musical form that was rooted in America, one must look forward eight years, to George Gershwin's *Porgy and Bess*.

George Gershwin (1898-1937) had started out as a 'song-plugger' and rehearsal pianist, playing other people's music. He started contributing songs to concocted revues and musicals, displaying from the start his interest in jazz, while his brother, Ira (1896-1983), was writing words to other people's tunes. Their initial collaboration produced *Lady Be Good* (1924) for another pair of siblings, Fred and Adele Astaire, but, reflecting the more serious mood of the Depression years, they worked toward shows with more social comment, producing, among others, *Of Thee I Sing*, the first musical play to be awarded a Pulitzer Prize for drama. It dealt with contemporary politics and led to the more pungent *Let 'Em Eat Cake*. On these shows, they had worked with George S. Kaufman, who as either co-writer, director or 'play-doctor' was one of the most successful collaborators in the history of Broadway.

Gershwin was also experimenting with serious compositions in the jazz idiom and had already written *Rhapsody in Blue* and *Concerto in F*, while still producing classic popular songs such as 'I Got Rhythm', 'Let's Call the Whole Thing Off' and 'They All Laughed'.

The *Porgy and Bess* project had begun as the novel *Porgy* by DuBose Heyward. With his wife, Dorothy, he dramatised the book about the crippled black Porgy for the ubiquitous Theatre Guild. There had been a suggestion that Jerome Kern should turn it into a musical vehicle for Al Jolson, blacked up. Fortunately Hayward declined what appeared to be the formula for infallible commercial success in favour of a score by George and lyrics by Ira Gershwin.

Porgy and Bess (1935) is claimed by opera buffs as the first American opera, as if they cannot accept that a popular 'Musical' could be *that* good, and it is true that it probably needs an opera company to do it justice; but it is musical theatre of the highest calibre written by a very successful, commercial song-writing team which just happened to be touched with genius. One of the Gershwins' fellow-inmates of the American Musical Hall of Fame, Alan Jay Lerner, explained the achievement:

> What Gershwin had done was taken the song form and given it a depth, a height and an emotional expansion that on the normal operatic stage would be achieved by aria. He called it a folk opera and that is precisely what it is. There was recitative, but there was also dialogue, which by strict definition was 'opera bouffe'. But intellectual distinctions in the case of *Porgy and Bess* seem irrelevant. It was the first of its kind and remains to this day the greatest triumph of modern musical theatre.[5]

And this from the co-author of *My Fair Lady* who had seen *Oklahoma!*, *South Pacific*, *West Side Story* and the rest!

In July 1938, at the age of just 38, George Gershwin died of a brain tumour; in the light of *Porgy and Bess* and *Rhapsody in Blue*, not to mention the many Tin Pan Alley standards that he wrote, America had lost its first composer of genius.

While it is not possible to attribute any great development in the field of Musical Theatre to him, mention must be made here of Cole Porter (1891-1964) whose songs, along with those by the Gershwins, Noel Coward and Irving Berlin, epitomised the 1930s. While his most successful musical *Kiss Me Kate* was not written until 1948, after the war and the 1937 riding accident which crippled him physically and also appeared to restrict him creatively, those pieces that contained his greatest songs – 'Night and Day' from *Gay Divorce*, 'I Get a Kick Out of You' and 'You're the Top' from *Anything Goes*, and 'My Heart Belongs to Daddy' from *Leave It To Me!* – belonged to the stylish, lighter-hearted time before the Second World War.

Among Porter's major competitors was the team of Richard Rodgers (1902-1979) and Lorenz Hart (1895-1943) who contributed considerably to Broadway's apparently insatiable appetite for musicals, although their only piece to provoke any controversy was *Pal Joey*. Hart wrote brilliant, often biting lyrics but their choice of 'books' was not particularly remarkable.

It was not until 1943, when Hart was too ill to collaborate on the transformation of a straight play, *Green Grow the Lilacs*, into a musical for the Theatre Guild, that it was suggested that Oscar Hammerstein II should take over the job. Hammerstein (1895-1960) had started writing lyrics while still at college, contributing the words for shows by both Herbert Stothart and Vincent Youmans. With *Showboat*, he showed that he was as dedicated as Kern to 'legitimising' the Musical, and his ideals were realised in this first partnership with Rodgers.

In its try-out in Boston, the new piece was called *Away We Go* but there a new song was added to the last act and its title adopted as the name of the show. *Oklahoma!* opened in 1943. As Howard Taubman wrote: 'It is impossible to guess the effect of the simple optimism of *Oklahoma!* on a nation receiving grim reports from battlefronts in North Africa, Europe and the Pacific, or the impact of its novelty.'[6]

The sincerity of the emotions that the piece displayed came to be a hallmark of Hammerstein's work, a thing that he insisted upon: 'There's nothing wrong with sentiment...The things people are sentimental about are the fundamental things in life. I don't deny the ugly and the tragic – but somebody has to keep saying that life's pretty wonderful too. Because it's true. I guess, I can't write anything without hope in it.'[7] It may appear cynical to say so but when Hammerstein listed 'My Favourite Things' in *The Sound of Music*, he probably meant every one of them.

Apart from the optimism and warm-heartedness of the piece, *Oklahoma!* broke new ground with its structure. Instead of the big opening number with the chorus and dancers leaping around, it started with an old woman churning butter on an empty stage and the opening song a solo, with the singer starting 'Oh, what a beautiful morning' off stage. One producer told the Guild that the show had little chance to succeed on Broadway because it was too clean, had no bawdy jokes or strip-tease girls, and would not appeal to the people who were crowding theatres that featured more raucous entertainment.[8] *Oklahoma!* ran for five years in New York.

There was an old 'showbiz' adage that given the usual scantily-clad dancing girls and the archetypal opening number 'the average businessman could tell whether he would or would not like a musical comedy before the curtain was halfway up'.[9] In *Oklahoma!*, the average businessman had a long wait, for the dancers were not introduced until the end of the first act and even then, only in a ballet, the influence of the choreographer, Agnes de Mille.

Another first was the killing of a character on stage; even though Jud was 'the baddy', the death an accident and the perpetrator, Curly, the hero, this action opened the way to more deliberate stage killings from the knife-fights of *West Side Story* to the orgy of 'de-gorging' in Sondheim's *Sweeney*

Todd; it also helped to ascribe the epithet 'serious' to the show.

The story was of a 1907 range war between cowmen and farmers, the former demanding open range for the cattle and the latter wanting fenced-in fields for their crops. Set against this are the classic comic elements and love interests, although in 'People will say we're in love', there is the clever reversal of the normal situation with a duet that insists that the pair do *not* love each other. The success of the piece was phenomenal, becoming the longest-running production in both New York and London, a record that was not to be surpassed until the arrival of *My Fair Lady*, some thirteen years later. Alan Jay Lerner, the co-author of the subsequent hit, is again more than generous in his evaluation:

> *Oklahoma!* was the most totally realized amalgamation of all the theatrical arts. The book was legitimate playwriting, every song flowed from the dramatic action, and Agnes de Mille's ballet at the end of Act 1…was one of the most imaginative uses of choreography yet seen in the theatre…Lyrically, *Oklahoma!* was a masterful work, lighter than Hammerstein had been before and with none of the 'poetic' excesses that…frequently marred some of his future writing. Dick's music adjusted itself to the new collaboration and together they produced a new voice and a style that was distinctly their own.[10]

The mould was broken and the way open to serious subjects in contemporary settings.

Nothing could be more serious nor more recent than the war, and by 1949 Rodgers and Hammerstein had succeeded in putting at least one theatre of that war onto stage. *South Pacific* was set in a war that had only been over for four years and had such a long run that the Korean War was underway before the show had closed, adding unintended poignancy to the final performances.

It was based on two stories from James Mitchener's collection *Tales from the South Pacific*, a body of work that had been turned down by MGM as film material but suggested by them as a musical, possibly on the grounds that you can sing what you cannot say! The main figure, Nellie Forbush, came from the story 'Our Heroine' which also provided the unorthodox male 'lead', the planter, Emile de Becque. He has two children by a previous marriage to a Polynesian and this offends the girl from 'Little Rock, ARK.' (thus providing Hammerstein with his first piece of social comment). The original production broke new ground by casting Ezio Pinza, a recognised bass-baritone star of the opera, as Emile de Becque; at the time, Broadway most definitely did not stretch as far as the Metropolitan Opera House. Nelly's opposition to Emile's previous marriage was easily overcome but the theme of the difficulty of cross-culture marriages was stressed far more strongly in the other story that was used as the basis for the 'book'.

'Fo' Dolla' introduced Lieutenant Cable, Liat and her mother, the Polynesian black-marketeer, 'Bloody Mary'. This is one of the most impressive characters to have appeared on the musical stage, combining the rough byplay of her dealings with the sailors with the lyrical 'Bali Ha'i' and 'Happy Talk', a song title that describes itself.

While there are no difficulties in the path of Nellie's happy ending, the prospects of a mixed marriage for Cable and Liat are spelled out in 'Carefully Taught', a blatant criticism by Hammerstein of the mentality of certain Americans and one which aroused considerable opposition from conservative elements in the southern States. The problems are romantically solved by Cable's death on an important mission.

From a technical point of view, the developments that the team made were considerable. They moved even further away from the classic 'chorus-line' concept; the vocal chorus was provided by the sailors and nurses who were integral to the story, there was no 'imposed' choreography and what little dancing there was evolved from the situation, as in the well-known transvestite concert-party scene where the sailors dress up as native girls and perform 'Honey-Bun'.

Not only were the 'show-biz' elements integral, the influence of the cinema was displayed by the fact that the various scenes flowed into each other without resorting to the deadly 'black-out' and much scene changing was done while the action was continuing on stage. It is true that the list of 'hit' songs is a long one, with each song a success in its own right and the whole demonstrating a remarkable variety of styles, but it is essentially the content of the piece and Hammerstein's ability to make a remarkable evening that was both entertaining and educational out of a serious subject, that makes *South Pacific* so special in the development of the *genre*.

Its major competitor for the awards in the 1948/49 season was Cole Porter's *Kiss Me Kate*. The songs are inevitably clever, as is the situation but the competiton was too great and *South Pacific* won both the Critics' Circle Award and the Pulitzer Prize for Drama.

What makes *Kiss Me Kate* of interest now is that it shows the range of the search for material for 'books'. While Rodgers and Hart had made tentative inroads on Shakespeare, using *The Comedy of Errors* as a starting point for *Boys from Syracuse* before the war, Porter's clever re-working of *The Taming of the Shrew* is probably the most effective attempt at employing the most prestigious – and most compliant – librettist that there is. Galt McDermot, under the direction of Joseph Papp's New York Shakespeare Festival, produced a rock version of *Two Gentlemen of Verona*, while Ray Poleman and Emile Dean Zogliby attempted to outdo both Verdi's *Otello* and Shakespeare's original with *Catch My Soul* but neither made a lasting impression. *West Side Story*, of course, has Shakespearean origins but is sufficiently distant from *Romeo and Juliet* to be considered in its own right.

Culture was invading the Musical. No sooner had the apparent 'realism' of *South Pacific* taken to the stage than *Guys and Dolls*, the paean in praise of Damon Runyon's stylised representation of the New York underworld, appeared. Runyon's stories feature gamblers, hoodlums and show girls in a sanitised, fantasy version of New York's criminals, couched in a language of esoteric slang and comic juxtaposition, unfaltering in its use of the present tense. Two examples from Runyon's stories refer to characters that reappear in *Guys and Dolls*:

> Angie the Ox is an importer himself, besides enjoying a splendid trade in other lines, including artichokes and extortion[11]

and;

> ...Nicely-Nicely is known far and wide as a character who dearly loves to commit eating.[12]

The characters that the authors of the 'book', Jo Swerling and Abe Burrows, and the producer, George Kaufman, concentrated on were Nathan Detroit with his apparently endless engagement with Miss Adelaide and equally endless search for a venue for his illegal crap-game (culminating in the superb sequence 'Luck, be a Lady' in the city sewers), and Miss Sarah Brown, her efforts to establish a 'Save-A-Soul' Mission on Broadway and her involvement with the ultimate gambler, Sky Masterson. Frank Loesser (1910-1969), the composer and lyricist, had earlier worked on a musical version of *Charley's Aunt*, called *Where's Charley?* which did not do justice to the original, but in the score that he wrote for *Guys and Dolls*, he was more than equal to the task. Ranging from the brash night-club numbers 'Bushel and a peck' and 'Take back your mink' to the beautiful 'I've never been in love' and 'I'll know', the score provided big production numbers like 'Sit down, you're rocking the boat' and 'Luck, be a lady', small comic pieces like 'Sue Me' and 'Miss Adelaide's Lament' and, most impressively, the music for the choereographed opening 'Runyonland' and the progressively wilder Cuba sequence where the dance rhythms reflect the growing intoxication of Miss Sarah. And all the time, whenever the music gave way to dialogue, there is always the idiosyncratic structure of Runyon's language to maintain or even heighten the pleasure.

There is no doubt that the structure is weak, hurrying through the final scenes to the double wedding at the end, but it takes either a close examination of the text or continual work on the show to notice such a flaw. In productions of the calibre of that by Richard Eyre for the British National Theatre in the early 1980s, finishing with the entire company tap dancing to the 'Guys and Dolls' reprise, it is impossible to bring such critical faculties to bear.

As stern a critic as Eric Bentley has selected *Guys and Dolls* as a worthy representative of the American drama and it was chosen as one of the best plays, not just musicals, of the 1950/51 season. It must be said that the film version, with Frank Sinatra and Marlon Brando, was very different from the stage show and in the minds of the champions of the musical, considerably inferior.

While producers were searching through Shakespeare and Runyon for suitable material for 'books', the most revered playwright of the twentieth century remained firmly opposed to the transformation of his work into musical theatre. George Bernard Shaw had allowed his *Arms and the Man* to be used by Rudolf Bernauer and Leopold Jacobson as the basis for *Der Tapfere Soldat* (1909), which was immediately adapted and translated by Oscar Straus and Stanislaus Stange as *The Chocolate Soldier*; Shaw had been so unimpressed that he had refused to give permission for anything else. However, after his death in 1950, his executors relented and released *Pygmalion*.

In the legend of Pygmalion and Galatea, the sculptor, Pygmalion, carves a most beautiful statue and falls in love with his creation, thus bringing it to life. In Shaw's version, the sculptor has become Professor Higgins, an expert phonologist who accepts the bet to transform the cockney flower seller, Eliza Doolittle, into one whose speech could pass for that of a duchess. Understandably, Shaw's version is pithier than the musical, where Eliza comes back to Higgins at the end; in Shaw, the creation turns on her Frankenstein and abandons him, threatening to set up her own school of phonology in opposition, to teach what she has had forced upon her.

The producer, Herman Levin, encouraged the partnership of Lerner and Loewe to work on *Pygmalion*. Alan Jay Lerner (1918-1986) was a well-to-do young man who had studied at the Juilliard School and Harvard and been weaned on Broadway. His collaborator, Frederick Loewe (1904-1988), was a classically trained Viennese musician who brought something of the old-fashioned operetta style to the partnership. Their first success had been *Brigadoon*, a rather fey fantasy about a magical Scottish village, reminiscent of J.M. Barrie's *Mary Rose*. After the more robust but less successful *Paint Your Wagon*, the partnership had split up but the prospect of working on the Shaw brought them back together again, and the product was *My Fair Lady*. Lerner must be credited with the considerable achievement of bringing the wit and humour of the original to the musical without succumbing to the inevitable temptation to 'improve' on it. With the exception of the ending, he is very faithful to Shaw, an intention that he expressed:

> The major factor that influenced us was – whether we were aware of it or not – the changing style of musicals. It now seemed feasible to preserve the text as much as possible without the addition of a secondary love story or choreographic integration. What *was* essential was that every song and every addition to the play should not violate the wit and intelligence of Shaw's work. He was the ideal

'collaborator' because there was so much oblique and unstated emotion that could be dramatized in music and lyrics.[13]

My Fair Lady provided Rex Harrison with the part of Professor Higgins in which he gave the definitive performance, a part with which he was to be associated ever since and which must have contributed considerably towards his knighthood in 1989. It also introduced Julie Andrews as a performer of 'star' quality and displayed the considerable strength of British character actors with supporting performances such as Robert Coote's Pickering and Stanley Holloway's Doolittle. While it cannot make any claims to innovation, it was probably the epitome of the lavish musical where even the costumes, designed by Cecil Beaton, won awards.

Its complete antithesis appeared a year later, in 1957, conceived by Jerome Robbins (b. 1918). As early as 1944, Robbins had adapted his classical ballet training to the commercial theatre, choreographing a piece by Leonard Bernstein, *Fancy Free*, which was to develop into the fully-fledged musical, *On the Town*. Bernstein (1918-1990) was restricted in his opportunities to compose for the musical theatre by his commitments as a conductor of world-wide esteem as well as a composer of more so-called 'serious' work, but in 1953 he wrote the score for *Wonderful Town* and, by 1956, produced the first of the many editions of his version of Voltaire's *Candide*, a project that seemed to have obsessed him ever since.

However, it was on their 1957 project that Robbins and Bernstein combined to create a revolutionary new work; they employed a protegé of Oscar Hammerstein's called Stephen Sondheim (b. 1930) as lyricist and the result was *West Side Story*.

The ploy of portraying two ethnically opposed New York street gangs, the Jets and the Sharks, as the twentieth-century versions of the Montagues and the Capulets has been criticised. Howard Taubman writes:

> ...I resented the romantic tragic style of *Romeo and Juliet* as imposed on a theme of contemporary urgency. To equate the conflict between races and nationalities with the romantic theme of a doomed love was to me a species of theatrical sentimentality. The problem was too serious for superficial and flamboyant parallels.[14]

However, such views can be contradicted by the opposite approach, that a modern parallel helped to highlight the universality of Shakespeare's theme and that internecine strife is as destructive as inter-racial conflict.

While some of Bernstein and Sondheim's songs, songs like 'Tonight', 'Maria', 'Somewhere' and 'America', have assumed classic status, the reaction to the whole work was initially not universally rapturous. The production portrayed the seamier side of American life; the splendid 'Gee, Officer Krupke', containing the immortal line: 'I'm depraved on account of I'm deprived', offended many who did not like to see a policeman, the only representative of the American state, being held up to ridicule. Sex and violence were all very well second-hand in the South Pacific, but to bring them straight off the streets of New York onto the Broadway stage offended many a delicate sensitivity.

Robbins' choreography to Bernstein's music was revolutionary. It introduced a style of theatre dance that owed much to the innovations of modern 'classical' dance companies and demanded an athleticism, especially in the men, that was unimaginable in productions like *South Pacific* or *My Fair Lady.* 'The entire cast...intrigued audiences for it was composed of dancers and singers whose lightning speed and catlike movements made the fighting ballet periods of breathless movement.'[15]

The more choreographic of Andrew Lloyd Webber's pieces are direct descendants of these innovations; indeed, with *Starlight Express* and *Cats*, the demand for a plot has been ignored in favour of choreographic pyrotechnics. Then, such things were unheard of:

> Today, the finger-snapping, crouching, lurching and leaping dancers of *West Side Story* have become familiar figures on the stage, but in 1957 these dances were excitingly new in the theater. The dance movements not only epitomised perfectly the tensions, the brutality, bravado and venomous hatred of the gang warriors, but also had sufficient variety in themselves to hold audiences spellbound.[16]

While Robbins continued to impose his magisterial direction and choreography on later productions, *West Side Story* was the last full-scale 'musical' that Bernstein wrote and the musical theatre lost a composer of genius to the concert hall.

Stephen Sondheim continued with the *genre* to become very much the major figure in musical theatre in the 1970s and 80s, assuming the role of composer as well as lyricist.

He created such works as *A Funny Thing Happened On the Way To The Forum* (based on Plautus), *Company*, *A Little Night Music* (based on Ingmar Bergman's film, *Smiles on a Summer Night*), *Pacific Overtures* (based on Japanese kabuki theatre), *Sweeney Todd* (based on the classic Victorian melodrama) and *Sunday in the Park with George* (based on the life and work of Georges Seurat) and it is possible to argue that the later work has become more and more cerebral, less accessible to the average audience and that his best body of lyrics was written in *West Side Story*.

With *South Pacific* and *West Side Story*, the serious musical had come of age and this trend was maintained in *Fiddler On The Roof* (1964). The piece was set in the 1900s in the Russian village of Anatevka during the pogroms against the Jews and was based upon Sholom Aleichem's stories about Tevye the milkman. With the final scene of the expulsion of the Jews from their homes, this work must have struck a responsive chord with many first and second generation Americans whose families had come to the New World with just such a send-off.

The Musical continued to be successful throughout the 1960s although works like *The Music Man, Gypsy, Camelot* and *Hello, Dolly* were nostalgic in content and unadventurous in style.

It was not until 1968, the era of student revolt, anti-war demonstrations and the 'flower-power' era of 'Make love, not war' that a completely new style of show appeared, the 'rock' musical.

Galt McDermot's *Hair* was, in its own way, as revolutionary as *Show-boat, Oklahoma!* or *West Side Story*; it epitomised an era, with the songs 'Hair' and 'Aquarius' becoming anthems for the generation that had been born after the Second World War and that was questioning everything that its conservative parents stood for.

Initially, in its 'Off-Broadway' form, the show was essentially American, being about the current dichotomy facing most young American males, whether they should accept the *status quo* and go to fight in an unwelcome war in Vietnam, or else commit a criminal act by burning their draft-cards. Eventually, the 'hero' goes to war and is killed.

On its transfer to Broadway, this slim framework had further songs on further issues added to it which tended to confuse the original theme. What was a simple anti-war vehicle was encumbered with attacks on pollution, or-ganised religion, the 'older generation' as well as hymns to free sex and soft drugs. Hardly surprisingly, *Hair* created a great deal of hostility in the more conservative elements of its audience while the younger, more liberal ele-ment loved it, with its 'revolutionary' ending whereby the cast invited the audience onto the stage to dance with them.

In Britain, *Hair* received invaluable publicity because it was the first pro-duction to open after the 'demise' of the Lord Chancellor's office, the government department responsible for censorship, which had powers to close down a show if it was deemed unsuitable. Cassandras forecast the opening of the floodgates of pornography, with *Hair* and its much-vaunted use of nudity to the fore. In fact, the 'nude' scene was not only tastefully handled, being no more erotic than an art school life class, but also had none of the coy prurience of the 'tableaux vivants' that had made the Windmill Theatre so renowned for so long.

Hair was billed as an 'American tribal love-rock musical' but not all the music was 'rock'; songs like 'Good Morning, Starshine' and 'Frank Mills' dis-played a gentle, lyrical touch. While it is true that the whole lacked a definite aim and was something of a *pot-pourri*, *Hair* was exciting, vibrant, apparent-ly sincere and evoked feelings of empathy and solidarity in those members of its audience that were of the same generation as its young cast. *Hair* seemed to be ethereal, an unlikely candidate for resurrection in the spate of revivals that has epitomised the musical theatre in the late 1980s but, indeed, there has been an updated version on tour in Britain in 1989. How the monetarist 'yuppies' of the 1980s will take to the communal 'hippies' of the 1960s remains to be seen, but it is difficult to imagine their sympathy.

Hair proved that not all successful American musicals have to be the product of Broadway 'megabucks' and vast technical resources, repeating the lesson of an earlier work. *The Fantasticks* had opened Off-Broadway in 1960, in the Sullivan Street Playhouse, Greenwich Village with a cast of five singers, two actors and a mime, and an 'orchestra' of piano, harp and drums. It ran for over 10,000 performances and became incredibly popular with both audiences and performers and legend has it that somewhere, be it in a college theatre or amateur production, there is always a production of *The Fantasticks* going on. Based on a Edmond Rostand play, *Les Romantiques*, it tells the story of two fathers who, wishing their son and daughter to marry, insist on them having nothing to do with each other, working on the concept that children will do the exact opposite of their parents' wishes. The music is by Harvey Schmidt and the 'book' and lyrics by Tom Jones, the best-known songs being 'Soon its gonna rain' and 'Try to remember the kind of September'. This team took the concept of the minimalist musical even further with *I Do, I Do* which had only two performers, but in *The Fantasticks* they created a miniature work that bears comparison with any other musical and deserves reconsidering by British managements.

There has often been a back-stage, 'show-biz' element in the 'book' of musicals, with *Showboat*, *Guys and Dolls* and *Gypsy* being among the most obvious; in *A Chorus Line* (1975), the whole piece is given over to the process of auditioning for the chorus of a musical. Based on Michael Bennett's taped interviews with actual dancers, the 'book' was produced by Nicholas Dante and James Kirkwood, to which Marvin Hamlisch and Edward Kleban added songs. This was the musical's version of 'cinéma vérité' and as well as producing such excellent numbers as 'One' and 'What I did for love', it also provided the ignorant audience with something of an insight into the dedication, hardships and heartbreaks inherent in the life of those members of the profession who were lucky enough to make it even as far as the chorus.

While the Broadway Musical may be the only uniquely American contribution to the canon of world theatre, it must not be forgotten that the British were also working in the field that Gilbert and Sullivan had once dominated. True, there was little produced in Britain to compare with the works from the American heyday of the *genre*; while Noel Coward's work displays a remarkable versatility, there is little depth to his music and his greatest achievements were comedies that included songs, like *Private Lives* (1930) and the pastiche operetta, *Bitter Sweet*, rather than fully-fledged musicals. Admittedly, he wrote whole revues, such as *On With The Dance* and *This Year of Grace* but they are essentially fragmented works that do not provide him with the chance to demonstrate the ability to handle a score on a scale and in the contemporary style of a Gershwin, Porter or Rodgers.

Ivor Novello's romantic pieces, while extremely popular in Britain, made little impact in the States and while America was seeing *South Pacific, Kiss Me Kate, Annie Get Your Gun* and *West Side Story*, Britain previewed the pastiche and nostalgia of Sandy Wilson's *The Boy Friend* and Julian Slade's *Salad Days*.

It was not until the influence of Joan Littlewood's Theatre Workshop began to be felt throughout British theatre that the British musical started to grow up. From her Stratford East music hall, Miss Littlewood's approach to Total Theatre had been seen in productions of such plays as Shelagh Delaney's *A Taste of Honey* and Brendan Behan's rumbustious *The Hostage*, and she encouraged the authors of new musicals as well. The height of her achievement was probably the show that the company evolved about the First World War, *Oh, What A Lovely War!* (1963), but she also introduced Frank Norman, an erstwhile petty criminal and current writer, to the budding composer, Lionel Bart. This collaboration produced *Fings Ain't Wot They Used T' Be* in 1959, capitalising on the rough cockney background of the two authors. It also started Bart searching for more London underworld stories to set to music, a search which culminated in the inclusion of Charles Dickens in the list of involuntary collaborators from literary history.

Oliver Twist provided Bart with ideal material but his version, *Oliver!*, provoked as many objections from the Dickensian purists as had *My Fair Lady* from the Shavians and *West Side Story* from the Shakespeareans. Literary critics complained about the sanitising of Dickens' social criticism and the cosmetic surgery done on the masterpiece, but it is also true that such telescoping of the action of a novel to suit the dictates of a musical was not surpassed until the recent filleting of Victor Hugo's *Les Misérables*. It is also true that the horrors of the workhouse were reduced by the winsomeness of songs like *Food* and *Where is Love?* and the comic nature of Mr and Mrs Bumble, who appear as grotesques in the original; the thuggishness of Sykes and the squalor of the thieves' den are played down while Fagin, described by Dickens in *Oliver Twist* as 'a very old shrivelled Jew, whose villainous-looking and repulsive face was obscured by a quantity of matted hair', becomes a lovable rogue and the star of the show.

That said, *Oliver!* is a remarkable achievement for any one man, considering that Bart wrote 'book', lyrics and a score that includes 'As long as he needs me', 'Consider yourself', 'You gotta pick a pocket or two', 'Oompah-pah', 'Who will buy?', while the original London production was further enhanced by a stage design of genius from Sean Kenny.

English literature continued to be plundered, with musical versions of *The Pickwick Papers* (*Pickwick*), H.G. Wells' *Kipps* (*Half a Sixpence*), *The Barretts of Wimpole Street* (*Robert and Elisabeth*) while J.M. Barrie's serious comedy *Admirable Crichton* was reduced to *Our Man, Crichton*.

Anthony Newly and Leslie Bricusse created vehicles for Newly in *Stop the World, I Want to Get Off* and *The Roar of the Greasepaint, the Smell of the Crowd*, but it was not until the late 1970s that Britain started to make a considerable impact on the world of the musical and not until the 1980s that the balance of power shifted from America to Europe, largely due to the efforts and achievements of one man.

Andrew Lloyd Webber (b. 1948) joined forces with Tim Rice (b. 1944) at an early age to write their first show, *Joseph and the Amazing Technicolour Dreamcoat*. It was initially written for a school performance but eventually reached the London professional stage in 1968. They stuck to the Bible as the source material for their next show, audaciously producing *Jesus Christ, Superstar* in 1970. While this is a clever enough work in the 'rock-opera' mode that had started with *Hair* and been given more impetus by Pete Townsend's *Tommy*, it was the subject matter of *Superstar* and one or two anachronistic touches, such as Herod played as an Elvis Presley look-alike, that made it special, rather than any innovations to the *genre*. At the same time, another Jesus musical *Godspell* was having considerable success in the aftermath of the 'peace and love' movement that the hippies had embodied and *Superstar* was simply equated with this.

It was not until Rice and Lloyd Webber turned to the unlikely subject matter of Eva Peron, the erstwhile sluttish nightclub singer, wife of a fascist Argentinian dictator, who was both revered as a saint and dismissed as a confidence trickster, that their influence was felt on both sides of the Atlantic.

They made two very astute moves in the presentation of *Evita* (1976); firstly they released the album of the music before the show opened, so that the audience knew the unusual hit song – 'Don't cry for me, Argentina' – before the curtain went up. They also employed as director Harold Prince, the *eminence grise* behind the sequence of Sondheim's concept musicals, all of which he had directed. The staging of *Evita* was as impressive as any other aspect of the show, with the rally sequence at the end of the first act an indelible memory. The employing of top-quality technicians has become a hallmark of Lloyd Webber's subsequent productions.

The mixture was apparently infallible, but Lloyd Webber moved on, changing his collaborators in his next work, *Cats*. If anything, the prospects for this enterprise looked even bleaker for he intended setting T.S. Eliot's collection of poems, *Old Possum's Book of Practical Cats*, to music; however, his eye for what is theatrical and an ear for infectious melodies combined with the involvement of the best technicians to produce another international success of enormous proportions. This time he employed Trevor Nunn from the Royal Shakespeare Company as director and Gillian Lynne as choreographer to produce a piece that has proved as innovative as *West Side Story* or *Oklahoma!* in its staging.

While music purists decry much of his work, dismissing him as derivative and repetitive, there can be no denying Lloyd Webber's feel for musical theatre and for unusual but effective sources. In *Starlight Express* (1984), he sets the performers on roller skates as they portray trains, while in *Phantom of the Opera* (1986), he employed the classic melodramatic tale of the masked and disfigured genius who acts as a Svengali-like figure on the singer, Christine, a story that had already made such an effective silent film. Proof that he can handle the chamber work as well as the full-sized epic was given in his *Tell Me On A Sunday*, a one-act solo setting of words by Don Black. That Andrew Lloyd Webber has taken on the mantle of apparent infallibility which Rodgers and Hammerstein wore in the 1950s was proved when his 1989 work *Aspects of Love* produced an advance box-office income of over £3 million in London alone before he had even finished writing the piece.

The only real opposition to him and his various collaborators is the French team, Alain Boublil and Claude-Michel Schonberg. While they may have decimated Victor Hugo's rambling novel, *Les Misérables* (1985), it has been argued that they improved on it, for the 'show' that resulted was undoubtedly successful. Employing a formula similar to that tested by Lloyd Webber, they dealt with a large-scale subject, staged with highly impressive technical skill, and restricted themselves to one or two simple musical themes that they repeated often. In 1989 their new work, *Miss Saigon*, again dealt with War, this time the war in Vietnam and its effect on the soldiers and the population; first signs suggest that they have a success equal to that of *Les Misérables*.

The fortunes made by Rice, Lloyd Webber, Boublil and Schonberg will continue to entice aspiring composers and lyricists to the *genre* despite the prohibitive costs of an initial production. The crop of revivals that was filling the theatres of both London and New York at the end of the 1980s implies that there is as large an audience as ever for musicals, but the fact that they *are* revivals and not new works proves that Andrew Lloyd Webbers are few and far between, while the comments of many young audiences coming out of these 1940s and 50s revivals, amazed by the quality of the lyrics and the quantity of good tunes, imply that a Richard Rodgers or an Oscar Hammerstein is even rarer.

Ten remarkable examples of the genre

1. Jerome Kern, Oscar Hammerstein II, *Showboat*
2. George and Ira Gershwin, *Porgy and Bess*
3. Rodgers and Hammerstein, *Oklahoma!*
4. Rodgers and Hammerstein, *South Pacific*
5. Loesser, Burrows and Swerling, *Guys and Dolls*

6. Leonard Bernstein, Stephen Sondheim, *West Side Story*
7. Lionel Bart, *Oliver!*
8. Galt McDermot, *Hair*
9. Stephen Sondheim, *A Little Night Music*
10. Andrew Lloyd Webber, Tim Rice, *Evita*

Notes

1. Abe Laufe, *Broadway's Greatest Musicals*, p. 7
2. Quoted in Richard Kislan, *The Musical*, pp. 99-100
3. ibid., p. 162
4. ibid., p. 110
5. Alan Jay Lerner, *The Musical Theatre*, p. 133
6. Howard Taubman, *The Making of the American Theatre*, p. 254
7. Kislan, op. cit., p. 137
8. Laufe, op. cit., p. 59
9. ibid., p. 60
10. Lerner, op. cit., p. 153
11. Runyon, *The Old Doll's House* in *Runyon on Broadway*, pp. 53-4
12. Runyon, *Lonely Heart*, in ibid., p. 379
13. Lerner, op. cit., p. 186
14. Taubman, op. cit., p. 314
15. Laufe, op. cit., pp. 223-4
16. ibid., p. 224

8: MILD AND BITTER

In 1962 John Russell Taylor published the first edition of his authoritative study, *Anger and After*, taking as the starting point for the supposedly new British drama the first performance of John Osborne's *Look Back In Anger* on 8 May 1956. Despite his opening statement:

> With practically any 'overnight revolution' it turns out, when one comes to look more closely, that the signs were there to be read by anyone with enough foresight and that the revolution proper was only the final culmination of a whole string of minor skirmishes with whatever party happened to be in control at the time,[1]

his enthusiastic study of the works of Arden, Wesker, Osborne, Pinter and the flood of new talent that followed in their wake did much to consolidate the view that twentieth-century English playwriting was born, fully grown, on that day in May.

While it may appear that the British theatre in the first half of the century did not offer work of startling originality, ignoring the revolutions in European theatre with the same 'sang-froid' that British statesmen employed towards European politics, there was a thriving commercial theatre and considerable innovative strides were eventually made, albeit in the wake of the reformers from across the Channel.

Much of what has been new in London theatre throughout the century has come from two theatres: the Royal Court and the Arts. For most 'aficionados', the Royal Court will mean the English Stage Company, George Devine, William Gaskill, Lindsay Anderson *et al.*, but just as the story of English theatre did not start with that company, so the Court itself has a longer history.

It was opened in Sloane Square in 1888 and taken over in 1904 by the actor, director and playwright, Harley Granville Barker, with J.E. Vedrenne to handle the business side of things. Granville Barker (1877-1946) had been a member of the Stage Society and adopted their aims of producing new, 'uncommercial' plays. By 'uncommercial', they meant works in the new naturalistic style and as well as bringing in some of the European experiments, the Society also provided a stage for eleven of Shaw's new plays; in fact, Shaw became something of a 'house' writer at the Royal Court, because a decade or so after Granville Barker's seasons, Sir Barry Jackson took over the theatre for a while, again to produce Shaw. Until the recent 'yuppification' of Sloane Square, the pub next door to the Royal Court was filled with photographs and giant murals of George Bernard Shaw.

Granville Barker also used his time at the Court for his own work, the most notable piece being *The Voysey Inheritance*, a play that is still produced today. This, like much of the early Shaw, deals with social problems in an upper-middle-class setting which, after all, was the background of the majority of the theatre-going audience.

In his 1906 season, Granville Barker staged *The Silver Box*, the first play by John Galsworthy (1867-1933), and in 1909 directed the same author's *Strife* at the Duke of York's and *Justice* in the same theatre the year after.

Galsworthy's move into the theatre is an interesting one; he is best known, and rightly so, for his sequence of novels, *The Forsyte Saga*, which was popularly televised in the 1960s. These are a delight to read and, on their own, sufficient cause for his 1932 Nobel Prize for Literature. However, he was persuaded to write for the stage and with some success, although the structure of his theatrical writing is reminiscent of the short-story format. Each play deals with a specific issue, with titles such as *Strife*, *Joy* and *Justice* leaving the audience in little doubt about the content. Rather than try to express these rather blatant morals in his novels which are delicately observed and intricately interwoven, Galsworthy presents them in plays which possess much of the force of a Zola or Hauptmann. In fact, *Strife* owes a great deal to the European writers both in its style and setting.

Dealing with the intransigence of both sides in a labour dispute in a tin mine in the Welsh marches, *Strife* has Capital represented by the Board of Directors, characters from the world of the Forsytes, while the workers' representatives, the miners and engineers, are reminiscent of Hauptmann's weavers; however, the characters are portrayed in a less partisan manner than that employed by Hauptmann, so that the leader of each side of the dispute, both Mr Anthony and David Roberts, are seen as intransigent, both eventually losing from the conflict. Anthony is deposed from his position as Chairman of the Board while Roberts' wife dies of hunger and deprivation.

In *Justice*, the moralising is less subtle and trappings of melodrama more evident than any innovation. Falder, a clerk in a firm of solicitors, has swindled his employers by altering a cheque, in order to help the woman he loves who is being abused by her drunken husband. Falder is discovered and sentenced to gaol. After serving his time, he is offered his job back at the firm provided he has nothing more to do with the woman; this he refuses to do, as his love for her was the only thing that had maintained him in prison. Rather than give her up, he jumps down the stairwell and breaks his neck. Galsworthy calls his play a tragedy but it is pathos rather than tragedy that he exploits, with Cokeson, the senior clerk, saying to Ruth, the woman:

No one'll touch him now! Never again! He's safe with gentle Jesus!

> (RUTH *stands as though turned to stone in the doorway staring at* COKESON, *who, bending humbly before her, holds out his hand as one would to a lost dog.*)[2]

While such effects are more suited to the nineteenth than the twentieth century, Galsworthy was both aware of the new currents in the theatre and conscious of the results that he was seeking:

> ...it can be understood how a dramatist, strongly and pitifully impressed by the circling pressure of modern environments, predisposed to the naturalistic method, and with something in him of the satirist, will neither create characters seven or even six feet high, nor write plays detached from the movements and problems of his times. He is not conscious, however, of any desire to solve these problems in his plays, or to effect direct reforms. His only ambition in drama, as in his other work, is to present truth as he sees it, and, gripping with it his readers or his audience, to produce in them a sort of mental and moral ferment, whereby vision may be enlarged, imagination livened, and understanding promoted.[3]

Despite his claims to the opposite, Galsworthy was instrumental in social reform because his portrayal of Falder in his cell in solitary confinement in Act III, scene iii of *Justice* was so shocking to his affluent, influential audience that it is said to have provided considerable impetus to prison reform.

It is quite understandable that novelists should have been attracted to the naturalistic style of theatre but there is no doubt that simply viewing the stage as another branch of the novel or short story limited its potential for experimental work. Edward Gordon Craig (1872-1966), the illegitimate son of one of the nineteenth century's finest actresses, Ellen Terry, was probably the most original dramatic theorist that Britain produced at that time; yet 1903 saw his last work in Britain and it was in the more fertile ground of Russia, Denmark, Germany and Italy that his theories on acting and stage design were to flourish.

While German reactions to the First World War were reflected in such expressionistic works as Goering's *Naval Conflict* and Kaiser's *Gas II*, the British retained their reserve in the theatre. While their poets were giving freer range to their emotions, playwrights stuck to traditional fare. Even R.C. Sherriff's *Journey's End* (1928), powerful though it undeniably is, remains within the realms of realism. The audience is taken into the front-line dugout, shown the hard-drinking Captain Stanhope and the idealistic young Raleigh, the benevolent, pipe-smoking 'uncle', the coward who is not quite a gentlemen and the salt-of-the-earth servant; Sherriff gives a fair impression of the mud and dirt and the interminable meals, but the death of the 'ingénu' at the end is as inevitable as the hero rescuing the heroine from the clutches of a melodramatic villain.

Some were aware of the limitations and, indeed, W. Somerset Maugham (1874-1965) expressed a possible remedy:

> The fashion of today prevents any reference on the stage to the great subjects of human life and the most profound thought of human beings. It is to this, I think, that may be ascribed the childishness with which the continental critics often charge the English drama. It does not seem to me that the French and German dramatists make so great a distinction as we do between the spoken and written word. It gives them the opportunity to treat of psychological states as we, trammelled by realism, may not.[4]

Given this awareness, then, it is unfortunate that Maugham did not feel able to put his theories into practice; indeed, shortly after writing this Preface, he was to abandon the theatre entirely.

Somerset Maugham had trained originally as a doctor and had qualified as a surgeon, and there is something of the surgeon's incisiveness about his work, coupled with that objective distancing that is necessary for a doctor to maintain his emotional stability, but which, in the playwright, tended to manifest itself in an irony and satire that often crossed the border into cynicism. It is difficult to believe that Maugham cares for any of his characters and nowhere is this more evident than in *For Services Rendered*, a piece often cited alongside *Journey's End* as actively opposing the war.

Where Sherriff might have been too sympathetic, Maugham lays all his characters bare beneath his microscope and is unable to find a redeeming feature in any of them. Mr Ardsley is too busy with his solicitor's practice, telling other people what to do, to notice that his family is disintegrating; his wife is dying of cancer and actually looking forward to it as a release; his eldest daughter goes mad with grief and frustration while his youngest decides to elope with an older man, oblivious to the effect that it will have on everybody else, simply to fleece her lover of his money:

> Has it never occurred to you what power it gives a woman when a man is madly in love with her and she doesn't care a row of pins for him?[5]

His middle daughter is married to a bore who believes that:

> I had the time of my life in the war. No responsibility and plenty of money. More than I'd ever had before or ever since. All the girls you wanted and all the whisky...I tell you it was a bitter day for me when they signed the armistice.[6]

The one man his eldest daughter loved commits suicide because of his inability to handle business after twenty years in the Navy and his son, Sidney, blinded in the war, admits that he capitalises on his disability, relying on emotional blackmail for attention. Maugham uses the cliché of the blind man as the one who can 'see' most clearly:

> ...I know we were the dupes of the incompetent fools who ruled the nations. I know we were sacrificed to their vanity, their greed and their stupidity...They muddle on, muddle on, and one of these days they'll muddle us all into another war. When that happens I'll tell you what I'm going to do. I'm going out into the streets and cry: Look at me; don't be a lot of damned fools; it's all bunk what they're saying to you, about honour and patriotism and glory, bunk, bunk, bunk.[7]

The only character who is even vaguely sympathetic is the doctor whose beneficial contribution is to ease the agony of cancer or the trauma of mental breakdown with hypodermic injections. There is a cynicism, a nihilism even, that makes this a profoundly disturbing play, more deserving than Ionesco or even Beckett of Peter Hall's epithet, 'The Theatre of Despair'. This inability to portray sympathetic characters may either be a reflection on Maugham's medical education, a reaction to Society's repressive and restrictive attitude towards homosexuals or a more general by-product of the emotional climate but it is interesting to note that other successful British playwrights on either side of the First War had a similar difficulty in handling emotional situations in a warm and yet adult manner.

In the case of J.M. Barrie (1860-1937), he avoided too close a contact with adult issues by cocooning them in escapist fantasy. While *Admirable Crichton* (1902) is a clever, funny play, dealing with the injustice of the class system and the preferability of meritocracy, the very act of setting the middle section on a desert island removes immediacy and emphasises the fact that it is a parable. Imaginary worlds play a major part in Barrie's most famous work, *Peter Pan* (1904), the story of the boy who would not grow up. Never-Never Land is an island populated by the stuff of fantasy, Lost Boys, Red Indians, the crocodile and Captain Hook's pirates and is reached by faery flight. The prominent part that flying plays in dreams was only then being examined by Freud and the flying, the rejection of adolescence and the condemnation of the father-figure, Mr Darling, to the dog-house would have been significant to very few members of Barrie's audience. The fact that Peter, in the tradition of British pantomime's principal boys, was, until the National's recent production, played *a travesti* can only have served to add to the sexual confusion. However, *Peter Pan* has deservedly become an annual classic and has probably introduced more children to the world of the theatre than any other play this century.

It is easy to dismiss Barrie as a repressed Victorian Scot whose psychological and emotional conflicts were sublimated into fey fantasies but that is to ignore the satirical content of plays like *What Every Woman Knows* (1908) and, more especially, *Dear Brutus* (1917).

Even though he is dealing with faults or at least flaws in the human char-

acter – arrogance in Lady Caroline, lack of ambition in Coade, unfaithfulness in Purdie, the death of ambition anaesthetised by alcohol in Dearth,
coquetry in Joanna – Barrie still resorts to the magical in *Dear Brutus*, his
own version of *A Midsummer Night's Dream*. Shakespeare's Puck appears
under one of his other names, Lob, here an ancient host to an Edwardian
house party to which he has invited the eight dissatisfied characters. Magi-
cally, the wood appears in Lob's back garden and, as in Shakespeare,
midsummer night in the wood provides the mortals with insight and education. While Barrie takes his moral and his title from *Julius Caesar*:

> The fault, dear Brutus, is not in our stars,
> But in ourselves, that we are underlings

perhaps Puck's words from the *Dream* would have been more apt:

> Lord, what fools these mortals be!

Fairy plays were something of a vogue before the First War; *The Gold-
fish* by Lila Field was one such, intended not only for an audience of children
but also for a juvenile cast. And, resplendent as Prince Mussel, the court jester to King Starfish in the 1911 production was a precocious twelve year-old,
one Noel Coward (1899-1973).

Coward, like Somerset Maugham before him and Alan Ayckbourn after
him, was a phenomenal commercial success; both in London and New York,
from *Hay Fever* in 1925 to *After the Ball* some thirty years later, he wrote,
composed, directed and acted in a remarkable number of pieces in an
equally remarkable number of styles. The brittle comedy of *Hay Fever* and
Private Lives has become his trademark and the witty, catchy songs from his
many revues have received a wider audience with the recording of his cabaret act in Las Vegas. There are also the overtly patriotic pieces like *This
Happy Breed* and his film of homage to Lord Mountbatten and HMS 'Kelly',
In Which We Serve, which understandably takes patriotism into the realms
of propaganda. Coward's old-fashioned devotion to his country manifested
itself in the exhaustive and exhausting tours that he made during the Second
World War, entertaining troups with just his pianist, Norman Hackforth, as
company. This again goes against the image of the perfectly-groomed aes-
thete, cigarette holder clamped betwen his teeth, clad in silk pyjamas,
dressing gown and cravat, tossing off his latest selection of *bons mots* between a late breakfast and cocktails.

The myth does not take into consideration the undertaking of vast projects like *Cavalcade*, the panoramic review of recent British history which
evoked from Coward, in his curtain speech, the oft-quoted phrase:

> I hope that this play has made you feel, in spite of the troublesome
> times we are living in, it is still pretty exciting to be English.

It does not consider one of his earliest plays, *The Vortex* (1924), which dealt

with drug addiction and incest and displayed its merit in a 1989 London revival with Maria Aitken and Rupert Everett in the Lillian Braithwaite/Noel
Coward roles. What it does reflect is the need in many actors to establish a
public façade that is both performance and protection. While Coward epitomised the successful, commercial face of the theatre between the wars, it
must not be thought that all experiment had been excluded by an excess of
french windows and moonlit terraces.

In 1927, the Arts Theatre Club had been founded in order to provide
'the amenities of a London club and a congenial place for those interested
in the theatre on both sides of the curtain'.[8] It provided a small stage and an
intimate auditorium with seating for about three hundred and fifty. Initially,
because of its club status, it could produce plays without a licence from the
Lord Chamberlain's office and so became the venue for experimental and
controversial work; new plays by John van Druten and Benn Levy received
their first performances there while productions of limited appeal, such as
Racine in French and Goethe in German, found an audience at the Arts. In
1931, La Compagnie des Quinze appeared there with Andre Obey's *Noah*
while British actors of the stature of Sybil Thorndike, Emlyn Williams, Gwen
Ffrangcon-Davies, Jean Forbes-Robertson and John Gielgud were prepared to work there for next to nothing.

As with anything of minority interest in the theatre, the Arts was continually in financial difficulties but there always seemed to be enough people
who considered the enterprise to be of sufficient importance to support it.
In 1942, Alec Clunes, one of the leading actors of his generation, took over
the direction of the Club to provide a service that he believed that London
needed:

> We believe that there is an audience in London eager for intelligent
> and entertaining plays; for a theatre whose policy, without being
> highbrow, is yet opposed to the monotony of the leg-show and the
> dullness of the average West End drawing room piece. We believe
> that this audience can be best served by a consistent policy of plays
> and personnel established at one central theatre premises.[9]

Among the remarkable achievements of Clunes' directorship was the 1946
production by the twenty-one year old Peter Brook of Sartre's *Huis Clos* with
a cast of Alec Guinness, Beatrix Lehmann and Betty Ann Davies, about
which J.C. Trewin wrote that: 'For years there had been nothing comparably
terrifying on the London stage', and the premiere of Christopher Fry's *The
Lady's Not For Burning* (1948).

By 1955, Peter Hall (b. 1930) had taken on the artistic directorship and
an astonishing list of works received their first British performances there.
O'Neill's *Mourning Becomes Electra*, Ugo Betti's *The Burnt Flowerbed*, Pirandello's *The Rules of the Game*, Ionesco's *The Lesson*, Anouilh's *The Waltz*

of the Toreadors and, most especially, on 3 August, Beckett's *Waiting for Godot*. While British playwrights are conspicuously absent from the list, it can be said that the Arts at least was doing its bit to keep London abreast with trends in world theatre.

Christopher Fry (b. 1907) was, with T.S. Eliot, in the vanguard of a movement that was to attempt a return to verse drama; with *A Phoenix Too Frequent* (1946), *The Lady's Not For Burning* (1948), *Venus Observed* (1950), and *The Dark is Light Enough* (1954), Fry was following Eliot's *Murder in the Cathedral* (1935) – a version of the Thomas à Becket story – and *The Family Reunion* (1939) in an attempt to employ a heightened poetic language, rather than the debased, colloquial style that, supported by the cinema, was appearing elsewhere. In *A Phoenix Too Frequent* (1946), Fry took a story from Petronius – little more than an extended joke – as the basis for his one-act play. Dynamene, the young and beautiful wife of Virilius, is waiting to grieve to death beside her husband's body, accompanied by her less fanciful maid, Doto. Tegeus, a corporal guarding the corpses of six hanged men, stumbles upon the two women in the tomb and persuades Dynamene to live for his sake; during this dalliance one of the corpses that he is supposed to be guarding is stolen and so he prepares to commit suicide for his inattention. However, Dynamene, rather than lose her new-found source of inspiration, suggests that they replace the missing corpse with that of Virilius, no longer any practical use to anyone else, and let the living continue happily.

In *Venus Observed* both the strengths and the weaknesses of Fry's work are evident. He has a fine ear for the comic:

BATES: I tell you,
     Miss, I knows an undesirable character
     When I sees one; I've been one myself for years,

while a speech from the Duke of Altair displays the poetry in the writing:

DUKE: Branches and boughs,
     Brown hills, the valleys faint with brume,
     A burnish on the lake; mile by mile
     It's all a unison of ageing,
     The Landscape's all in time, in a falling cadence
     All decaying.

However, the story, that of the Duke in the autumn of his years falling for a young girl, Perpetua, is slight, almost fey and even in his strongest piece, *The Lady's Not For Burning* (1948), where he deals with the same subjects of witchcraft and bigotry that Arthur Miller was to examine in *The Crucible*, it has to be said that the stylised language was too subtle a taste for most people. With the exception of pantomime doggerel – perhaps even because of it – dramatic verse had not been in vogue in Britain since the Jacobeans and audiences are essentially conservative. Fry is now perhaps best known for his beautiful translations of plays like Giraudoux's *La Guerre de Troie N'Aura Pas Lieu* which he called *Tiger at the Gates* and Anouilh's *L'Invitation au Chateau*, which he transformed into *Ring Round The Moon*.

Despite the views of some actors and directors, London does not have a monopoly on the British theatre; beginning with Miss Annie Horniman's financing of the Abbey Theatre in Dublin in 1904, a number of now-famous repertory companies were founded throughout the country, initially by philanthropic benefactors and eventually, after the Second World War, by public money from the newly-established Arts Council.

Miss Horniman's money came from the tea trade and, having met W.B. Yeats in London, she became the financial force behind the founding of the Abbey. After one of the schisms that seem to characterise that theatre's history, Miss Horniman left Dublin in 1907 and established a small but influential repertory company in the Gaiety Theatre, Manchester. It provided a home for the work of writers like Harold Brighouse, whose *Hobson's Choice* appeared in 1915 and is still played today, a fortune shared by Stanley Houghton's earlier play *Hindle Wakes*. Like the theatre, the plays were 'regional' and the Gaiety became the centre of a Manchester school of writing. Miss Horniman's company only survived until 1920 but its influence was considerable and there is no doubt that her shade will be smiling enthusiastically on her successors in Manchester, the Royal Exchange Company.

Sir Barry Jackson brought a similar philanthropic attitude to Birmingham where, in 1913, he financed the building of the Birmingham Repertory Theatre. As well as owning the theatre, he became its artistic director, with a particular devotion to the works of Shaw. This also manifested itself in his establishing the Malvern Theatre Festival which was dedicated to Shaw's work; in Jackson's temporary management of the Royal Court to present some of Shaw's new plays; and in the staging, at Birmingham, of the vast 'pentateuch', *Back to Methuselah*. As appears to be the case with even the most philanthropical 'angel', Sir Barry eventually became disillusioned with the lack of public support and passed the Birmingham Rep over to a civic management.

In Liverpool, the Repertory Playhouse was not indebted to a sole benefactor for its instigation, which is probably why it has survived. Hardly surprisingly in such a commercially enterprising city, it was established in 1912 by a company of some 900 shareholders, under the artistic direction of Basil Dean.

In the case of Glasgow, it was James Bridie who was the motivating force behind the foundation of the Citizens' Theatre (1943); Bridie (1881-1951) was a playwright whose Biblical comedies such as *Tobias and the Angel* (1930) and *Jonah and the Whale* (1932) had had considerable success before the war; in the Citizens', he was hoping not only for a regional but a national theatre where the work of Scottish playwrights could be promoted, a policy which, while still adhered to by the present management of Giles Havergal and Philip Prowse, has been broadened to encompass European work as well.

Given its geographical position, the Memorial Theatre at Stratford-upon-Avon can be regarded as a regional 'rep'. Founded in 1879 by the Flowers family of brewers, it was an even earlier example of benign patronage from the world of enlightened commerce. The original theatre was burned down and the present building opened in 1932. It was Anthony Quayle who brought about the move of bringing famous actors from London to play a season at Stratford at a time when Britain was blessed with possibly its finest generation of actors ever. Olivier, Gielgud, Ralph Richardson, Michael Redrave, Paul Schofield, Alec Guinness, not to mention Quayle himself, were at the height of their powers while Diana Wynyard, Barbara Jefford, Peggy Ashcroft, Vivien Leigh and Rachel Kempson more than matched their male counterparts.

In 1960, Peter Hall took over from Glen Byam Shaw as director and instigated the changes that took Stratford from being the Shakespeare Memorial Theatre to the Royal Shakespeare Company, from a seasonal, occasional company playing in the one house in Stratford to a permanent repertory company with a London venue and three performing spaces in Stratford. It must be said that some of the more recent developments, under the directorships of Trevor Nunn and Terry Hands, where the RSC appears to be assuming the trappings of a commercial production company with very little relevance to Shakespeare, are confusing and the ideals of Fordham Flowers, Anthony Quayle and Peter Hall seem to have been lost in a welter of misdirected aspiration.

The Theatre Royal in Bristol, the oldest working theatre in Britain, became the home of the Bristol Old Vic Theatre Company in 1946. It was established under the direction of Hugh Hunt and as well as borrowing the name of its illustrious counterpart in London's Waterloo, it also opened a drama school, emulating Michel Saint-Denis' establishment. New repertory companies also flourished in Nottingham and Coventry, where the Belgrade was the first new theatre to be purpose-built after the war.

The idea of a repertory company running for a season with the same actors seen in a sequence of plays has fallen into abeyance recently; many of the small repertory companies, particularly those based in the sea-side towns, have closed and the major theatres now look upon themselves as regional production houses with more than one eye on what has proved successful in London, while the concept of joint productions that can be seen in more than one theatre has become increasingly popular.

While new companies in new theatres were beginning to appear after the Second World War, there was not a brave new world of dramatic writing for them to play. Arnold Hinchliffe has described the theatre in 1955 as looking like Harrods at Christmas, while John Elsom is more specific about its poverty:

> In terms of theatre, Britain suffered from a bad balance of payments deficit after the war. We owed so much to movements which had been imported. We looked to Broadway for the best commercial theatre (the musicals), elsewhere in New York for the best acting school (The Method) and the most challenging naturalistic drama (the plays of Arthur Miller and Tennessee Williams). We looked to Paris for the most influential philosopher-dramatist (Jean-Paul Sartre), the best boulevard dramatist (Jean Anouilh), for the best mimes (such as Marcel Marceau), for the most stimulating 'avantgarde' drama...and the most prestigious example of a national theatre (the Comédie-Française) of a type we lacked. In addition, we looked to the Moscow Art Theatre for the best ensemble (naturalistic) acting and the most recent 'classics'.[10]

True, Terence Rattigan (1911-1977) had developed from the light comedies like his enormous first success *French Without Tears* (1936) to more serious post-war topics such as justice in *The Winslow Boy* (1946) and the study of the repressed school master, Crocker Harris, in *The Browning Version* (1948), but pieces like *The Deep Blue Sea* (1952) display considerable restriction of structure and dialogue. It was not until 1960 – after the 'revolution', as it were – when he was able to portray the more sensitive subject of T.E. Lawrence's homosexuality in *Ross* that the freedom of content was also reflected in the expansion of structure and setting.

However, reflecting the old cliché about the darkest hour, dawn was about to come up like thunder. The Labour government that had instigated the Arts Council and the National Health Service after the war also intended improving the nation's education. Stemming from the Butler 1944 Education Act which had radically improved secondary schooling, insisting on a thorough education for all and a reconstruction of the higher education system, the ideal of a more literate society was beginning to be realised by the beginning of the 1950s. The growth of the so-called 'red brick' (not to mention Jimmy Porter's 'white-tile') universities meant an inevitable increase in articulate, committed graduates, by no means all of them in the upper-middle-class, public schoolboy, 'Oxbridge' mould. And it was as a spokesman for this new generation that Jimmy Porter appeared in John Osborne's *Look Back In Anger*, produced by the English Stage Company at the Royal Court in 1956.

The English Stage Company was the brain-child of Ronald Duncan, the librettist for Benjamin Britten's *Rape of Lucrece*. With other enthusiasts, he had founded the Taw and Torridge Festival in North Devon; he had experienced difficulty in finding producers who were willing to mount small-scale productions that would suit the Festival and so set about establishing a man-agement company that would put on plays with the inevitable description of 'non-commercial'. As with so much in the theatrical world, this company eventually became based in London and with the financial backing of Ne-ville Blond, a wealthy businessman, set about looking for premises. Originally, they were to take over the derelict Kingsway Theatre but Blond managed to secure a three-year lease on the Royal Court.

George Devine (1910-1965) had been working with Michel Saint-Denis at the Old Vic school but when it closed in 1951, he returned to freelance acting and directing. He was appointed with Tony Richardson to run the new company at the Court and, in a first season that included Arthur Miller's *The Crucible*, they also produced the script written by an actor, John Osborne.

Look Back In Anger does not stand up to particularly close re-examination nowadays; Jimmy seems to be suffering from pique rather than heart-felt anger, an impression enhanced if one reads it with the intonation of Jimmy Porter's contemporary, Tony Hancock. Essentially, Osborne (b. 1929) strings together a sequence of ranting monologues that are not particularly dramatic, although his ear for invective is impressive. Despite his acting pedigree, he did not appear to have learned much about con-struction and falls into the trap set by Shaw of putting much of his best writing into his stage directions, while at the same time imposing unhelpful and impossible expectations on his actors. When describing the entry of Helen, he writes:

> *Now and again, when she allows her rather judicial expression of alert-ness to soften, she is very attractive. Her sense of matriarchal authority makes most men who meet her anxious, not only to please but to im-press, as if she were the gracious representative of visiting royalty. In this case the royalty of that middle-class womanhood, which is so emi-nently secure in its divine rights, that it can afford to tolerate the parliament, and reasonably free assembly of its menfolk.*

And the bears and squirrels game that Alison and Jimmy play is positively embarrassing.

That said, however, Osborne's subsequent plays, in particular *The En-tertainer* (1957), *Luther* (1961), *Inadmissible Evidence* (1964) and *A Patriot For Me* (1965), have shown that Devine was right in recognising genius even if it was not totally realised in the early work.

The later plays are not only interesting theatrically, they also provide 'thumping great roles' for a main actor. Albert Finney consolidated his reputation in *Luther* where the first act is a fine examination of the doubts of the young idealistic monk, while the panoramic 'epic' setting shows a remarkable development in structural capability with more than a little indebtedness to Brecht. *Inadmissible Evidence*, the portrait of a lawyer on 'self-destruct', displayed Nicol Williamson's star quality and helped to re-establish it in the 1981 revival, while Maximilian Schell played Reidl in *Patriot*. However, it was *The Entertainer* that was the most remarkable in that it provided Laurence Olivier with a vehicle that transported him from the heart of the establishment right into the revolutionaries' camp.

The Entertainer is the story of Archie Rice, a fading stand-up comic, whose world is in decline, reflecting the state of contemporary Britain. With the use of Archie's 'spots', monologues to the play's audience as if they were the audience at the girlie show in which he is working, interspersed with the scenes at home, we are not only shown a more subtle and hence more effective portrait than Jimmy Porter's but the whole makes a far more remarkable piece of theatre. Had Osborne written nothing else, *The Entertainer* would have justified those Messianic claims made for him that *Look Back In Anger* cannot maintain.

In a collection of essays commemorating twenty-five years of the English Stage Company, Olivier wrote of that time:

> When my most dear George Devine started his thrilling new policy there in 1956 I became immediately fascinated by the work that was being done. I followed it avidly and, I should confess, enviously. After seeing *Look Back In Anger* for the second time [in his autobiography, Olivier admits that it took Arthur Miller to point out its merits to him on first viewing] I took pains to express my admiration to John Osborne, daring to hope that perhaps it might just occur to him to think of me for some future possibilities. His modest reception of this idea and his obviously brimming enthusiasm for it delighted me in the extreme.[12]

The combination of Olivier and Osborne at the Royal Court not only made for 'a good show' but, more especially, provided a bridge between what had been two opposing, if not actively hostile, camps. There was the commercially successful world inhabited by the theatrical knights and their ladies and there was the Court, a teeming den of young writers. By providing a vehicle for the most charismatic actor of one generation and the 'hottest' playwright of the next, Devine, consciously or not, united British theatre and his contribution to the new company and hence to the revitalising of the British theatre cannot be overstated. Osborne explains:

> ...hardly anyone in the theatre or outside realised then just how much he was doing, how he hated the administrative load, how much it was weighing him down. He was picking up people all the time and putting them on their feet again. He had this terrible phrase, 'I wish everyone would just stop swinging on my tits, day after day'. But they did. 'I never want to talk to another actor's agent or draw up another contract', he would say. But he did. He had to.[13]

In the nine years between 1956 and Devine's death in 1965, a list of authors whose work was produced now reads like the membership of a theatrical elite: Arthur Miller's *The Crucible*; Osborne's *Look Back In Anger*, *The Entertainer* etc.; Eric Bentley's translation of Brecht's *The Good Person Of Setzuan*; Beckett's *Endgame*, *Act Without Words*, *Krapp's Last Tape*; Ionesco's *The Chairs*, *The Lesson* and *Rhinoceros* with Olivier as 'Berenger'; Ann Jellicoe, Arnold Wesker, John Arden, Willis Hall, Errol John, N.F. Simpson, Harold Pinter, Jean Genet's *The Blacks*, Sean O'Casey, Henry Livings, Charles Wood, David Halliwell's anarchic *Little Malcolm and his Struggle Against The Eunuchs*; even Noel Coward, initially looked upon as the arch-enemy, was represented with *Look After Lulu*, his adaptation of Feydeau's *Occupe-toi d'Amélie*.

The young writers were discovering their voices and had a home in which to try them out. Osborne acknowledges his debt:

> For ten years, thanks to George, I had a professional life there that I'd most certainly never had before and haven't since. You were part of a family, which accepted all your frailties and imperfections, a family that most of us don't have any longer.[14]

Arnold Wesker is more specific:

> ...four elements – the base, international spotlight, writer's group and, especially, the team – all culminated in the fifth element: self-confidence.[15]

Wesker (b. 1932) portrayed his Jewish, East End, working-class background in his first play to interest the English Stage Company, *Chicken Soup with Barley* (1958). It focuses on the Kahn family with special attention paid to the mother, Sarah. Although there are elements of the traditional Yiddish 'momma' in her character, these are never caricatured and it is her aspirations towards education, both for herself and her children, that are emphasised. Harry, the father (given a memorable first performance by Frank Finlay) is a weak and, in the final scenes, pathetic man, but Sarah's strength is shown to be sufficient to motivate them all. At the end of *Chicken Soup*, Sarah says to Ronnie, arguably the author-figure in the play: 'You've got to care or you'll die', a line that sums up her intensity.

Two further plays deal with characters that are either members of the Kahn family or touched by them. *Roots* is set in East Anglia in the home of Beatie who, at the outset, is supposed to be marrying Ronnie, whom she has met in London. Because of her experiences in the capital, she has become dissatisfied with her rural, rustic family, but initially, can only express that dissatisfaction in clichés learned from Ronnie. When it becomes clear that Ronnie is not going to come to marry her, the experience is shown to be liberating because, at last, she can articulate her own emotions:

> I'm talking, I'm not quoting any more...I'm beginning, on my own
> two feet – I'm beginning!

a curtain line reminiscent of Clifford Odets' pre-war moralising.

In *I'm Talking About Jerusalem*, the last of what has come to be called
the *Wesker Trilogy*, the idyll dies. Sarah's daughter and son-in-law, Ada and
Dave, try to set up in the country away from the city in a move that was to
anticipate the self-sufficiency trend by some fifteen years. Dave loses his job
because he steals some linoleum and even his attempts at running his own
business, initially so gratifying as he made furniture by hand, are frustrated
by cost-effectiveness and mass production. An element of Jewish stoicism is
revealed in the final scenes, with Ronnie's final lines being: 'We must be
bloody mad to cry', but the vision of building a new Jerusalem has died and
the disillusionment of the author as well as his characters cannot be hidden.

In *The Kitchen* (1959) and *Chips with Everything* (1962), Wesker again
draws on his own experiences to create two plays that are interesting as much
for their style as their content. *The Kitchen* is very much a 'slice-of-life'
drama, where Wesker handles the considerable number of chefs and waiters
and their respective stories with the same dexterity that he would have employed as the pastry chef he had once been. In *Chips with Everything*, the style
changes drastically from the naturalism of *The Kitchen* to a cinematic, 'epic'
montage style depicting life in the Air Force for National Servicemen; despite this development, it must be admitted that Wesker resorts to comic
stereotypes in some of his characterisation, although whether it is the style
or the content that forces this on him is debatable.

These early plays display a socialist idealism that is as evident as Wesker's theatrical talent and it was this idealism that was to motivate his next
move, the attempt to establish Centre 42, a Trade Union-orientated arts
centre at the Round House. Unfortunately, not every trade unionist shared
Wesker's vision for this erstwhile engine-shed in Chalk Farm, North London
and this dream, like Dave and Ada's, failed. Wesker has continued writing
but, so far, nothing has proved as powerful, or as significant, as his autobiographical trilogy which at its time of writing was so unusual that it needed a
try-out at the Belgrade Theatre, Coventry, before George Devine would accept it at the Royal Court.

Anne Jellicoe (b. 1927) had been teaching and directing at the Central
School of Speech and Drama and was founding director of the Cockpit theatre
when she 'composed' her first full-length play, *The Sport of My Mad Mother*
(1956). It came equal third in a competition sponsored by the *Observer* and
was staged at the Royal Court with Jellicoe and George Devine as co-direc-
tors. Although not a commercial success, it gave Jellicoe the encouragement
to join the writers' group that was based at the Court and, in 1961, her next
play *The Knack* marked the advent of a new era, the 'Swinging' 60s.

Shelagh Delaney (b. 1939) had already opened the door for women to write about sex in her touching play, *A Taste of Honey*, which Joan Littlewood had produced with great effect at Stratford East in 1958. This challenged a number of taboo subjects for it not only featured Jo, the unmarried teenage mother, her black boyfriend and slatternly mother, Helen, but also the 'maternal', homosexual art student, Geoffrey. Compared with this, perhaps *The Knack* with its subtitle *or how to get it* was less revolutionary, but it did display the ebullience of youth and the burgeoning sense that the epoch of the 'young ones' had arrived.

Miss Jellicoe has continued to reflect the mood of the times. In the 70s she founded the Colway Theatre Trust in Dorset to promote large-scale, essentially amateur community plays in places like Lyme Regis and Dorchester and, again as a sign of the times, resigned in 1985 because of government cuts in funding.

John Arden (b. 1930) is the other playwright whose early work is especially associated with the early years of the English Stage Company at the Royal Court. His first play to be staged there, *The Waters of Babylon*, received a Sunday evening production without setting and is very reminiscent of early Brecht. The 'hero', Krank, – no allegorical pun, apparently – is an amoral exploitative landlord and pimp who would not have been out of place in *Baal*, while *In the Jungle of the Cities* would have been a perfectly acceptable subtitle for the play. In *Live Like Pigs* (1957), Arden begins to find something of an individual voice; this tells of the Sawney family, a group of 'travellers' forced by the Welfare State to abandon their gypsy ways and move into a real house, next door to the Jacksons. Led by 'Sailor' – a triumphant performance was given by Wilfred Lawson in the original production – the Sawneys amply demonstrate that lower-middle-class values and a housing-estate lifestyle do not suit them and eventually they are evicted by the same council that installed them in the first place. While obviously political, it was not partisan for, as Arden, in his Preface to *Live Like Pigs*, has written: 'On the one hand, I was accused by the Left of attacking the Welfare State: on the other, the play was hailed as a defence of anarchy and amorality.' This situation seems wholly admirable for there cannot be much wrong with a play that manages to antagonise both sides in an argument. He goes on to clarify his point: 'I approve outright neither of the Sawneys nor of the Jacksons. Both groups uphold standards of conduct which are incompatible, but which are both valid in their correct context.'

The Happy Haven was essentially written as an acting exercise for the students at Bristol University and is of interest because of the unsentimental view it offers of old people and, technically, because of the use of masks in portraying the characters. While it is an obvious way for young actors to portray old people without resorting to the usual Crewe Junctions of tramlines and crows' feet in black grease-paint all over the place, the masks can also imply an intransigence of character in the old people.

However, it is probably on *Serjeant Musgrave's Dance* that Arden's fame is most securely based, not least because it must feature alongside *Our Town* and *A Man For All Seasons* at the top of many a school teacher's list of favoured texts. The story is set in the late nineteenth century and tells of a group of redcoats that arrives in a northern town; the inhabitants take them for a recruiting team but in fact they are deserters, trying in vain to teach the civilians of the horrors of war. The plot is complex, featuring as it does a striking work-force, arresting dragoons and the 'coup de théâtre' of the skeleton of a local lad, killed abroad and carried back by Musgrave. The deserters fail in their futile bid to rouse the town and are arrested, prompting an inevitable conclusion that pacifism is ineffective. This, of course, is not Arden's point, for he is essentially anti-war in his outlook; it is another example of his examination of an emotive situation in which neither side is 'right'; the complexity of the issue heightens the dramatic impact and by avoiding the sort of simplistic approach that a Brecht might have employed, Arden has created a disturbing and intriguing play. He uses verse and song as well as rough dialogue and, while demonstrating elements of Brecht's influence, shows how far he had developed in the few years that separated *Musgrave* from *The Waters of Babylon*.

And one only has to compare *Serjeant Musgrave's Dance* with a play that is equally opposed to war, Somerset Maugham's *For Services Rendered*, written a mere thirty years earlier, to discover the remarkable strides that British theatre had made towards catching up with our European counterparts in the technical aspects of playwriting. Shakespeare may have been writing powerful, panoramic pieces three hundred and fifty years previously but the English drawing-room had cabined, cribbed and confined such power. Now, Osborne and Arden were freeing the genie.

The 1950s and early 60s cannot be left without acknowledging the most idiosyncratic and original voice of the era, a playwright who, more than any of his contemporaries, evolved a style that has become recognised as unique. Harold Pinter (b. 1930) has produced a body of work that has not only prompted more discussion and partisan debate than that of any other contemporary British writer but which, even at this short distance, seems likely to have proved both most lasting and most influential. 'Pinteresque' has already entered the language as an adjective that describes the elliptical, enigmatic, apparently banal style of his early writing while the theme of those plays can flippantly be summarised as 'the inability of a number of people in a room to get on with each other'.

The Room (1957) was indeed the title of his first play, which was not a success. Neither, surprisingly, was his next, *The Birthday Party*; surprisingly, because now the images of the simple Meg with her 'nice' cornflakes and fried bread, of Petey and his deck-chairs, of the oleaginous Goldberg and the terrified Stanley, his glasses smashed and his foot in the toy drum, and most particularly – especially when portrayed by Patrick Magee – the sight and sound of McCann tearing immaculate strips of newspaper as he waits to torment Sidney have entered into the theatrical consciousness of a generation of audiences.

Equally evocative – and probably the piece that has done most to establish the received idea of a Pinter play – is *The Caretaker* (1960). Here there is the solitary room, the same nameless threat of mindless violence, this time portrayed by the more 'normal' brother, Mick; there is the same pathetic victim – this time the tramp, Davies – and there is a similar intimation of mental illness, although Aston's mesmeric description of electro-shock therapy at the end of the first act is more specific than anything that Meg had said. It is Davies' continual harping on his 'papers' in Sidcup, and the story of the shoes at the monastery that has become archetypal, 'essential' Pinter, intentionally comic but profound.

Pinter progressed with the decade, away from the apparent obsession with enigmatic violence that had reached a peak in *The Homecoming* (1965) and started to examine other complex matters, such as time and memory. In 1975, he wrote *No Man's Land* where Gielgud and Richardson reunited the double act that had been so successful five years earlier in David Storey's *Home*.

More than any other of the 'angry' young pioneers of the 1950s, Pinter continues to write, impress and entertain; however, far from being an outsider any more, he has now become one of the select few that can be called the National Theatre's 'resident' writers.

Osborne, Arden, Wesker and Pinter, although often bracketed together, display an enormous variety of styles and themes in their writing. What they can be accredited with collectively, though, is the creation of a healthy climate in which the crop of talented writers that was developing behind them could flourish and grow.

Ten plays for further consideration

1. John Galsworthy, *Strife*
2. J.M. Barrie, *Admirable Crichton*
3. R.C. Sherriff, *Journey's End*
4. Noel Coward, *Private Lives*
5. Christopher Fry, *The Lady's Not For Burning*
6. Terence Rattigan, *Ross*
7. John Osborne, *The Entertainer*
8. Arnold Wesker, *The Wesker Trilogy*
9. John Arden, *Serjeant Musgrave's Dance*

10. Harold Pinter, *The Birthday Party*

Notes

1. John Russell Taylor, *Anger and After*, p. 17
2. John Galsworthy, *Justice*, final speech and stage directions
3. John Galsworthy, introduction to *Collected Plays*, p. xi
4. W. Somerset Maugham, preface to *Collected Plays*, p. xii
5. W. Somerset Maugham, *For Services Rendered*
6. ibid.
7. ibid.
8. Quoted in W. and J.C. Trewin, *Arts Theatre*, p. 1
9. ibid., p. 12
10. John Elsom, *Post War British Drama, 1940-80*
11. John Osborne, *Look Back In Anger*, Act II, stage directions
12. Olivier in R. Findlater, *At the Royal Court: 25 Years of the English Stage Company*, p. 40
13. John Osborne, ibid., p. 26
14. ibid., p. 26
15. Wesker, ibid., p. 82

9: EVERYBODY'S DOING IT

Of all the social, cultural and economic elements that contributed to the excitement of the 1960s (and early 70s), the explosion in playwriting talent in Britain is perhaps the most remarkable. Twenty or more children born in the 1930s have produced serious, considerable bodies of work of international standing, work which first began to appear on the experimental, commercial and 'Fringe' stages in the 60s; this then paved the way for a handful of *enfants terribles*, born soon after the Second World War, whose work was appearing in the early years of the 70s, more often than not in small, 'portable' companies of their own foundation. The children of the 1930s should have all been subjected to the new secondary educational system and it may have proved gratifying to the authors of the 1944 Bill that, of this new generation of playwrights, more than two thirds had been to university and most of those to Oxford or Cambridge.

The most remarkable, however, had not. Joe Orton (1933-1967) was born in Leicester and trained as a clerk. In 1951 he went to R.A.D.A. where he met Kenneth Halliwell, an older but less gifted student. Their homosexual relationship lasted for the rest of their lives, ending when Halliwell, jealous of Orton's success, battered the sleeping Orton to death and then took an overdose. Their 'collaboration' was restricted to defacing library books, for which they were both briefly imprisoned, but, despite Halliwell's hysterical and eventually homicidal protestations to the contrary, the originality was all Orton's.

Although there is an early radio play, *Ruffian on the Stair*, and three television plays, *Erpingham Camp, The Good and Faithful Servant* and *Funeral Games*, it is on the stage plays, *Entertaining Mr Sloane* (1964), *Loot* (1966) and, most especially, *What the Butler Saw* (1969), that Orton's fame is based.

Simple summaries of the plots reduce the work to celebrations of bad taste. While it is more than likely that Orton *did* set out to offend, he does so with such expertise of technique and mastery of language that comparisons with Wilde, Feydeau and Shaw are not misplaced and he himself is now a considerable and evident influence on subsequent writers.

His epigrams are delightful:

I'd the upbringing a nun would envy and that's the truth. Until I was fifteen I was more familiar with Africa than my own body.[1]

> Reading isn't an occupation we encourage among police officers. We try to keep the paper work down to a minimum.[2]

and:

> This is a boy, sir. Not a girl. If you're baffled by the difference it might as be well to approach both with caution.[3]

while his farce technique, first demonstrated in *Loot* and masterfully displayed in *What the Butler Saw*, shows what a great loss to British theatre his premature death was.

Orton's influence appears in one of David Storey's later plays, *Mother's Day* (1976), an unworthy and atypical sample of a remarkable writer's work. In the theatre, it is best epitomised by his 'job of work' plays (*The Contractor* and *The Changing Room*) while *Home* remains a unique and remarkable achievement. Storey (b. 1933) is the son of a Yorkshire miner and an archetype of the 1950s and 60s phenomenon of the man uprooted and hence disorientated by education. Not only did the grammar school remove him from his immediate background but his eventual studying at the Slade School of Fine Art in London necessitated a complete move away, an upheaval reflected in a number of his novels and in plays like *In Celebration* (1969).

Storey's first success came with his novel *This Sporting Life* (1960), about the life of a rugby league player. Storey had indeed played professionally for Leeds and he came back to this subject in *The Changing Room* (1971), one of a sequence of plays that are apparently very 'realistic', reflecting activities in Storey's past. In *The Contractor* (1969), a firm of marquee erectors put up a tent for a wedding reception; in *Life Class* (1974), Storey's art training is in evidence, while his years as a school teacher in Islington provided him with the raw material for his first play, *The Restoration of Arnold Middleton* (1966). In these plays, much of the audience's initial attention was taken up by the realistic detail. The cast in the second actually erected a tent on the stage of the Royal Court while in the first, 'all that really happened' was the team changing before and after the match, with the half-time break in the middle. However, underneath the apparently banal action, the inter-relationship of the characters is subtly and intricately established.

Nowhere is this better done than in his beautiful study of institutional life, *Home*. This first appeared at the Royal Court under Lindsay Anderson's direction in 1970 with Sir John Gielgud as Harry and Sir Ralph Richardson as Jack. Gielgud has written of it:

> The text of *Home* naturally intrigued but also somewhat mystified me. Construction, situation, dialogue – all was quite unlike anything I had ever been asked to tackle...and once I began to work, the atmosphere of rehearsals began to become enormously sympathetic and exciting, especially as my old friend Ralph Richardson was in

the play, as well as two brilliant actresses, Mona Washbourne and Dandy Nichols.[4]

The cast was completed by Warren Clarke as the simpleton, Alfred; anyone lucky enough to have seen this production will remember a magical creation. The text is made up of apparently aimless snatches of conversation between the two old men, occasionally interrupted by incursions from the more boisterous, bawdy women as they kill time in the garden of the 'home'. Comparisons have been drawn with Pinter's style of non-sequential dialogue but this is unfair to Storey's unique achievement. Towards the end, Harry and Jack are still seated in the garden:

JACK: Moral Fibre. Set to a task, never complete it. Find some way to back out.

HARRY: Oh, yes.

JACK: The sea is extraordinary...

HARRY: Oh, yes.

JACK: Cousin of mine...

HARRY: See the church.

[*They gaze off*]

JACK: Shouldn't wonder. He's disappointed [*Looks up*]

HARRY: Oh yes.[5]

The final tableau of the two old men weeping for no apparent reason was not only very moving but also, in the hands of Gielgud and Richardson, a 'tour de force' of understated playing.

Storey continues to write both novels and plays, recently continuing the story of the Shaw family whom he introduced in *In Celebration*. The novels, particularly *Pasmore* and *Radcliffe*, display the same sensitivity as *Home* but are far more complex pieces. It is as though Storey, like Galsworthy before him, uses the theatre to develop single ideas while saving his more complex work for the larger canvas of the novel.

While the middle-class 'literati' expressed amazement that a professional rugby league player could actually write, they were even more amazed to discover that the work of a taxi-driver was being presented at the Royal Court. However, when Edward Bond's *Saved* appeared in 1965, with its notorious scene of the stoning of a baby in its pram, some must have been confirmed in their conviction that educating the 'masses' had gone too far.

Bond was born in 1934, left school at 14, supported himself by factory work and driving taxis and, early in the sixties, joined the writers circle centred on the Royal Court. It is possible to argue that Bond set out with intentions similar to Orton's, to shock his audiences into reconsidering their opinions, but where Orton was more interested in revealing sexual hypocrisy, Bond's work portrays an increasing interest in social and therefore political morality, often expressed through violence. Apart from the stoning in *Saved*, there is cannibalism in his fantasy *Early Morning*, the harakiri in *Narrow Road To the Deep North*, the killings in *Lear*, drowning in *The Sea* and so on.

In his Preface to *Lear*, Bond provides us with an impassioned defence of his work to accompany the evidence of the plays themselves:

> I write about violence as naturally as Jane Austen wrote about manners. Violence shapes and obsesses our society, and if we do not stop being violent we have no future. People who do not want writers to write about violence want them to stop writing about us and our time. It would be immoral not to write about violence.[6]

His use of violence is neither gratuitous nor imbalanced. A speech from his *Lear* who, like Shakespeare's, learns through suffering, voices a view that might well be the author's:

> If a God had made the world, might would always be right, that would be so wise, we'd be spared so much suffering. But we made the world – out of our smallness and weakness. Our lives are awkward and fragile and we have only one thing to keep us sane: pity, and the man without pity is mad.[7]

It has been said that Bond's is an 'uncompromising, pitiless view of man, that strips him of his last shred of nobility' but this is impossible to equate with Bond's own words which are worth quoting at length because they demonstrate the philosopher within a playwright who is one of the most powerful authors to have emerged in Britain this century:

> What ought we to do? Live justly. But what is justice? Justice is allowing people to live in the way for which they evolved. Human beings have an emotional and physical need to do so, it is their biological expectation. They *can* only live this way, or all the time struggle consciously or unconsciously to do so. That is the essential thing I want to say because it means that in fact our society and its morality, which deny this, and its technology which more and more prevents it, all the time whispers into people's ears 'You have no right to live'. That is what lies under the splendour of the modern world. Equality, freedom and fraternity must be reinterpreted in the light of this – otherwise real revolutionary change is impossible.
>
> We can express this basic need in many ways: aesthetic, intellectual, the need to love, create, protect and enjoy. These are not higher things that can be added when more basic needs are met. *They* are basic. They must be the way in which we express all our existence, and if they do not control our daily life then we cannot function as human beings at all. They are not weaknesses, but they have nothing to do with the caricatures that pass for strengths in our society

– the hysterical old maids who become sergeant majors, the disguised Peeping Toms who become moralists, the immature social misfits who become judges. Society pays lip service to these needs, but it has no real interest in them, and they are of course incompatible with the strident competitiveness of a commercial culture. So really we deny them. Like ghosts we teach a dead religion, build a few more prisons to worship Caesar in, and leave it at that. Blake said that when we try to become more than men we become less than beasts, and that is what we have done. Our human emotions and intellects are not things that stand apart from the long development of evolution; it is as animals we make our highest demands and in responding to them as men, we create our deepest human experience.[8]

While much of his work portrays destruction and degeneration, it must not be assumed that Bond's vision is totally negative. The positive element is there in the very act of creation, of stimulation and while the range of styles with which Bond has experimented makes any attempt at categorising his work a difficult, even pointless task, it is possible to argue that he has shown that tragedy on a human scale might still exist in post-war drama. There is a nice incongruity to the fact that a taxi-driver who left school at fourteen should adopt the mantle of philosopher-tragedian while the university graduates content themselves with comedies of manners.

Simon Gray (b. 1936) is the playwright who can most easily be accused of voluntary confinement to an ivory tower which he then proceeds to embellish. He was educated at Dalhousie University, Canada and Trinity College, Cambridge where he also did postgraduate research. Since 1966, he has been a Lecturer in English at Queen Mary College, London and it is this world of the Oxbridge arts graduate that has been the setting for much of his work.

Although his first stage play was an Orton-esque comedy, *Wise Child* (1967) with Sir Alec Guinness as a criminal who dresses up a woman to avoid detection, his first real success came with *Butley*, in which Harold Pinter directed Alan Bates, a collaboration that has since been repeated on a number of occasions.

Butley was set in the world of academia and dealt with a character that many took to be Gray. As he has written:

The set...was taken, down to details, from my office at Queen Mary College, London, which made the experience of sitting at my own desk in private more disorientating than seeing Alan Bates doing it in public. There was a period when people asked me whether I'd based Butley on myself. I now realise that it was far more likely that, for a time at least, I based myself on Butley – or more precisely, Alan Bates' performance in it.[9]

Otherwise Engaged (1975) deals with the emotional and sexual merry-go-round of a group of 'arts' or 'media' people, a setting that he returns to in *The Common Pursuit* (1984). *Quartermaine's Terms* (1981) deals sympathetically with a lonely teacher whose entire, degenerating life centres on the Cambridge language school in which he teaches and from which he is eventually sacked.

While it is possible to criticise these examples of Gray's work as being limited in their scope, the same criticism could be levelled at Restoration Comedy, a body of work that provides not only entertainment but a valuable examination of a certain element of a specific society.

Alan Bennett's success stems, famously, from his university days. *Beyond the Fringe*, the revue that opened at the Edinburgh Festival in 1960 with Bennett (b. 1934), Jonathan Miller, Peter Cook and Dudley Moore, had its origins in the Cambridge University 'Footlights' revue club and Oxford college 'smokers'. Moore and Bennett were Oxford educated while Cook and Miller came from 'the other place'. Prior to *Beyond the Fringe*, the popular image of revue had been a light concoction of songs, dances and sketches as epitomised by the productions of C.B. Cochran and performed by artistes like Noel Coward, Jack Buchanan and Beatrice Lillie. *Beyond the Fringe* herald-ed the death of that format and the move of satire from the novel to the stage.

While Peter Cook and Dudley Moore quickly went on to fame in television light entertainment (with Moore an unlikely film star and sex symbol of the 80s) and Miller has become one of the most respected directors in world theatre, Bennett's initial success after *Beyond the Fringe* was muted, being restricted to appearances in other people's plays. However, in 1968, things changed when his first full-length play, *Forty Years On*, was produced. While his roots in revue are obvious in the format of the piece – it is the school play for 'Albion House', a minor public school in the Home Counties and consists of a sequence of sketches performed by the staff – the whole adds up to a review of Britain up to and including the Second World War, (with Albion House an image of Britain). Sir John Gielgud performed a virtual parody of himself as the Headmaster, while Bennett appeared as Tempest, the young teacher who wrote and acted in 'the play'. The sketches included a hilarious confirmation class, a 'spoof' on the Bloomsbury Group, one on T.E. Lawrence and another on Bertrand Russell ('I have led a very sheltered life. I had no contact with my own body until the spring of 1887, when I suddenly found my feet. I deduced the rest logically'. While the first part may be reminiscent of Orton's line from *Entertaining Mr Sloane*, quoted above, the word play and parody in the second is particularly Bennett's). But the play also contained touching evocations of grief at the death of 'old boys' in the Second World War and the passing of former values. The whole displayed Bennet's ability to juxtapose comedy with pathos, an aspect that has appeared in much of his subsequent work. As he said afterwards:

> Within the framework of *Forty Years On* I was able to be both sad
> and funny. Critics prefer you to be one or the other, but audiences
> have no objection if you manage to be both.

Subsequent stage plays have included *Getting On* (1971), the rather
uneven *Habeas Corpus* (1974) about sexual permissiveness, *The Old Country*
(1977) and *Enjoy* (1980). He has written screen plays and television plays,
the most recent successes being the script for *Prick Up Your Ears*, based on
John Lahr's biography of Joe Orton, and the remarkable sequence of monologues for television, *Talking Heads* (1988). These epitomised the
development in Bennett's work in that they display his acute observation of
people, especially from the genteel world of the lower-middle-classes, his
enormous capacity for sympathy, at the same time exhibiting his ability to
combine the comic with, if not the tragic in the 'Aristotelian' meaning of the
word, then certainly the 'tragic' in its every-day usage.

'Tragic' is an adjective that has been applied to what is arguably Peter
Shaffer's finest play, *Equus*. Shaffer (b. 1926) was educated at Trinity College, Cambridge and was a music critic before his early theatrical success,
Five Finger Exercise. His work falls into two categories, the earlier, small-
scale one-act comedies and the large, 'epic' discursive pieces.

The best example of the first is *Black Comedy* (1965), a brilliant little
farce based on the simple idea of reversing light and dark, so that the action
happens in the dark but the audience can see it. In the course of the piece,
all the furniture has to be moved from one room to another while Shaffer
constantly employs the classic farce maxim of bringing on the last person in
the world that the protagonist would actually want to see – or not see, in this
case.

His three major plays each employ a remarkable theatrical idea as its
focal point, after which Shaffer tends to allow his predilection for over-dis-
cursive dialogue to take over. In *The Royal Hunt of the Sun* (1964), the image
is the sun throne of Atahuallpa, the Sun King of the Incas. The play deals
with the invasion by Pizarro of Peru and the conflict of moralities and faiths.
The use of colour (in particular gold), mime and sound in the original production coupled with the powerful, physical performance of Robert
Stephens as the Sun God made it a remarkable experience that Artaud would
have applauded, but like Shaffer's subsequent play *Equus* (1973) it demands
a very high standard of production to disguise, or perhaps manage, the convolutions of the dialogue.

Equus has, if anything, an even more memorable 'coup de théâtre', the
blinding of the horses by Alan, the seventeen year old boy who worships the
animals, seeing a Christ-like element in them. The stylised staging of the horses is another example of Shaffer's instinctive feel for the theatre but the

same verbosity that unbalanced *The Royal Hunt of the Sun* is not helped in *Equus* by the setting which resembles a lecture theatre or court room.

Amadeus (1979) has received a very wide audience in its film version which differs considerably from the stage play. The gossiping whisperers of the play are removed in the film which is narrated by Salieri, as he watches, envies and eventually hounds to death the precocious genius of Mozart. There is no doubting the power of the film but the play went through considerable 'growing pains' before it reached a satisfactory and effective form.

In the three major plays – his *Yonadab* (1985) was not a great success – Shaffer has displayed a remarkable feel for effective theatrical spectacle and an interest in serious philosophical issues but it must be said that the two have not always 'married' in a totally successful manner.

Of a different generation the most precocious example of the 'Varsity scribe' is Christopher Hampton (b. 1946). His first play *When Did You Last See My Mother?* (1964) was written before he had even gone up to Oxford to study Modern Languages and has something of the confessional, 'could-be' autobiographical elements that have distinguished so many undergraduate plays. *Total Eclipse*, his second play, was staged in 1968 at the Royal Court where he has become 'Resident Dramatist', a grand title for what was essentially a dogs-body.

It is a considerable improvement on the earlier work and reflects Hampton's Modern Language education, in that it is an examination of the relationship between the two French poets, the young Arthur Rimbaud and the older, married Paul Verlaine. While it may betray the predilections of a linguist, this play has a vitality and sympathy that deserves reconsideration. Hampton's next play, *The Philanthropist* (1970), marked the end of his stay at the Royal Court, an unremarkable departure in that Hampton's work reflects neither the mood, the politics nor the house style of the English Stage Company at the Court at that time.

The Philanthropist, with its inverted acknowledgement of Molière's *Le Misanthrope*, is very much in Simon Gray land; full of semantic juggling and philosophical fencing, it is set in a university environment where, after the intentionally shocking opening scene of a student's suicide, the characters indulge in a sequence of word games to keep reality at bay:

> ...I always divide people into two groups. Those who live by what they know to be a lie, and those who live by what they believe, falsely, to be true.[10]

while in the final monologue on the telephone, after which the audience is led to believe that the main character might repeat the suicide but he simply lights a cigarette instead, Philip delivers a line that sums up Hampton's cerebral games:

> I thought of a new anagram today...'imagine the theatre as real'

...it's an anagram of 'I hate thee, sterile anagram'.[11]

Although he has gone on to display a certain originality in *Savages* (1973), *Treats* (1976) and *After Mercer* (1980), much of his more recent work has been in translating and adapting European works for the English-speaking stage, the most successful of which being his initial dramatising of Laclos' *Les Liasons Dangereuses* and the subsequent screen play for the highly successful film version of the same (1988).

The most popularly cerebral of this generation of writers, however, did not go to university. Tom Stoppard was born in Czechoslovakia in 1937; his family emigrated first to Singapore and then to Britain and this 'displaced' childhood has been seen by some critics as sufficient justification to couple his name with the older Parisian 'emigrés' whose work has been called 'absurd'. However, while there may be certain 'absurdist' echoes – Rosencrantz and Guildenstern in *Rosencrantz and Guildenstern are Dead* can be seen as more accessible decendants of Vladimir and Estragon – Stoppard's plays disguise any existential 'angst' that he may feel with a brilliant display of wit and intellectual gymnastics.

Stoppard's early writing was done on Bristol's *Western Daily Press* and his first successful play *Rosencrantz and Guildenstern are Dead* was staged by the Oxford Theatre Group at the 1966 Edinburgh Festival; like much of Stoppard's subsequent work, it is based on an original 'theatrical' idea that has the simplicity of genius. Here, he concentrates on the two minor attendants in *Hamlet*, hypothesising on their actions while out of the main-stream action, into which they are periodically and helplessly swept up and from which, just as swiftly, they are rejected. Working from the Player's summary of an actor's life one says: 'We do on the stage the things that are supposed to happen off. Which is a kind of integrity, if you look on every exit being an entrance somewhere else', Stoppard has his two pawns killing time with word-games and the interminable tossing of coins with which he opens the play so skillfully.

There are some who dismiss the piece as undergraduate silliness while others read into it an excessive significance which it does not deserve. It is a most enjoyable and stimulating piece of entertainment, full of philosophical niceties, such as 'Eternity's a terrible thought. I mean, where's it going to end?' and 'Life is a gamble, at terrible odds – if it was a bet, you wouldn't take it,' but by the end when the two little men simply disappear ('Now you see me, now you – ') the sad farce that Stoppard's characters have played out can be seen as a telling parable of man's insignificance.

A lack of control over the 'real' world coupled with gymnastics that are both physical and verbal epitomised Stoppard's next play – *Jumpers* (1972); the central character of the philosophy don, 'a' George Moore (rather than *the* George Moore), provided Sir Michael Hordern with a custom-made role to suit his inimitable brand of comic characterisation. While it may appear that we are back in the realms of *Butley* and *The Philanthropist*, the marked difference between Stoppard and his British colleagues is the absence of agonising over relationships, sexual or otherwise. George's wife simply gets on with her convoluted – and athletic – affairs while he gets on with matters of the mind. The content of the 'jokes' reflects this difference:

> The result was, as I will now demonstrate, that though an arrow is always approaching its target, it never quite gets there, and Saint Sebastian died of fright.

> To attempt to sustain the attention of rival schools of academics by argument alone is tantamount to constructing a Gothic arch out of junket,

while Stoppard allows his character a moment of simplistic philosophising that reflects a true 'British' compromise:

> …millions of children grow up without suffering deprivation, and millions, while deprived, grow up without suffering cruelties, and millions, while deprived and cruelly treated, none the less grow up.
> No laughter is sad and many tears are joyful.

Travesties (1974) continued the rarified examination of ideas, being set in Zurich in 1917 where Lenin, Joyce and the 'Dadaist' Tristan Tzara are all ignored by the main character Henry Carr, who is more interested in the British Consulate's 'am-dram' production of *The Importance of Being Earnest*. While this continued to display Stoppard's erudition and remarkable ability with words, it must be admitted that the piece was unbalanced structurally and one tended to admire the occasional dexterity rather than become involved in the whole.

More recently, Stoppard has begun to experiment with form, with *Dirty Linen* (1976) being a 'Whitehall' farce and *The Real Thing* (1982) an examination of the nature of reality. In 1977, in collaboration with André Previn and the London Symphony Orchestra, he wrote *Every Good Boy Deserves Favour* about political prisoners in Eastern Europe. What made it of particular interest was the integral involvement of 'live', classical music – the protagonist being a musician who was attempting to retain his sanity by remembering the music – and the move towards more serious, political content was continued with *Night and Day* (1978).

Like Hampton, Stoppard has looked to Europe for material to translate and adapt, choosing the same Nestroy comedy, *Einen Jux will er sich machen,* for his *On the Razzle* (1981) that Thornton Wilder used as the basis for his *Merchant of Yonkers*; despite a 'star' cast assembled by the National Theatre for its production, one cannot say that the enterprise was a total success.

It may be that, in the twenty years that he has been writing plays,

Stoppard has 'written himself out'. The evidence of *On the Razzle* might suggest this but, if so, it would mean the silencing of one of the wittiest, most original voices to be heard in Britain this century.

Stoppard's contemporary in Bristol, Peter Nichols, has recently abandoned the theatre, not through lack of inspiration but because of disillusionment with the realities of collaboration.

Nichols was born in 1927 in Bristol which has been the setting for a number of his 'autobiographical' plays; after National Service, he trained as an actor at the Bristol Old Vic Theatre School. This education is of considerable importance because Nichols is one of the most 'theatrical' playwrights of recent times, using 'show-biz' elements of song, dance and pantomime to put across some of his most serious subjects.

This juxtaposition, the comic presentation of 'tragic' subject matter, is evident in Nichols' first stage-play, *A Day in the Death of Joe Egg* (1967). It tells of a teacher and his wife who employ music-hall routines, jokes and comic patter to cope with the harrowing experience of caring for their severely handicapped spastic little girl (the 'Joe Egg' of the title). Nichols had been a teacher and he and his wife had a spastic child so the autobiographical parallels were obvious. What makes the play remarkable is that the combination of protective comedy and black despair, rather than being 'sick', is extremely successful and the moment in the piece when, in a fantasy sequence, the little girl, whom the audience has only seen as a 'vegetable', skips and smiles like any 'normal' child is very powerful.

Nichols' plays after *Joe Egg* appear to separate the two elements of the autobiographical and the theatrical; *Forget-Me-Not Lane* (1971) and *Born in the Gardens*(1979) deal with his attitudes towards his parents (*Forget-Me-Not Lane* making particularly effective use of 'flash-backs' into the protagonist's adolescence) while *Chez Nous* (1974) and *Passion Play* (1981) examine the relationship between husband and wife, with the latter employing two actors to play each of the partners, one presenting the public 'persona', Nichols' own version of the 'doppelganger'.

The less personal the plays, the more theatrical their structure; in his second stage play, *The National Health, or Nurse Norton's Affair* (1969), Nichols parodied the television soap-opera to deal with the death of a patient, again using comedy to help cope with a serious topic, and had the character 'Barnet' as a chorus/narrator figure, reminiscent of The Common Man in Robert Bolt's *A Man For All Seasons*.

Privates On Parade (1977) dealt with Communist insurrection in Malaya in 1948 but by setting it in an Army Concert Party such as Nichols had served in during National Service, interspersing the action with songs and routines from the 'camp' show, Nichols was able to make his comments on authority, honesty and imperialism in the best way possible, by causing the audience to laugh first and then consider what it was they were laughing at.

Nichols attempted to take this technique of education through entertainment even further in his last work to date, *Poppy* (1982).

The idea is excellent, in that a didactic pantomime seems to combine the very elements of sugaring serious pills with 'show-biz' glitter that Nichols has used from *Joe Egg*, through *National Health* to *Privates On Parade* and beyond. Unfortunately, *Poppy*, which sought to expose the British involvement in the Opium Wars and was presented as a Victorian Pantomime, Principal Boy and all, did not work. Whether it was simply the fault of 'a wholly inappropriate production' or whether Nichols was getting too far away from experience into theoretical dogma is a matter of opinion; what is definite is Nichols' disgust with the theatre:

> I've had enough of sacrificing my work to directors' whims, trusting it to inexpert actors and being trampled on by philistine managements.[12]

While it may be possible to argue that a playwright's conception of his work and a director's realisation are bound to differ, with the latter often falling short of the former because of human fallibility, it is also true that, with the present dearth of 'theatrical' writers with a feel for their medium, Nichols' withdrawal from the theatre is a loss that it can scarce afford.

The answer to Nichols' objections could be that adopted by Alan Ayckbourn, namely to direct his own plays. This, of course, is not as simple as it sounds but if, like Ayckbourn, you run the theatre company that you write for, then much of that difficulty disappears. Alan Ayckbourn (b. 1939) started young in the theatre, as the archetypal lowest of the low, the walking-on Assistant Stage Manager. By 1962, he had joined Stephen Joseph who was experimenting with the 'theatre-in-the-round' with companies in Scarborough and Stoke-on-Trent. After working as a radio drama producer for the BBC and at the newly-formed Victoria Theatre, Stoke-on-Trent, Ayckbourn returned to Scarborough in 1970 to run the theatre that had been established there as a memorial to Joseph, who had died in 1967.

All of Ayckbourn's earlier plays were written with the Scarborough theatre in mind, the first half-dozen especially for the summer holiday-makers. The first real success was *Relatively Speaking* which appeared in Scarborough in 1965 and London in 1967. It is essentially a farce based on mistaken identity and immediately displayed Ayckbourn's feel for comic situations. These evolved through *How The Other Half Loves* (1970) with two separate homes being on stage at the same time and the high-light being two dinner parties played concurrently, with the same guests but two separate sets of hosts.

Ayckbourn continued to display his growing mastery of the *genre* with *Bedroom Farce* (1977) where the action is going on in three different rooms at the same time, while with *The Norman Conquests* (1974), he deals with the same action in three separate plays, seen from the point of view of three different characters.

As Ayckbourn's work has progressed, there has been a marked development towards sharp, even bitter observation about people, essentially middle-class, progressively middle-aged, married people and their inability to achieve happiness. This progression is distinctly marked in *Just Between Ourselves* (1976), the first play that the Scarborough theatre had presented in their move away from being a summer 'rep.' towards a permanent, year-round company. Ayckbourn writes:

> As is customary, I wrote mainly at night – but this was my first experience of tackling a play whilst the North Sea storms hurtled round the house...Not surprisingly, the result was a rather sad (some say a rather savage) play with themes concerned with total lack of understanding, with growing old and with spiritual and mental collapse.

This does not sound the stuff that comedies are made of, but Ayckbourn's major and most remarkable achievement is that he can write about the most fraught human conditions and still make them extremely funny, whereupon, as with Nichols, the audience then is forced to consider what it has been laughing at. The plays are usually constructed around supposedly 'sociable' activities, such as meals, Christmas, or, as in the case of *Just Between Ourselves*, birthdays, for Ayckbourn is aware that the most destructive tensions surface during these periods of enforced proximity.

To reproduce his remarkable list of successes is unnecessary but it is important to note that, although he has been one of the most 'commercial' playwrights of the second half of the century with several plays running simultaneously in the West End, he is not the 'boulevard' hack that some critics make him out to be. Ayckbourn has managed the unique achievement of continually writing plays that people want to see – the new Ayckbourn being anticipated with much pleasure – and yet filling those plays with observations about human failings, anxieties and stresses that are as acute as any in Chekhov or the greatest 'naturalistic' novelists. Such has been the quality of his work that he is now an Associate Director of the British National Theatre.

While Ayckbourn had his Scarborough theatre in which to practise his craft, other younger writers were not so fortunate and so, towards the end of the 1960s, there was a move towards the founding of new, 'portable' companies, touring university campuses and arts centres with material written especially for the young actors by this new generation of playwrights.

It is no coincidence that the growth of these young, essentially political companies began in 1968, the year of student unrest and activity throughout Europe and America. That Britain did not experience the riots of Paris or Kent State is more a reflection on British character than an absence of commitment; the feelings manifested themselves in the fact that many influential new companies started that year, including the Pip Simmons Group, Ed Berman's Inter-Action, The Red Ladder Theatre and David Hare's Portable Theatre. By 1971, the Hull Truck Company, which is still functioning today under John Godber, and John McGrath's 7:84 Company were established, the name of the latter originating in the statistic that seven per cent of the population owned eighty-four per cent of the wealth.

Not everything was politically orientated; The Ken Campbell Road Show was also 'en route' by 1971 and they concentrated on fairground-style stunts, tricks, songs and 'mad-cap' humour, featuring the remarkable talents of Sylvester McCoy whose nude escapology and attempts on the world record for live ferrets down the trousers were a refreshing antidote at a time when the theatre was in danger of taking itself too seriously.

John McGrath (b. 1935) is of a different generation from most of the founders of, and authors for, these 'Alternative' theatre companies. He started writing while at Oxford, and served his apprenticeship writing material for television, including that forcing ground for new writing and acting talent, *Z Cars*. His first major success reflected his National Service experiences; *Events While Guarding the Bofors Gun* (1966) is exactly what the title says, a 'slice-of-life' play in the Wesker tradition, about army life. By 1971, McGrath had founded the 7:84 and his play, *Trees in the Wind*, was *the* thing to see on the Edinburgh Festival Fringe that year. By 1972, the company had started its nomadic existence, touring with John Arden and Margaretta D'Arcy's *The Ballygombeen Bequest* and McGrath's highly entertaining trilogy of short plays, *Plugged into History*, which proved that political theatre did not have to be boring or portentous.

This ability to present what is essentially 'agitprop' in a popular theatrical manner was best displayed in his 1973 play for 7:84 (Scotland), after they had separated into two companies, one that was to tour England and one for Scotland. In *The Cheviot, the Stag and the Black, Black Oil*, McGrath dealt with the long history of commercial exploitation of the Highlands and Islands, from the notorious 'clearances', the expulsion of the crofting population in order to capitalise on sheep, to the recent development of the off-shore oil. While this may appear to be 'heavy' subject matter, McGrath presented it as a local village hall entertainment, with song, dance and broad, Music Hall humour; the show toured throughout the areas that were depicted in the piece, so that the company travelled some 17,000 miles playing to over 30,000 people.

David Edgar (b. 1948) also started writing for a small touring company with a political bias, the General Will. As much of this material was topical satire, Edgar's early shows were ephemeral, with *Dick Deterred* (1974), dealing with Richard Nixon and the Watergate scandal in the style of *Richard III*, being the best known.

However, in 1974, 'alternative' theatre was embraced by the establishment when the Royal Shakespeare Company opened its small theatre, the Other Place, in Stratford, where Edgar's *Destiny* was performed in 1976. This dealt with the more lasting issues of race relations and neo-fascism and demonstrated Edgar's development as a playwright able to handle a broad, intricate canvas rather than small-scale, monochrome cartoons.

This ability was manifestly displayed in the enormously successful Royal Shakespeare Company's 1980 production of Edgar's dramatisation of that most theatrical of Dickens' novels, *Nicholas Nickleby*, and in his own *Maydays* (1983) which dealt with the rise and fall of socialist optimism over a period of some forty years. This development from hard-line socialism to a more humanitarian view has characterised a number of Edgar's contemporaries although it is doubtful if the claim can be made of Howard Brenton.

Brenton (b. 1942) wrote his first plays while still at Cambridge but it was with the Portable Theatre company that he had his first success, indeed his first *succès de scandale*. *Christie in Love* was performed in 1969 about a mass murderer who, under interrogation, re-enacts a number of his crimes in an attempt to explain them.

He produced an enormous body of work in the 1970s including *Brassneck* at the Nottingham Playhouse, *Magnificence* for the Royal Court, *The Churchill Play* which started life at Nottingham but was adopted by the Royal Shakespeare Company, *Epsom Downs* for Joint Stock and *Weapons of Happiness* for the newly opened National Theatre, in a style summed up by Philip Barnes:

> At his best Brenton writes forceful plays which are quick-moving, energetic, full of verbal and non-verbal jokes and which criticise people's tendencies to live on illusions in a society which restricts freedom of expression.[14]

There is a nice irony about this in that Brenton's most controversial play, *Romans In Britain* (1980), evoked storms of protest and litigation from the forces of the righteous who, without seeing the play, condemned it as offensive and depraving. It is true that a scene of homosexual rape sounds worthy of such criticism but only if the context, a Roman soldier 'invading' the body of a Briton, and the analogous comparison with modern Britain and Northen Ireland are ignored.

As with others of his contemporaries, Brenton has worked on translations of European works and it may be a reflection of his philosophy to note that he has chosen Büchner's *Danton's Death*, dealing with disillusionment with revolutionary politics, and Brecht's *Galileo*, again with its defeat of the idealist, as his source material. Parallel to Brenton's career and inextricably involved with it has been that of David Hare.

Hare (b. 1947) is another of the Cambridge graduates who have played such a significant part in British drama in the 1970s and 80s. His experimental touring company, Portable Theatre, which he founded with Tony Bicat in 1968 was one of the setters of a trend that was to expand to some fifty companies by the end of the 70s; his second play *Slag* was produced in 1970 at the Hampstead Theatre Club, one of the earliest London 'Fringe' theatres and for three years, he worked at the Royal Court, still the theatre for innovative new writing for the stage, by then under William Gaskill's direction. In 1974 he, Gaskill and Max Stafford-Clarke founded the Joint Stock Theatre Company, which 'evolved' new plays in workshops that included the actors as well as the director and playwright and which eventually was looked upon by many as a touring branch of the English Stage Company.

Much of Hare's early work reflected the state of Britain in decline, so that, while he was not perhaps as overtly political as some of his contemporaries, there is a definite feeling that Hare, Edgar, Brenton and other writers like Trevor Griffiths constitute something of a 'school'.

Hare was Resident Dramatist at the Nottingham Playhouse in 1973 under the new direction of Richard Eyre and while there he directed and wrote, with Howard Brenton, *Brassneck*, again on the theme of decline, this time of Nottingham, under the influence of misdirected capitalism.

With *Knuckle* (1974), Hare demonstrated his ability to impose a certain theatricality onto his political tract, employing a 'spoof' thriller *genre* and it is this 'theatricising' of serious political subjects that has marked the work of this school of colleagues and collaborators that centred firstly on Nottingham and then on Joint Stock.

One of the writers to benefit from the development of Joint Stock has been Caryl Churchill. Born in 1938 and educated at Lady Margaret Hall, Oxford, Churchill has admitted that her work falls into two periods, early material essentially for the radio, and the stage work, stemming from *Owners*, produced at the Theatre Upstairs at the Royal Court in 1972. She herself admits that, prior to writing *Owners*, she had recently re-read Joe Orton's *Entertaining Mr Sloane* and it shows in the characterisation – Worsely's preoccupation with committing suicide is treated as a joke – and the general air of amorality, although in *Owners* Churchill appears to be interested more in economic than sexual morality.

It appears that a subsequent sub-division in the categorisation of her work can be made, stemming from the period of collaboration with Joint Stock for whom she wrote *Light Shining In Buckinghamshire* (1976). She writes:

> My habit of solitary working and shyness at showing what I wrote at an early stage had been wiped out by the...self-exposure in Joint Stock's method of work in which, through talk, reading, games and improvisation, we tried to get closer to the issues and the people.[15]

Churchill employed the same technique when writing *Vinegar Tom*, a play about witch hunts for Monstrous Regiment, the feminist touring company established in the early 1970s. *Cloud Nine* (1979) also had its origins in the workshop method adopted by Joint Stock; here she is dealing with the subject of sexual stereotypes and employs transvestism and anachronous history in a style that suggests a collaboration between Joe Orton and Edward Bond. To represent the repressive, white, male-orientated, perverse world of colonial Victorian Britain:

> Betty, Clive's wife is played by a man because she wants to be what men want her to be, and, in the same way, Joshua, the black servant is played by a white man because he wants to be what whites want him to be. Betty does not value herself as a woman, nor does Joshua value himself as a black. Edward, Clive's son, is played by a woman for a different reason – partly to do with the stage convention of having boys played by women – and partly with highlighting the way Clive tries to impose traditional male behaviour on him.[16]

It has to be admitted, also, that Edward played as a woman makes the homosexual overtures made by Harry as convoluted as anything in the original all-male *As You Like It* !

From the fantastic Victorian world of the first act, the action moves to the present day, with the same characters, only twenty-five years older. The sexual casting is almost straightforward, although the child Cathy is played by a man. Churchill provides a number of reasons for this:

> …partly as a simple reversal of Edward being played by a woman, partly because the size and presence of a man on stage seemed appropriate to the emotional force of young children, and partly, as with Edward, to show more clearly the issues in learning what is considered correct behaviour for a girl.

To this one might add expediency, for there is an actor spare from the first act and it would be expensive to employ an extra actress just for the second half.

In 1982, *Top Girls* again employs historical anachronism in a cleverly sustained 'jeu d'esprit' of a number of women from different periods in history meeting over dinner to discuss the role of women through history. With plays like *Softcops* (1984) and, most recently, *Serious Money* (1987), Churchill has demonstrated those benefits of the Joint Stock method of collaboration, establishing herself as one of Britain's finest contemporary playwrights.

While Max Stafford-Clarke moved from Joint Stock to the Royal Court, David Hare also moved on. After the success of *Teeth 'n' Smiles* (1975), in which Helen Mirren played a drunken rock singer at a Cambridge University May Ball where Hare examined the adoption of the 'radical' views of the

1960s by the establishment of the 70s, he himself suffered a similar fate, in that he, like Ayckbourn, was embraced by the National Theatre. *Plenty* appeared there in 1978, he directed his own *A Map of the World* in 1983 and in 1985 Hare renewed his collaboration with Howard Brenton for the extremely successful *Pravda* about a power-mad, antipodean newspaper tycoon, although the authors made their monster South African to avoid any misconceptions that might have arisen. In 1984, Hare was made an Associate Director of the National Theatre, where, in 1986, Richard Eyre, his old 'boss' from the heady Nottingham Playhouse days, was appointed Artistic Director.

The wheel has gone full circle; as often happens, the revolutionaries have become established or, to be less cynical, those young talents of any worth have survived and developed until they, quite rightly, reach positions of authority and influence over the subsequent generations and can encourage the aspirants, either to imitation or opposition. What needs to be seen is whether there are any young turks who are not so much willing – youth will always be ambitious – but more properly, able to depose them.

Twelve plays for further consideration

(This period is so fertile that a list twice the size would not do it justice)
1. Joe Orton, *What the Butler Saw*
2. David Storey, *Home*
3. Edward Bond, *Lear*
4. Simon Gray, *Otherwise Engaged*
5. Christopher Hampton, *Total Eclipse*
6. Tom Stoppard, *Jumpers*
7. Peter Nichols, *Private On Parade*
8. David Egdar, *Destiny*
9. Howard Brenton, *Romans in Britain*
10. David Hare, *Teeth 'n' Smiles*
11. Hare and Brenton, *Pravda*
12. Caryl Churchill, *Cloud Nine*

Notes

1. Joe Orton, *Entertaining Mr Sloane*
2. Orton, *Loot*
3. Orton, *What the Butler Saw*
4. *At the Royal Court: 25 Years of the English Stage Company*, vol. 6, p. 137

5. David Storey, *Home*, p. 78

6. Edward Bond, Preface to *Lear*, p. v

7. Bond, *Lear*

8. Bond, Preface to *Lear*, p. xii

9. Introduction to *Plays: One-Gray*, p. ix

10. Christopher Hampton, *The Philanthropist*

11. ibid.

12. Quoted in Philip Barnes, *A Companion to Post-War British Theatre*, p. 167

13. Alan Ayckbourn, Preface to *Three Plays*, p. 7

14. Barnes, op. cit., p. 47

15. Caryl Churchill, Preface to *Plays*

16. Churchill, Preface to *Cloud Nine*, p. 246

10: AND GO WE KNOW NOT WHERE

Most people who work in the Theatre share broadly similar aims; very few go into the business of acting, directing or writing with the express aim of making money; motivating all but the most commercially-minded is some ideal that they are trying to realise.

Constance Cummings has called the Theatre her 'religion' where the communion between the audience and the actors equates with, or even surpasses, any mystical exchange experienced in church. Arthur Miller wrote that 'the function of the play is to reveal him [a member of the audience] to himself so that he may touch others by virtue of the revelation of his mutuality with them. If only for this reason I regard the theatre as a serious business, one that makes or should make man more human...'[1]

The Catalan company, Els Comediants, have claimed that their aim is to provide 'a sensation', 'an electric current' with all the galvanic power that that implies, while Graham Devlin, director of 'Major Road', has summed up the aim of all who work in the theatre as a desire to provide their audience with 'extraordinary moments', experiences that raise the audience, no matter how briefly, above the mundane.

While the cinema and television are immensely popular, they are essentially different from the theatre, both in the content and style of the entertainment that they provide and, most especially, in the relationship between the audience and the artist. This difference has been described, perhaps rather sensationally, as the difference between making love and masturbation and while too close a pursuit of this analogy may produce some dubious comparisons, there is no doubting the efficacy of the image. Its aptness depends entirely upon the reader's preferred medium.

While Theatre may be a universal art form, it is sad to have to relate that the attitudes towards it, both popularly and politically, are distinctly varied. In France, ever since De Gaulle's appointment of André Malraux as Minister of Culture in 1959, there has been a conscious movement toward supporting and decentralising the theatre. With the formation of the Maisons de Culture, a network of regional theatres was established, funded jointly by central and local government. It is true that this ideal became tarnished in its realisation, when petty politics played too important a role in the administration so that the 70s saw a period of stagnation, sending the innovators to work elsewhere, but by the 1980s, under the Mitterrand government, major infusions of money helped to re-establish the health of the nation's theatres.

The year 1968 saw a great upheaval in all aspects of French life and, for the theatre, the climax was reached when the students forced Jean-Louis Barrault from his theatre, the Odéon. The *manifestations* were taking place in the streets, so the newly politicised performers soon joined their potential audience there. 'Street Theatre' and 'Café-Theatre' became popular throughout Europe and America, providing instant, cheap, 'popular', political and usually communally-devised entertainment. Perhaps the finest and most lasting of the companies to establish themselves in France at this time was Ariane Mnouchkine's 'Théâtre du Soleil', whose *1789* played in a vast warehouse in a 'promenade' style, with the action occurring on a number of raised stages and the audience walking between, very much in the style of the medieval morality plays, performed on a procession of carts or floats.

The content of the shows performed by these peripatetic companies displays an approach to the theatre that is remarkably similar to that suggested by Copeau and Artaud nearly half a century before and it is interesting to note that, whenever the theatre appears to be going through a crisis, the inevitable salvation is a return to the basics of the clown and the circus. Lenora Champagne sums up the solution chosen by various 'alternative' companies:

> The development of popular forms became one of the dominant features of the young theatre. On the one hand, Jerome Savary's Grand Magic Circus, relying heavily on props, tricks, and special effects, attempted to simulate the atmosphere of festival and spontaneity reminiscent of circus and burlesque...On the other hand, troupes such as the Théâtre du Soleil...have tended to emphasise the body and creative means of the actor by training themselves in techniques of *commedia dell-arte*, clowns or Chinese Theatre.[2]

However, the honeymoon of collective creativity for a popular audience did not last for long and the move in the 1980s has been back towards text-based productions, often of classics, with the director's interpretations being the 'authorship' that interests critics and performers alike. The investment in the arts has returned under a socialist President and, perhaps inevitably with the removal of any obvious target, the move has been away from a 'political' theatre towards a philosophical one, ever a favourite with the French mentality.

What has been noted though, is a shift of emphasis in the potential audience. The ideal of a popular audience has died and the inevitability of theatre being an elitist medium accepted. As Champagne writes: 'this kind of active seeking of a popular audience is rare today. Even Mnouchkine's Shakespeare cycle is more dense and visually stunning – and much longer – than her early work. Her theatre is always filled, but not with workers.'[3] However, this has not stopped the government supporting the theatre, with centralised financing of decentralised theatres and active encouragement of new playwrights' work.

Unfortunately, not every government is as enlightened as the French; not every government views the theatre as essential to the cultural well-being of a nation, preferring to consider it a luxury to be touted in the market place. Those European countries that have lived through a period of fascist dictatorship have reacted to the experience in ways that reflect the individuality of their national temperament, rather than the communality of the experience.

There appears to be a lack of concerted effort in promoting an integral Italian theatre, an impression encouraged by both the individualistic Italian character and the ephemeral life-spans of successive Italian governments. The theatre has been dominated by individuals, be they actor/director/authors like de Filippo or 'outsiders' like Visconti who occasionally took sabbaticals from the cinema to work in the theatre, concentrating in particular on the works of Goldoni (1707-1798).

The experiences of the current major influence, Dario Fo, have been related elsewhere but his is essentially an anarchic, ego-centric theatre where one man's genius sets him above his collaborators and eliminates the possibility for a realisation of otherwise admirable ideals. His split from the left-wing company, Nuova Scena, reflected this dichotomy, as does the fact that two of his most famous pieces, *Mistero Buffo* and *Female Parts* are for one performer only, himself in the case of the former and his wife, Franca Rame, in the latter. They have made definite attempts to broaden the social basis of their audiences, playing once again to a more bourgeois, less working-class audience and one hopes that this expansion is for ethical rather than simply financial reasons. However, it may be that *Mistero Buffo* is an apposite reflection on the present state of the Italian theatre, a brilliant virtuoso, yet solo display.

In the chapter called 'The rough theatre' in his book, *The Empty Space*, Peter Brook describes a visit to Germany immediately after the Second World War:

> In a Hamburg garret I once saw a production of *Crime and Punishment* and that evening became...one of the most striking theatre experiences that I have ever had. By sheer necessity, all problems of theatre style vanished: here was the real main stream, the essence of an art that stems from the storyteller looking round his audience and beginning to speak. All the theatres in the town had been destroyed, but here in this attic...we were gripped by living theatre.[4]

While Brook uses this and other stories of Hamburg in 1946 to illustrate the intrinsic, essential 'hunger' that human nature has for the theatre, these specific stories also reflect the immediate re-emergence of a German spirit, that spirit which has rebuilt West Germany so successfully.

There has been a very definite, perhaps inevitable seriousness about the content and style of much of the subsequent German theatre, epitomised in the work of Rolf Hochhuth (b. 1931) and Peter Weiss (1916-1982). The 'Folk Play' has been used to examine social and economic subjects while the 'Documentary Drama' employs a comic-strip style to deal with more political topics.

The Berliner Ensemble, started by Brecht and his wife, Helene Weigel, on their return to Germany in 1949, has been an enormous influence throughout the theatrical world, with its tours abroad in the 1950s and '60s opening the eyes of many subsequent disciples to the 'Brechtian' style. Not only has the Ensemble promoted Brecht's own plays but has demonstrated, with its production of other works, particularly by Shakespeare, that this vision of the theatre can be universally effective. It has to be said, though, that the theatre in both Germanies has subsequently and inevitably lived in the shadow of both Brecht and his company and that everything is, either consciously or unconsciously, weighed in the Brechtian balance. One possible reaction to such a theatrical writer was the 'anti-theatre' of Peter Handke (b. 1942) whose *Offending the Audience* (1966) and *The Ride Across Lake Constance* (1970) question many of the conventional theatrical concepts. These are, though, like Brecht's plays, essentially cerebral exercises and one cannot imagine a German performer with the exuberance of a Fo, nor for that matter an Italian company with the dedication of a Berliner Ensemble.

It is, perhaps, no coincidence that the country that has most recently been released from the constraints of a restrictive regime, Spain, is the liveliest and most enthusiastic for both renovation and innovation.

The death of Franco in 1975 and the return of democracy under the monarchy has signalled a remarkable growth in theatrical activity. The new regime has permitted and even encouraged the expression of regional culture, which means that the national government has financed the development of regional drama centres, while the optimism that flourished as a result of the political changes continues to be expressed in the 'popular' manifestations of street theatre and cabaret. The Catalonian companies, Els Joglars and Els Comediants, have received international acclaim for their processional, multi-discipline spectacles, while playwrights like Alfonso Sastre (b. 1926) and Antonio Buero Vallejo (b. 1916) have a chance to express themselves without the restrictions of the clumsy code of censorship under Franco. It is hardly surprising that the removal of restrictions should bring about a burst of liberated creativity; what will be interesting to observe over the final decade of the century will be whether this dynamic exuberance can be maintained and channelled into any sort of internationally-recognised 'renaissance', a second Golden Age of Spanish theatrical literature.

Given the inordinately large number of universities and colleges in

America, each with its own Drama Department and Theatre courses, it is impossible to know if the seeds of revival are not at the moment germinating somewhere. From a distance, however, it appears that the problems of cost and the competition with television could have strangled playwriting in the States. Of course, New York is not a fair reflection of the general condition of the American theatre but, in 1986, Alan Jay Lerner wrote:

> History is replete with dire predictions about the future of the New York theatre...This time the malaise may indeed be terminal...half the theatres in New York are dark and with little prospect of future occupants...without an infusion of young talent, who is going to fill them?[5]

And his concern about the absence of youth among the authors and actors is equally valid for the audience whose average age, it has been estimated, is forty-four years old!

Lerner's view of the British theatre, while slightly less pessimistic, still carried dire warnings:

> ...the reduction in governmental grant (is) a destructive act in itself, but typical of the calculated indifference to the performing arts of conservative governments in general, and the Thatcher one in particular.[6]

Ideally, a government's attitude to the arts should not affect the health of that culture but, inevitably, it does. In Britain, with the improvement in education that stemmed from the 1944 Education Act, with the introduction of the National Health Service and the inception of the Arts Council of Great Britain in 1946, there followed an inevitable feeling that 'the Government', whoever they might be, were taking care of the welfare of the nation, and that the Arts were included in that cradle. When, however, the atmosphere changes and many essential services are put out to tender, becoming answerable to balance sheets, and the unprofitable is 'trimmed away', the motto of 'Art for Art's sake' is in danger of being drowned by the cry of 'Money, for the sake of Mammon'.

In Britain, in the mid 1970s, some fifty 'portable' theatre companies were funded by the Arts Council; at the end of the 80s, that figure is less than twenty; included in the more notable of the recent demises is the Joint Stock Theatre Company, instrumental in bringing the work of David Hare, Howard Brenton and Caryl Churchill – amongst others – to an audience outside London.

The removal of government subsidy is not the only reason for the death of the companies; there is no point in giving a grant to something that no-one wants to see and among the surviving touring companies, there is the double worry, firstly about the paucity of the material being submitted by aspiring writers and secondly, about the absence of audiences interested enough to bother patronising whatever it is they do offer.

Graham Devlin founded 'Major Road', one of the battalion of small companies to take to 'the road' in the early 1970s, and he still directs the company, now based in Bradford. On grounds of longevity, at the very least, he is viewed as the 'Grand Old Man' of 'portable' theatres, and he has expressed the opinion that television is not only attracting what young writers there may be away from the theatre because of the money that it can offer but that actors prefer to wait in London for a chance to make a commercial rather than commit themselves to a poorly-paid regional tour that could take them away from the telephone at that all-important moment. Television, enhanced by the infinite potential of the home video, is also keeping the audience comfortably and safely at home in its own armchair, rather than venturing out to see an unknown play in an uncertain venue.

Richard Eyre at the National takes the argument further, saying that most of the new plays received by their Script Department – some forty a week – betray television influence, either being consciously written for that medium or unconsciously affected by it. Television scripts are essentially naturalistic, filled with scenes of no more than thirty seconds duration and often including climaxes and breaks to suit the incursions of commercials; plays for the stage should be essentially 'theatrical', concentrating on stimulating the audience's intellect rather than their interest in an advertiser's product.

This bleak view is not reflected everywhere, however; the artistic directors of the regional theatres all have their stable of writers and, indeed, Robert Hamlin at the Belgrade Theatre, Coventry implies that the London-based companies arc out of touch with the wider theatre-going audiences. He offers a list of over a dozen writers that he has produced at Coventry, making particular mention of Julian Garner; he also remarks that 'the regional theatres keep generating new work, often with a strongly regional voice, or a voice which makes connections with a regional audience, rather than the London-based media or theatrical establishment. That regional energy is exciting.'

Everyone in the regional centres expressed an interest in encouraging new talent. Braham Murray, one of the quartet of Artistic Directors at the Royal Exchange, Manchester – a company that can vie with any in the country – writes:

> The question that has faced us has been how to construct a magnet that will attract it. We have been fortunate in being able to hold our International Playwriting competitions, sponsored by Mobil, and that has unearthed a significant percentage of new talent – in some cases people who have never before thought of writing for the theatre. This has, in turn, led to the commissioning of new work from those writers, and it is hoped that by compound interest the stable

of writers will grow into a formidable team.

The Royal Exchange produced some twenty-four new plays in the years between 1982 and 1989, six of which were adaptations or translations.

Murray's mention of sponsorship raises a vexed issue; commercial sponsors will want a return for their investment. No one is in the business of philanthropy and any company that puts money into a theatre will want to be seen to be doing so. Financing a competition presents a 'high profile' and can probably be included in the advertising budget; sponsoring an individual production so that the sponsor's name can be seen on the posters and programmes again puts the company in the public eye and is justifiable, as long as there is an individual executive prepared to push for this use of company money.

However, sponsorship is by no means an automatic, guaranteed source of income and for the theatres, it is essentially cosmetic. In the financial year 1987-8, the Arts Council of Great Britain provided financial help to approximately a hundred different companies and projects, from the National Theatre with their grant of almost £8 million, to the 'Not The National Theatre' with a grant of £4,000. The total income generated by all these companies was approximately £72 million; half of this came from ticket sales; £26.5 million came from Arts Council grants; £8 million came from Local Authorities and 'Other Public Subsidy'. The total sum provided by sponsorship was less than £1.5 million.

When questioned about this, the business world varies in its answer, from the evasive to the blunt. From a down-to-earth Midlands builder comes the reply 'there's no money in it' and what his customers want from 'corporate entertainment' is a night on the tiles, not an evening in the stalls. Others see the maintenance of a healthy culture as a responsibility of central government rather than private enterprise, and cannot understand why the National Theatre, for instance, should be forced to expend valuable energy on worrying about subsistence, rather than the pursuit of excellence.

Despite the impression received from the commercial theatre, where the 'hi-tech' musicals can cost millions to stage, it is not the production costs that are restricting the public theatres. Maintenance and administration of the buildings, without an actor or a set appearing on stage, is taking up to half the theatre's income and Richard Eyre has expressed a forlorn wish that the Government might take on the cost and administration of the buildings and leave the theatre companies free to concentrate on what they do and know best.

Reactions to the state of British theatre at the end of the 1980s vary considerably; one has to be honest and state that the majority of people would never even consider the question, for theatre-going is a minority activity and a fair proportion of the few who *do* go to the theatre would limit their visits

to revivals, Lloyd Webber musicals and the bastardised versions of the pantomime that fill our large theatres around Christmas, considered by most as
a winter version of the sea-side summer variety show. From those who are
sincerely interested, the dearth in new writing talent is viewed with equal
variety. John Adams at the Birmingham Repertory Theatre says that they
can rarely afford new work and so its absence it not so noticeable. At the
Royal Court, where the English Stage Company is still devoted to promoting new work, Max Stafford-Clarke's outlook is bleak:

> Fifteen years ago we were producing 16 plays each year, now we
> struggle to produce five. Inevitably, this means that fewer writers
> from this generation can emerge. This does not mean that the new
> talent is not there...the problem is that there is simply not enough
> money left in theatre to bring these new writers up through the
> ranks.

Graham Watkins, Artistic Director of the Redgrave Theatre, Farnham is
positively apocalyptic in his outlook:

> ...the pressures to balance the books are so acute...that to take a
> chance on a new play is an *enormous* risk possibly jeopardising the
> very future of the theatre.
> Under these circumstances the real loser is our culture as a whole.
> The great promise which British theatre showed after the creation
> of the Arts Council and which theatre practitioners responded to
> so magnificently, raising a beautiful statue on the horizon of world
> art, is rotting away. The nose is gone, the arms are eroded, the ears
> stolen and the very plinth so badly eaten by vermin that the whole
> thing looks to topple over soon. Our Ozimandias was built of papier
> mâché, because in our society it appears, the price of a piece of gra-
> nite is too much. (One more submarine is a more valuable property
> than fifty years of British Theatre.) Playwrights will have ideas, they
> will write, but the people who can bring their work before the pub-
> lic are under so much counter-productive pressure that the
> marriage is all too often unconsummated.

This vivid response reflects a dismay expressed by a number of those responsible for theatre companies, from Graham Devlin with his small touring
company to Richard Eyre at the National, who foresees a 'withering away of
a subsidised theatre'.

Paul Unwin, the young director of the Bristol Old Vic Company, while
adamant that the writers exist, says that: 'one of the great disadvantages of
the current theatre environment – with particular reference to public funding – is that new writers, young or old, have very little chance of getting their
first step on the ladder.'

And this seems to be an attitude that permeates many in the business;
financial worries are creating an atmosphere of resignation which cannot be

conducive to exciting work. In a society where monetarist values have become prevalent, so that the amount of money that a job will pay is of more interest than the work required, where consumerism and credit-funded hedonism are vaunted and spiritual values ignored, those who try to promote something more than sensation and spectacle are daunted by the problems of financing even the classics, without the added worry of the uncertain quality of new work. In the current financial climate, people cannot afford the luxury of failure and so dangerous experiments are 'out'.

Unwin adds: '...the position of new writing remains precarious and...is getting worse. Writers need engagement in the art of theatre and need contact with an audience. The most exciting writing, to my mind, has emerged because it has been forged by a debate with an audience, or at least some kind of conflict of views.' When a generation of potential audiences is more interested in the performance of its Porsche than the performance of an actor, more interested in the appreciation in the value of its Dockland flat than in appreciating a new work of art, when part of that audience has been priced out of theatre-going by its income from education or nursing, the debate is going to be at the best sterile and, more likely, non-existent. What is most worrying, as Richard Eyre has said, is that the Conservative Government under Margaret Thatcher gave the impression that all the theatres in the country could close tomorrow without worrying them in the slightest, without them being *aware* of what the country would be losing.

This is ironic, Eyre maintains, because the theatre was the first 'enterprising' business that set out to 'market' itself and is one of the few that still regularly meet the demands made by 'market forces' by providing its wares on time and at the price originally quoted!

That said, optimism and idealism are essentially youthful traits; drama schools are inundated with applications, with over a hundred hopefuls competing for every available place. While there is no doubt that some are entering with stars in their eyes, intending to be big-earning 'megastars', the majority of aspiring actors recognise that they will work rarely, very hard and for very little money and, despite these home truths, they still desperately want to become communicants in the mystery of live theatre.

The theatre has survived for thousands of years; it may well be that it has outgrown its present potential audience, at least in Britain and America, and that a period of recession, of natural selection, may be in order. The fact that the standard of new writing is in decline is, eventually, matters little. There are great gaps on the map of European playwriting when nothing of note has been produced, the middle of the nineteenth century being a prime example. Thousands of plays were written in that time and virtually nothing has lasted, except as museum pieces. A fallow period will not seriously damage the progression and growth of an art form. In the absence of major new plays, we have a 'directocracy' which continues to create stimulating new pro- ductions of old plays, and the impetus in the last decade of the century may continue to come from that quarter. In Britain we have been spoiled by the phenomenon of the thirty or more authors whose work first saw the light of stage during the twenty years between 1956 and 1976 and we expect this unnatural glut to continue. Reasons for the decline differ; a member of that phenomenal group, David Hare, says that: 'the young writers don't give the impression that much is at stake for them, whereas there's still an urgency about the importance of things in older generations.' One of the younger generation, Paul Unwin, says that 'writers are, nowadays, so nervous of surviving that perhaps they are somehow becoming timorous'.

In 1956, John Osborne had Jimmy Porter say that 'there aren't any good, brave causes left', but the subsequent generation, Osborne included, found plenty to write about. The present financial and political climate reflects a hedonistic complacency and it may be inevitable that, for a while, this will affect what appears on stage. Directors of subsidised theatres fear for the State of the Art of playwriting in general and for their theatres in particular. With the decline in individual patronage of autocratic monarchies, it is the responsibility of democratic governments to fulfil that role; this, obviously, is not being done in Britain to the satisfaction of the theatre practitioners. If democratically-elected governments present philistine policies, this may well be a reflection on the state of the nation and the adage of 'getting the theatre you deserve' applies.

Whatever the present short-term prospects, there is no doubting that the twentieth century has been the most progressive and productive era in the history of Man and that the theatre, one of the many areas of achievement that raises Man above the beasts, has never witnessed a more fertile period. True, it may be facing financial problems in a capitalist world but the absence of money has always been the bane of the theatre's existence. Burbage's 'Theatre' doubled as a cockpit, the income from which helped to subsidise Shakespeare's plays; Molière's first company, the 'Illustre-Théâtre' went bankrupt, Molière spent time in a debtors' prison and thirteen years 'on the road', living a communal, hand-to-mouth existence before attracting the patronage of Monsieur, the king's brother. Büchner never heard a word of his plays performed, while the Provincetown Players built their own theatres in attics and warehouses to give the first performances of O'Neill's plays. It will be anathema to the present generation of actors, directors and writers, but an element of this adversity may not be counter-productive. Graham Watkins writes that: 'a young playwright cannot mount productions him or herself' but that is exactly what many of the present-day establishment figures did in the late 60s and early 70s with their 'portable' theatres.

Unfortunately, while the spirit may be willing it does appear that the audiences simply are not there nowadays and so 'retrenchment' may be the watchword at the beginning of the 90s. However, just as no Golden Age lasts for ever, so no government, benevolent or philistine, lasts for ever. One of the main conclusions drawn from this survey of apparently diverse and opposing works is that revolutions in the theatre are the sort that go full circle, rather than erupt. The wheel turns and the next great writer or influential school soon appears, if it is not already doing so somewhere at the moment.

As with much that he did, Strindberg exaggerated when he claimed in 1880 that the theatre was dead. It will take more than a surfeit of 'the Deadly theatre', Peter Brook's term for melodrama and spectacle – as prevalent now as it was when Strindberg was writing – to kill the Theatre; it will take more than money-orientated Philistinism to starve it, although that philosophy may well cause current practitioners to despair. The inspiration that drew competitors to the Dionysian festivals in the fifth century BC, that prompted the early tragedies, comedies and satyr plays is as integral a part of human nature as the search for the belief in a higher being or the desire to impose order on chaos. Of course, Theatre has modulated over the centuries and, unable to read the future, we inevitably look back nostalgically but the basis of all man's 'higher' achievements is faith, a belief in the potential of human nature. Fortunately, the theatre is an expression of that faith and not of government policies. As David Hare wrote, 'The theatre won't atrophy; it's like those children's candles that you can't blow out. Because at some level people will always need it'.

Notes

1. Arthur Miller, introduction to *Collected Plays*
2. Lenora Champagne, *French Theatre Experiment since 1968*, p. 28
3. ibid., pp. 101-2
4. Peter Brook, *The Empty Space*, pp. 89-90
5. Alan Jay Lerner, *The Musical Theatre*, pp. 235-6
6. ibid., p. 235

BIBLIOGRAPHY

Allen, J., *Theatre in Europe* (John Offord Publications Ltd, 1981)

Artaud, A., *The Theatre and Its Double* trans. Victor Corti (John Calder, 1970)

Ayckbourn, A., *Three Plays* (Chatto and Windus, 1979)

Bair, D., *Samuel Beckett: A Biography* (Cape, 1978)

Barnes, P., *A Companion to Post-War British Theatre* (Croom Helm, 1986)

Barrault, J-L., *Souvenirs Pour Demain* (Editions du Seuil, 1972)

Behl, C.F.W., *Gerhart Hauptmann* (Holzner Verlag, Wurzberg, 1956)

Benson, R., *German Expressionist Drama* (Macmillan, 1984)

Bentley, E., *The Dramatic Event* (Beacon Press, Boston, 1977)

Betti, U., *Three Plays* (Gollancz, 1958)

Bigsby, C., *David Mamet* (Methuen, 1985)

Bird, A., *Plays of Oscar Wilde* (Vision Press, 1977)

Boa, E., *The Sexual Circus* (Basil Blackwell, 1987)

Bond, E., *Lear* (Methuen, 1972)

Booth, M., *English Melodrama* (Jenkins, 1965)

Boucicault, D., *The Dolmen Boucicault* (Dolmen, 1964)

Bradby, D., *Modern French Drama from 1940 to 1989* (Cambridge University Press, 1984)

Brook, P., *The Empty Space* (MacGibbon and Kee, 1968)

Büchner, G., *Danton's Death, Woyzeck* ed. M. Jacobs (Manchester University Press, 1971)
———— *Plays*, trans. Victor Price (Oxford University Press, 1971)

Champagne, L., *French Theatre Experiment since 1968* (UMI Research Press, Michigan, 1984)

Chekhov, A.P., *Collected Letters* ed. Benjamin Blom (Friedland, 1974)
———— *The Cherry Orchard*, trans. J. Gielgud, introduction, M. St Denis (Heinemann, 1963)

Churchill, C., *Plays* (Methuen, 1985)

De Filippo, E., *Saturday, Sunday, Monday* (Heinemann, 1974)

Elsom, J., *Post War British Theatre* (Routledge and Kegan Paul, 1979)

Findlater, R., *At the Royal Court: 25 Years of the English Stage Company* (Amber Lane Press, 1981)

Fitz-Simon, C., *The Irish Theatre* (Thames and Hudson, 1983)

Fo, D., *Trumpets and Raspberries* (Pluto Plays, 1984)

Friel, B., *Selected Plays*, introduction, S. Dean (Faber, 1984)

Furness, R.S., *Expressionism* (Methuen, 1973)

Galsworthy, J., *Ten Famous Plays* (Duckworth, 1929)

Garcia Lorca, F., *Three Tragedies* (Secker & Warburg, 1959)

Gelb, B. and A., *Eugene O'Neill* (Dell Publishing, 1965)

Goering, R., 'Naval Encounter' in J.M. Ritchie (ed.) *Vision and Aftermath* (John Calder, 1968)

Goll, I., 'Methusalem' in J.M. Ritchie (ed.) *Seven Expressionist Plays* (John Calder, 1968)

Granville Barker, H., *The Exemplary Theatre* (Chatto and Windus, 1922)

Guicharnaud, T., *Modern French Theatre from Giraudoux to Genet* (Yale, 1967)

Hauptmann, C., 'War, a Te Deum' in J.M. Ritchie (ed.) *Vision and Aftermath* (John Calder, 1968)

Hayman, R., *Artaud and After* (Oxford University Press, 1977)

Hinchcliffe, A.P., *British Theatre, 1950-1970* (Blackwells, 1974)

———— *The Absurd* (Methuen, 1969)

Hobson, H., *French Theatre Since 1830* (John Calder, 1978)

Hunt, H., *The Abbey* (Gill and Macmillan, 1979)

Ibsen, H., *Brand*, trans. Gathorne-Hardy (George Allen and Unwin, 1966)

———— *An Enemy of the People*, trans. Faber, introduction, M. Esslin (Heinemann, 1967)

Kaiser, G., *From Morn to Midnight*, trans. Ashley Dukes (Henderson's, 1920)

Kearney, C., *The Writings of Brendan Behan* (Gill and Macmillan, 1977)

Kenworthy, B.J., *Georg Kaiser* (Modern Language Studies, Blackwells, 1957)

Kislan, R., *The Musical* (Prentice-Hall, Englewood Cliffs, N.J., 1980)

Laufe, A., *Broadway's Greatest Musicals* (David and Charles, 1978)

Lerner, A.J., *The Musical Theatre* (Collins, 1986)

Maugham, W.S., *Collected Plays* (Heinemann, 1931)

McIntyre, H.G., *The Theatre of Jean Anouilh* (Harrap, 1981)

Miller, A., *Collected Plays* (Secker & Warburg, 1967)

Mitchell, T., *Dario Fo – The People's Court Jester* (Methuen, 1984)

Nelson, B., *Tennessee Williams* (Ivan Obolensky inc., N.Y., 1961)

Nicolls, A., *A History of English Drama* (Cambridge University Press, 1952)

O'Casey, S., *Selected Plays* (Macmillan, 1949)

O'Connor, G., *French Theatre Today* (Pitman Publishing, 1975)

O'Connor, P., *Five Plays of Protest from the Franco Era* (Sociedad General Espanola de Librera, Avda de Valdeparra, Alconendas, Madrid, 1981)

Odetts, C., *Six Plays* (Methuen, 1979)

O'hAodha, M., *Theatre in Ireland* (Blackwells, 1974)

Orton, J., *Plays* (Methuen, 1973)

Papajewski, H., *Thornton Wilder* (Frederick Ungar Publishing, 1968)

Pirandello, L., *Three Plays*, introduction, John Lindstrum (Methuen, 1985)

Rattigan, T., 'Deep Blue Sea' in *Famous Plays of Today* (Gollancz, 1952)

Richards, L., 'Teatro del grottesco' in M. Banham (ed.) *Cambridge Guide to World Theatre* (Cambridge University Press, 1988)

Ritchie, J.M., *German Expressionist Drama* (Twayne Publishing, Boston, 1976)

Rowell, G., *Theatre in the Age of Irving* (Blackwells, 1981)

Runyon, D., *Runyon on Broadway* (Picador, 1975)

Russell Taylor, J., *Anger and After* (University Paperback, 1962)

Shepard, S., *Angel City and Other Plays* (Faber and Faber, 1978)

Spalter, M., *Brecht's Tradition* (Johns Hopkins University Press, Baltimore, 1967)

Starkie, W., *Luigi Pirandello* (University of California Press, 1937; new edn, 1965)

Sternheim, C., *Scenes from the Heroic Lives of the Middle Classes* (John Calder, 1968)

Storey, D., *Home* (Jonathan Cape, 1970)

Strindberg, A., *Collected Works*, trans. and introduction by M. Meyer (Secker & Warburg, 1964)

Taubman, H., *The Making of the American Theatre* (Longmans, 1967)

Trewin, W. and J.C., *The Arts Theatre, London, 1927-1981* (Society for Theatre Research, 1986)

Wedekind, F., 'Earth Spirit', in Stephen Spender (trans.), *The Lulu Plays* (John Calder, 1977)

———— 'Pandora's Box', in Stephen Spender (trans.), *The Lulu Plays* (John Calder, 1977)

Wellwarth, G.E., *The New Wave Spanish Drama* (New York University Press, 1970)

Willett, J., *The Theatre of Brecht* (Methuen, 1967)

INDEX